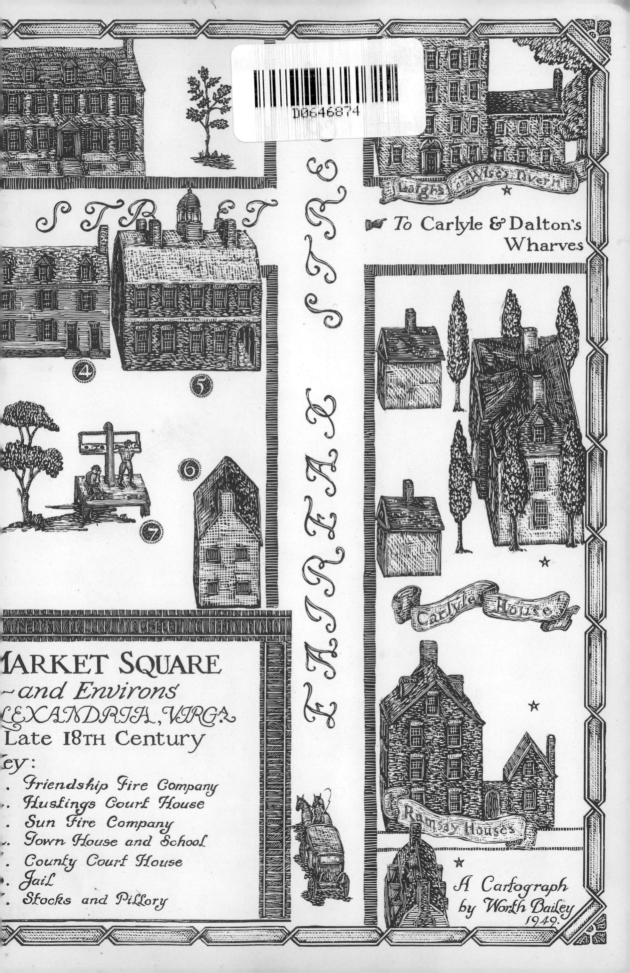

S T R E E T

FAIRFAX

To Carlyle & Dalton's Wharves

Laigh's of Wise's Tavern ✶

④

⑤

⑥

⑦

Carlyle House ✶

Ramsay Houses ✶

MARKET SQUARE
~and Environs
ALEXANDRIA, VIRGA.
Late 18TH Century

Key:

. Friendship Fire Company
. Hustings Court House
. Sun Fire Company
. Town House and School
. County Court House
. Jail
. Stocks and Pillory

A Cartograph
by Worth Bailey
1949.

SEAPORT IN VIRGINIA

Jun Graham Taylor

1952

GEORGE WASHINGTON

By Dr. Elisha Cullen Dick. A painting in oil after a pastel by
James Sharples. *(Courtesy Mount Vernon Ladies' Association)*

Seaport in Virginia

George Washington's Alexandria

By

GAY MONTAGUE MOORE

DRAWINGS BY WORTH BAILEY
PHOTOGRAPHS BY WALTER WILCOX

RICHMOND·VIRGINIA
GARRETT AND MASSIE·INCORPORATED

TO MY HUSBAND

CHARLES BEATTY MOORE

TOGETHER WE HAVE DELVED INTO WHAT RECORDS
WE COULD FIND THAT MIGHT THROW UPON THE
SCREEN SOME SHADOW OF THOSE WHO BUILT
AND LIVED IN THE OLD HOUSES IN
ALEXANDRIA

PREFACE

Twenty years ago on a hot and sultry July afternoon, my husband and I started to Mount Vernon to spend the day. On our return to Washington, we lazily drove through the old and historic town of Alexandria —and bought a house!

The town at once became of vital interest to us. We spent months and years going through every vacant building into which we could force an entrance. Our setter dogs could point an empty doorway as well as a covey of quail, and seemed as curious about the interiors as we were ourselves. I became obsessed with a desire to know the age of these buildings and something of those early Alexandrians who had lived in them.

Old maps and records littered my desk. Out of the past appeared clerks on high stools wielding quill pens and inscribing beautiful script for me to transpose into the story of one of America's most romantic and historic towns. It has been impossible to write about every house in Alexandria—even about every historic house. I tried to recall the old town as a whole. A succession of hatters, joiners, ships' carpenters, silversmiths, peruke makers, brewers, bakers, sea captains, merchants, doctors and gentlemen, schoolteachers, dentists, artisans, artists and actors, began to fill my empty houses. Ships, sail lofts, ropewalks, horses, pigs, and fire engines took their proper places, and the town lived again as of yore—in my imagination.

Everywhere I turned I found General Washington: as a little boy on his brother Lawrence's barge bringing Mount Vernon tobacco to the Hunting Creek warehouse; on horseback riding to the village of Belle Haven; as an embryo surveyor carrying the chain to plot the streets and lots. He was dancing at the balls, visiting the young ladies, drilling the militia, racing horses, launching vessels, engaging workmen, dining at this house or that, importing asses, horses, and dogs, running for office, sitting as justice; sponsoring the Friendship Fire Company, a free school, the Alexandria Canal, or other civic enterprises. He was pewholder of

Christ Church and master of the Masonic lodge. To town he came to collect his mail, to cast his ballot, to have his silver or his carriage repaired, to sell his tobacco or his wheat, to join the citizenry in celebrating Independence. His closest friends and daily companions were Alexandrians. The dwellings, wharves, and warehouses of the town were as familiar to him as his Mount Vernon farm.

In Alexandria Washington took command of his first troops. From the steps of Gadsby's Tavern he received his last military review, a display of his neighbors' martial spirit in a salute from the town's militia. An Alexandrian closed his eyes, and Alexandrians carried his pall.

Washington belongs to Alexandria as Alexandria belongs to him. This is *George Washington's Alexandria*.

GAY MONTAGUE MOORE.

Alexandria, Virginia
September 1949

CONTENTS

CHAPTER DRAWINGS

PART ONE: PROLOGUE

An Account of the First Century of
The Seaport of Alexandria

A typical Alexandria shipping merchant's home: Bernard Chequire, called the "count," built his dwelling and storeroom under the same roof

SITE AND ANTECEDENTS

In the middle of the seventeenth century when the English King, Charles II, was generously settling Virginia land upon loyal subjects, what is now the port of Alexandria was part of six thousand acres granted by the Royal Governor, Sir William Berkeley, in the name of His Majesty, to Robert Howsing. The grant was made in 1669 as a reward for bringing into the colony one hundred and twenty persons "to inhabit."

Howsing did not want this land but John Alexander did. He had surveyed the tract and knew its worth. Howsing doubtless thought himself well out of it when Alexander paid six hundredweight of tobacco and took it off his hands within a month.[1]

The growth and development of the colony of Virginia into a great agricultural population occupied in the cultivation of tobacco was not at all what the London Company had in mind. It visualized a colony of towns. But the possibilities offered by the great rivers emptying into Chesapeake Bay and the development of the tobacco trade were responsible for a civilization unique to Englishmen. True that the establishment of towns as trading centers was a recognized need—generally agitated by the Burgesses and planters from interested motives—but little came of it. Planters whose lands and domiciles lined the Virginia waterways found the direct trade with English ships a facile, if expensive, convenience. It was so easy to dispose of a cargo of tobacco and receive at one's door in return delivery of a neat London sofa, greatcoat, or a coach and harness. So instead of towns, great tobacco warehouses were built at convenient centers where tobacco was collected, inspected, and shipped. Such a warehouse was established by act of Assembly in 1730 and 1732[2] at the mouth of Great Hunting Creek, where it empties into the Potomac River, on the land of Hugh West, Sr. (a member of the Alexander clan) and where there was already a ferry to the Maryland side of the river. Almost immediately a little village grew up—a group of small houses and a school—known then as Belle Haven.

Tobacco was currency in the colony, tendered as such, and it constituted the first wealth. Salaries and fees were paid in tobacco, fines were levied in tobacco; it was the medium of exchange in England as well as in Virginia. When the colonists wrote the word, they used a capital T!

His Majesty's government of the New World was much occupied with the cultivation, housing, and transportation of this natural weed. The importance attached to tobacco is best illustrated by a most extraordinary law. When Englishmen, whose homes are their castles, permitted the right of search of citizens' private dwellings, some idea of the value of this commodity may be realized. The Burgesses resolved early "that any Justice of Peace who shall know or be informed of any Package of Tobacco of less than —weight made up for shipping off, shall have power to enter any suspected House, and by night or by day and so search for, and finding any such Package, to seize and destroy the same; and moreover the Person in whose Possession the same shall be found, shall be liable to a Penalty."[3] Inspectors of tobacco held their appointments under the King; theirs was the responsibility of watching the crop, estimating its yield and weight, maintaining the standard of quality and inspecting the packing. Moreover, no tobacco could be "bought or sold, but by Inspector's Notes, under a Penalty both upon the Buyer and Seller."[4]

In 1742 the Burgesses, lower house of Virginia's Parliament, in session at Williamsburg, became exercised about the tobacco trade and "Resolved, That an humble address of this house be presented to His Majesty, and a Petition to the Parliament of Great Britain; representing the distressed state and decay of our Tobacco Trade, occasioned by the Restraint on our Export; which must, if not speedily remedied, destroy our Staple; and there being no other expedient left for Preservation of this Valuable Branch of the British Commerce, to beseech His Majesty and His Parliament, to take the same into Consideration; and that His Majesty may be graciously pleased to grant unto his subjects of this Colony, a Free Export of their Tobacco to Foreign Markets directly, under such Limitations, as to His Majesty's Wisdom, shall appear Necessary."[5]

THE TOWN SPONSORED

From 1742 a series of petitions from the inhabitants of Prince William and Fairfax[6] counties, asking authority from the Assembly at Williamsburg to erect towns in the county, were presented to the Burgesses. Several years passed before any notice was taken of these requests.

At a General Assembly, begun and held at the College in Williamsburg on Tuesday, November 1, 1748 (sixteen years after the establishment of the warehouse at Hunting Creek) in the twenty-second year of the reign of George II, a petition was presented from "the inhabitants of Fairfax in Behalf of Themselves and others praying that a Town may be established at Hunting Creek Ware House on Potomack River."[7] On Tuesday, April 11, 1749, a bill for establishing a town at Hunting Creek Warehouse, in Fairfax County, was read for the first time.

The bill went through the regular proceedings and was referred to Messrs. Ludwell, Woodbridge, Hedgeman, Lawrence Washington, Richard Osborne, William Waller, and Thomas Harrison. On April 22, the ingrossed bill was read the third time, and it was "resolved that the Bill do pass. Ordered, that Mr. Washington do carry the Bill to the Council for their concurrence."[8] On May 2, 1749 the bill came back from the Council (the upper house) with additional amendments to which the Council desired the house's concurrence. Washington was again sent up to the Council with the approved amendments, and on Thursday, May 11, 1749, Governor Gooch commanded the immediate attendance of the house in the Council chamber. The Speaker, with the house, went up accordingly; and the Governor was pleased to give his assent to the bill "for erecting a town at Hunting Creek Ware House, in the County of Fairfax."[9]

The act stated that such a town "would be commodious for trade and navigation, and tend greatly to the best advantage of frontier inhabitants."[10] Within four months after passage of the act, sixty acres of land belonging to Philip Alexander, John Alexander, and Hugh West, "situate, lying and being on the South side of Potomac River, about the mouth of Great Hunting Creek, and in the County of Fairfax, shall be surveyed and laid out by the surveyor of the said County . . . and vested in the Right Honorable Thomas, Lord Fairfax, the Honorable William Fairfax, Esq., George Fairfax, Richard Osborne, Lawrence Washington, William Ramsay, John Carlyle, John Pagan, Gerard Alexander, and Hugh West, of the said County of Fairfax, Gentlemen, and

Philip Alexander of the County of Stafford, Gentleman, and their successors in trust for the several purposes hereinafter mentioned."[11]

These same gentlemen were "constituted and appointed directors and trustees, for designing, building . . . the town"[12] and the trustees and directors or any six of them were to have the power to "Meet as often as they shall think necessary, and shall lay out the said sixty acres into lots and streets not exceeding half an acre of ground in each lot; and also set apart such portions of the said land for a market place, and public landing as to them shall seem convenient; and when the said town shall be so laid out, the said directors and trustees shall have full power and authority to sell all the said lots, by public sale or auction, from time to time, to the highest bidder so as no person shall have more than two lots."[13] The money arising from the sale was to be paid to the two Alexanders and to Hugh West, the proprietors.

It was further enacted that purchasers of every lot or lots should "within two years next after the date of the conveyance for the same, erect, build and finish on each lot so conveyed, one house of brick, stone or wood, well framed of the dimensions of twenty feet square, and nine feet pitch, at the least or proportionably thereto if such grantee shall have two lots contiguous, with a brick or stone chimney . . . and if the owner of any such lot shall fail to pursue and comply with the directions herein prescribed for the building and finishing one or more house or houses thereon, then such lots upon which such houses shall not be so built and finished shall be revested in the said trustees, and shall and may be sold and conveyed to any other persons whatsoever, in the manner before directed, and shall revest and be sold as often as the owner or owners shall fail to perform, obey and fulfill the directions aforesaid, and the money arising from the sale of such lots as shall be revested and sold applied to such public use for the common benefit of the inhabitants of the said town as to them shall seem most proper; and if the said inhabitants of said town shall fail to obey and pursue the rules and orders of the said directors in repairing and mending the streets, landing, and public wharfs, they shall be liable to the same penalties as are inflicted for not repairing the highways in this Colony."[14]

The county surveyor wrote on July 18, 1749:

By Virtue of an Act of the General Assembly . . . I, the Subscriber did Survey and lay off sixty acres of land to be for the said town, and divided the same into lotts, streets, etc., as per the plan thereof   JOHN WEST, JR.
                                                                                                           Dept. S.F.C.[15]

THE TOWN FOUNDED

George Washington had been living with his half-brother, Lawrence, at Mount Vernon for some time and studying engineering under Mrs. Lawrence Washington's brother, Colonel George William Fairfax. It is a safe assumption that the three young men sailed up the Potomac numerous times to see the layout for the prospective new town; or, that wanting an afternoon's ride, they set their horses towards Belle Haven. It was not a strange journey. For years the Hunting Creek warehouse had handled tobacco from Mount Vernon, Belvoir, Gunston Hall, and the neighboring estates. Tradition has it in Alexandria that Washington aided John West when he was struggling through the underbrush and tree stumps staking out the lots. So familiar did the embryo engineer become with the future town site that he drew a map, and added the names of lot purchasers to the side of his drawing.[16]

News traveled throughout the colony, from the Tidewater to the Shenandoah, of the town to be built near the Hunting Creek warehouses. Advertisements were inserted in the colony's gazettes. Auction of lots was to take place on the site, in the month of July, on the thirteenth day.

On the morning of the sale people on horseback began pouring into the village of Belle Haven from all the nearby plantations and estates. Tidewater was represented by Ralph Wormley of Rosegill in Middlesex; from Westmoreland came Augustine Washington; from Fredericksburg, William Fitzhugh; from Gunston Hall, George Mason; from Belvoir, the two Colonels Fairfax; and from Mount Vernon, young George Washington and his half-brother, Augustine, up for the proceedings.

Lawrence Washington was not present, possibly away in England at the time. His brother, Augustine, however, stood proxy and the letter in which he reported the day's proceedings throws a new light upon the sale. It is believed never to have been published; here is the portion relating to the Alexandria auction:

Mount Vernon July 19th 1749

Dr Brother

I have this day returned from Goose Creek, and the Vessel by whom this comes being under way alows one but a short time to write. As to your family I need only to say that they are well as my Sister &c wrote to you by the same ship whilst I was up the Country. You have a very fine prospect for a Crop of Corn & I am in hopes you have made a worse Crop of Tob° than you'll make this year if the fall is Seasonable, but that depends very much upon the fall. As to Belhaven or Alexandria I understand my Brother George has left much to say upon that head. I purchased you two lots near the water upon the Main street, as every one along the rode will be trough that street. I thought they would be as agreeable to you as any, as M[r] Chapman was determined upon having the Lot on the point. I had a Plan & a Copy of the Sale of the Lots to send you, but as my Broth[r] has sent both & I am [torn] very exact, I need not trouble you with any more; you will see by the amount of the Sale that your part cleared three hundred & eighty three pistoles [torn] sensible if Alexander had Stood to the sale of them he would not have made half the Sum by th [torn] every one seem'd to encourage the thing, upon y[r] and M[r] Chapman's account, as they were sensible what you did was through a Publick Spirit & n [torn] of interest; the reason the lots sold so high was River side ones being sett up first which were purchased at a very extravagant price by the prop [illegible] Your two, M[r] Carlyles M[r] Dortons M[r] Ramseys [illegible] M[r] Chapmans sold at different prices, as you may se by the Sale, but we agreed before the Sale to give any Price for them & to strike them upon an average so that by adding them up & dividing them by five you will se what your two lots Cost. M[r] Chapman was obliged to pay Phil Alexander the money for your & his bond last Stafford Court (before the Sale) or other wise was to have George the Second upon his back. M[r] Chapman took into Partnership M[r] Ramsey Carlyle & Dorton, Ramsey has a fourth, Dorton & Carlyle the other fourth . . .

The price is £10 12s. 10d.

Here assuredly are the circumstances surrounding the plan of the town in the youthful George Washington's hand, still preserved among the Washington papers in the Library of Congress, as indeed is the relevant letter. If this was not the actual map sent by George to Lawrence, it most certainly was the copy which he retained for his personal files of the eighty-four lots divided by seven streets running east and west; and three north and south, checkerboard fashion, which comprised the contemplated town.

The bell was rung. Business got under way. John West was crier and announced that the lots put up would be sold within five minutes. The hot crowd pressed in to hear and see all that took place. The disturbed dust blanketed man and beast.

Bidding was brisk; and twenty-four lots were sold in short order. Among the first day's purchasers, besides those mentioned above, were William Fitzhugh, the Honorable William Fairfax, and Colonel George Fairfax.

The trustees met again the next day, July 14, and wasted no time. At once seventeen lots were sold. The trustees agreed to adjourn "till 20th of September next,"[17] at which time the "deeds are to be executed for the above lots and the remaining lots to be sold, and that the Clerk prepare blank deeds for the same."[18]

As for the prices paid for the lots—it is surprising to find a foreign coin, the Spanish *pistole,* as the basic unit of currency. This was due to a situation where hard money was seriously lacking in colonial Virginia. As early as 1714 a general act had been passed to attract foreign specie, which was declared *current* according to weight. Thus the legal valuation of the *pistole* was slightly in excess of 21s. or approximately $4.34.[19] Its purchasing power in the eighteenth century was about five times as great as today. Lots purchased at auction on the first day brought from 16 to 56½ *pistoles.* On the second day, they went for as little as six *pistoles,* the highest bidder for that day being Henry Salkeld, who purchased lots Nos. 38 and 39 for 23 *pistoles* (present-day normal evaluation about $282.00).

THE TOWN BUILT

For many months the trustees were primarily concerned with the disposal of the lots and "advertisements were set up to that purpose,"[20] in the gazettes. Sales were numerous, houses began to go up speedily. By January 1750, eighty lots had been sold with two lots set apart for the town house and market square. In August 1751, Colonel Carlyle was "appointed to have a good road cleared down to Point Lumley and to see the streets kept in repair."[21] On July 18, 1752, the trustees "Ordered on Coll. George Fairfaxe's motion that all dwelling houses from this day not begun or to be built hereafter shall be built on the front and be in a line with the street as chief of the houses now are, and that no gable or end of such house be on or next to the street, except an angle or where two streets cross, otherwise to be pulled down."[22]

While the trustees were feverishly building the new port, the Assembly at Williamsburg was discharging the purchasers of marsh lots from the necessity of building on and improving them; approving the proposition "for appointing fairs to be kept in the Town of Alexandria."[23] Fairs and lotteries were the principal source of municipal income in early years; the journals of the House of Burgesses contain frequent requests for such from many of the Virginia towns.

On March 10, 1752, a committee reporting to the House of Burgesses

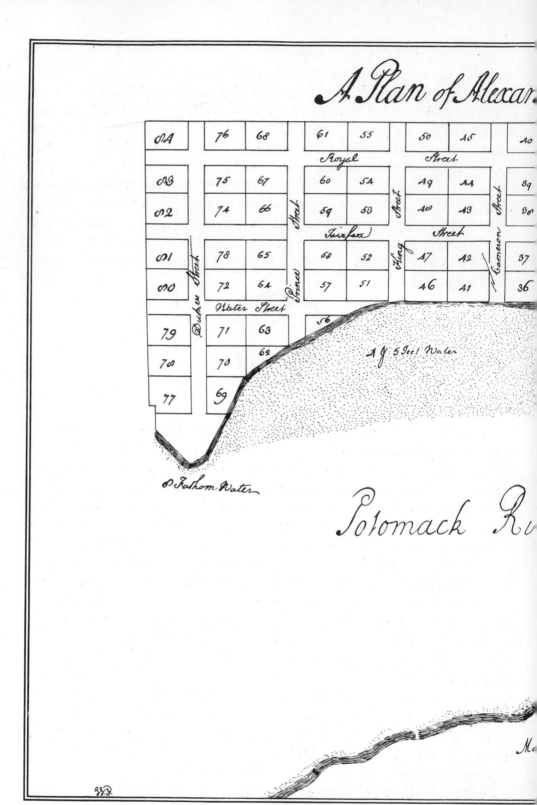

A Plan of Alexar.

| 84 | 76 | 68 | 61 | 55 | 50 | 45 | 40 |
Royal Street

| 83 | 75 | 67 | 60 | 54 | 49 | 44 | 39 |
| 82 | 74 | 66 | 59 | 53 | 48 | 43 | 38 |
Fairfax Street

| 81 | 73 | 65 | 58 | 52 | 47 | 42 | 37 |
| 80 | 72 | 64 | 57 | 51 | 46 | 41 | 36 |

Water Street

79	71	63	56
70	70	62
77	69

A of 5 feet Water

8 Fathom Water

Potomack Ru

Ma

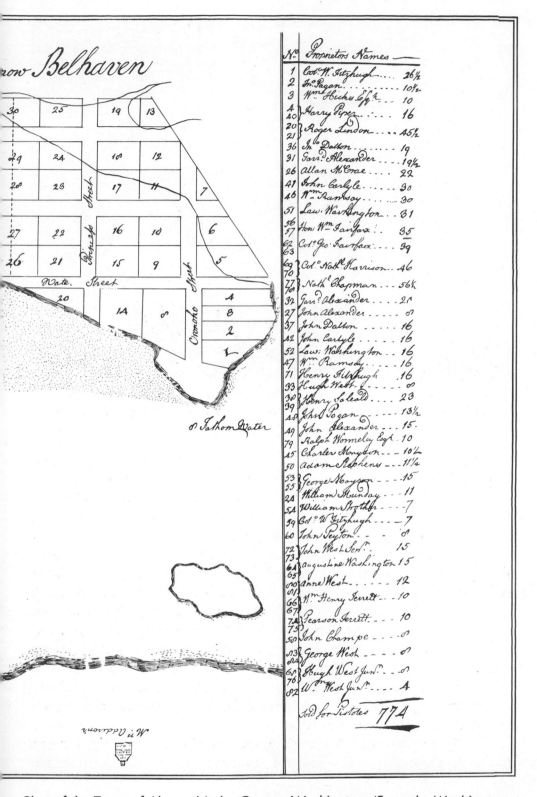

Plan of the Town of Alexandria by George Washington. *(From the Washington Papers in the Library of Congress)*

The good ship *Metamora* of Alexandria, John Hunter, builder and owner. He was the founder of Hunter's Shipyard, "the most complete private establishment of the kind in the country."

"Resolved That it is the opinion of the Committee that the Proposition from the County of Fairfax, in opposition to the proposition from that county, for appointing the Court of the said County to be held at the Town of Belhaven, be rejected."[24] A somewhat complicated manner of ordering the court to be held at Alexandria.

Four days later the Burgesses rejected "the proposition from the Town of Alexandria for altering the name of that town to Belhaven."[25] There had been much talk about this, and for long "The Town at Hunting Creek" was the only designation. The Alexander family, which was both numerous and important (the head of the clan bearing the title Lord Stirling), and the bulk of the land upon which the town was built having been a part of its patent,[26] it was deemed appropriate to name the new town Alexandria. Save for an occasional slip in some old letter (Washington dated some letters Bellehaven) Alexandria is the name by which the town was called since this time.

By 1753 a village had become a town with the market place located exactly in the middle. The first courthouse of frame was built on the east side of lot No. 43, at the intersection of Cameron and Fairfax Streets. South of the Town House on Fairfax stood the jail, stocks, and whipping post for the use of those who failed to keep the law. Directly behind these buildings the market square, or green, occupied all of lot No. 44. Here the town militia drilled, here were held the carnivals, and public gatherings, and here was the larder of Alexandria. To this day the market square caters to the appetites of hungry townsmen. Across Royal Street, facing the square, stood the City Tavern or Coffee House; southward on the same side of the street was the Royal George, after the Revolution called George Tavern. Already substantial wharves and warehouses appeared along the water front, and private houses and stores were beginning to fill the empty lots.[27]

HEADQUARTERS AND PORT OF SUPPLY

As the passage of four years marked physical growth in Alexandria, so it made a difference between a lad barely seventeen and an officer in His Majesty's Militia. Early in November 1753, Major George Washington, aged twenty-one, and an Adjutant General of the Colony, was sent by the Royal Governor to the Ohio to "visit" the commandant of the French forces and deliver a letter asking him to withdraw from the lands "known to be the property of the Crown of Great Britain." Up to town came Major Washington to busy himself acquiring the "necessaries" for the expedition. Once equipped, he set out from Alexandria and was gone about two months, returning on January 11, 1754. January 16 found him in Williamsburg making his report to the Governor. The report was of such a nature that His Excellency alerted the Virginia troops; it was deemed of such importance as to be published in both Williamsburg and London gazettes.

When Washington returned he carried a commission from His Excellency of a lieutenant colonelcy in the Virginia regiment "whereof Joshua Fry, Esquire, was Colonel," and joined his command in Alexandria. The market square took on a militant atmosphere. "Two Companies of Foot, commanded by Captain Peter Hog and Lieutenant Jacob Van Braam, five subalterns, two Sergeants, six Corporals, one Drummer and one hundred and twenty Soldiers, one Surgeon, one Swedish Gentleman, who was a volunteer, two wagons, guarded by one Lieutenant, Sergeant, Corporal and twenty-five soldiers," were all under the command of Lieutenant Colonel Washington.[28]

Many brave young men newly outfitted in the colorful uniforms of His Majesty's Militia, short clothes and white wigs, drilling in the market square, swaggering around the town, filling up the new City Tavern. Dances and dinners for the officers were the order of the day. Then came the command for Washington to join Fry in defending British possessions against the French, who had continued their depredations despite the earlier diplomatic parley, and had not removed from the lands claimed as the property of Great Britain.

Came April 2, and from the market place crowded with citizens, "Every thing being ready," the commander, aged twenty-two, gave the order and the company set forth to the strident beats of one drummer.[29] As the creaking wheels of the two wagons and the tramp of marching feet faded out of hearing, Alexandria had sent her sons off to her first war.

While Lieutenant Colonel Washington was occupied in so spectacular a fashion, the town trustees were not without their troubles, also. People were delinquent about complying with the Assembly laws. In June 1754, the trustees ordered that various lots not built upon be put up at auction and sold to the highest bidder. They were in earnest about this dereliction on the part of purchasers, and seven lots were forfeited at this time. Among those paying such a penalty was George Washington's half-brother, Augustine Washington.

By December 1754, public buildings were well under way, the courthouse lot was ordered "paled in with Posts and Rails in a workman-like manner," and John Carlyle, John Dalton, George Johnston and William Ramsay were appointed to see what was necessary to be done to the finishing of the courthouse.

Within the year, his expedition defeated, Washington was back at Mount Vernon, and very irritated by army orders demoting colonials of the same grade and rank below the British regulars. Despite a vote of commendation by the Burgesses and the sum of £50 voted for his services, he threw up his commission.

The French continued hostilities, stirring up the Indians and causing no end of trouble. His Majesty's government became sufficiently exercised to dispatch an officer of the line, Major General Edward Braddock, two warships in which were stowed a fine arsenal of powder, rifles, and cannon, and two regiments of regulars. Word reached Alexandria in February of Braddock's arrival in Williamsburg and that he and the Governor were in conference. The first result of this conference was a letter to "Mr. George Washington" written on March 2, 1755, and dispatched in the person of General Braddock's aide-de-camp, Lieutenant Robert Orme, requesting the presence of *Mr.* Washington as a member of the General's military family. This, thought the Governor and the General, would do away with any unpleasantness due to difference in rank. A second decision reached in Williamsburg was one that resounded along the Atlantic seaboard—to call a conference of the colonial governors to consider ways, and especially means, of waging the coming campaign. Alexandria was chosen as a meeting place and the day set was April 14, 1755.

In the meantime, the English warships *Sea Horse* and *Nightingale* under command of Admiral Keppel arrived in Alexandria. Two of His Majesty's regiments disembarked from the sea-grimed ships and the Redcoats in formation marched to the "northwest of the town" led by Colonel Sir Peter Halket and Colonel Dunbar. The humbler citizens had never seen such a sight; neither had the Redcoats, and up went British noses for all things Colonial. The regulars promptly dubbed the militia "Bobtails."

After the exchange of several letters, Colonel Washington "volunteered" to go unpaid with General Braddock on the campaign, and he came to Alexandria to attend the governors' conference and whip his militia into shape. Again he occupied the City Tavern as headquarters.

All at once the town was overrun with governors, His Majesty's royal representatives. From Williamsburg came Dinwiddie; from Maryland, Governor Sharpe; from Massachusetts, Governor Shirley; from New York, Governor De Lancey; and from Pennsylvania, Governor Morris. Neither dress nor ceremony had yet been curtailed by the drabness of Democracy. Each governor arrived with a retinue of secretaries, attendants, and aides; each by coach, decorated in gilded scrolls and colorful arms, drawn by four to six horses; each governor resplendent in wig and powder, silken hose, coats of brocade, velvet or broadcloth, waistcoats of satin or damask, embroidered and braided, shirts of finest linen, betucked and belaced, and attended by servants in livery as colorful as their masters. The town was packed. Taverns were full, and private houses were put at the disposal of these visitors. Dinners and balls followed the serious councils of the day, which lasted until eleven or twelve o'clock at night. The market place rang with the continuous drilling of the Bobtails. Redcoats were everywhere. The ladies of the town vied with one another in presents of potted woodcock and delicious cake to the distinguished guests.

It has been one hundred and ninety-four years since the citizens of Alexandria were treated to the panoply of five of His Majesty's royal governors, two warships, and the presence of Major General Edward Braddock with Mr. George Washington as part of his military family. These days established the little seaport in history and furnished sights and subjects resulting in tales and traditions more firmly established than the printed word. Amid the scratching of quills and the dipping of snuff, the destiny, not only of this hemisphere but of the world, was changed, for the five governors assembled decided to tax the colonies to support Braddock's expedition. It was not a popular decision, and great difficulties arose in collecting the allotted sums. It was a fateful step which led eventually to revolt by the colonies.

The conference over, pomp and pageantry departed, but not before Mr. Washington and General Braddock had disagreed heartily on the fashion of waging warfare. The heavy cannon brought by the British were dumped overboard, notwithstanding, or were otherwise abandoned as too cumbersome for the long trek west. General Braddock purchased from Governor Sharpe of Maryland "an old English chariot and six horses" for the march.

On April 20 the Redcoats and Bobtails (six companies, two from Alexandria and the nearby countryside) set out. To Sir Peter Halket's regiment were assigned Captain Stephens', Captain Peyronny's and Captain Cock's Company of Rangers, and Captain Polson's Company of Artificers. The heavy coach lumbered over the rough country roads, shaking poor General Braddock almost to pieces and "greatly increased his discomfort." Mr. Washington, desiring time to arrange his private affairs at Mount Vernon, was unable to depart with his military family for eight days after they left.

This tragically ill-fated expedition resulted in heavy casualties. On July 9, Braddock was attacked unexpectedly near Fort Du Quesne by a body of French and Indians, some three hundred strong, which so surprised the British regulars they were struck with a "deadly panic" and ignominiously fled. "The officers behaved with incomparable bravery . . . there being near 60 killed and wounded. The Virginian Companies behaved like men and died like Soldiers . . . scarce 30 were left alive

... The General was wounded behind in the shoulder and into the Breast, of which he died three days after."[30] George Washington miraculously saved the army from complete rout. He afterwards collected his decimated Virginians and marched them back to the market square in Alexandria. The reception was a sad one.

EARLY GROWTH

The minutes of the trustees for 1755 announced that by this time the first frame courthouse was fenced—it had taken two years—and the gentlemen justices of Fairfax County, sitting on November 17, 1756, ordered John West, John Carlyle, and William Ramsay, Gentlemen, to be paid five thousand pounds of tobacco; John Doonas, Alexandria's first policeman, was to receive 120 pounds for patrolling twelve days.

For the next hundred years the great municipal interests were to be tobacco, wheat, and ships; the rapid and proper dispatching of the produce stored in the great warehouses occupying the river front; the housing and sale of the vast diversity of goods coming to anchor with each new sail. But in these earliest days, tobacco and ships to transport it were the motivating forces of the town.

Turning the pages of a journal of long ago, one gets this glimpse of the fit setting:

In the evening we returned down the river about fifteen miles to Alexandria or Belhaven, a small trading place in one of the finest situations imaginable. The Potomac above and below the town is not more than a mile broad, but it here opens into a large circular bay of at least twice that diameter. The town is built upon an arc of this bay; at one extremity of which is a wharf; at the other a dock for building ships; with water sufficiently deep to launch a vessel of any rate or magnitude.[31]

On May 19, 1760, George Washington "went to Alexandria to see Captn. Litterdale's ship launched, wch. went off extreamely well."[32] Again on October 5, 1768, he "went up to Alexandria after an early dinner to see a ship [the *Jenny*] launched, but was disappointed and came home."[33] Next day, the 6th, he "went up again, saw the ship

launched; stayd all night to a Ball and set up all Night."[34] His expense
account shows a loss of 19 shillings at cards for the evening.

Alexandria's importance as a seaport was phenomenal and after a few
years it was ranking third in the New World—greater than New York,
the rival of Boston. Master shipbuilders turned out vessels to sail any
sea—manned, owned, and operated by Alexandrians. Down the ways of
Alexandria shipyards glided as good vessels as could be built. From her
ropewalks came the rope to hoist the sails made in her sail lofts. Chem-
ists' shops specialized in fitting out ships' medicine boxes for the long
voyages, and bakeshops packed daily thousands of ships' biscuits. Ship
chandlers forsook older ports for the new one; planters rolled in tobacco
in ever increasing bulk to fill the vessels crowding the harbor. With
greater wealth came the means to fill the need and desire of Alexandrians
for good clothes and fine furnishings. And so back to England with each
cargo went orders for the newest taste and the latest fashion.

It took months, sometimes longer than a year, to complete an order for
goods. Each voyage was a stupendous adventure. Ships with full cargoes
often disappeared and were neither seen nor heard of again. George
Washington's writings serve as a good history of Alexandria. His
voluminous letters reveal what our first citizens needed, bought, and
used, what various articles cost, and how business details were handled:

November 30, 1759

To Robert Cary & Company

Gentn: By the George and Captns Richardson and Nicks who saild with the
Fleet in September last I sent invoices of such Goods as were wanting for
myself Estate etc, but knowing that the latter unfortunately foundered at Sea
soon after her departure from Virginia and that the former may probably have
suffered by that Storm or some other accident, by which means my Letters &c
would miscarry I take this oppertunity by way of Bristol of addressing Copies
of them, and over and above the things there wrote for to desire the favour of
you to send me a neat Grait (for Coal or small Faggots) in the newest taste
and of a size to fit a Chimney abt. 3 feet wide and two Deep, and a fender
suited to Ditto. Steel I believe are most used at present; also send me a New
Market Great Coat with a loose hood to be made of Blew Drab or broad cloth
with Straps before according to the present taste, let it be made of such cloth
as will turn a good shower of Rain and made long, and fit in other respects for
a Man full 6 feet high and proportionately made, possibly the Measure sent
for my other cloths may be a good direction to these. Please to add also to
the things ordered for Mrs. Dandridge 12 yds of Silver cold Armozeen or
Ducape and cause it to be packed up with the Rest of her things charged with
them. &ca.

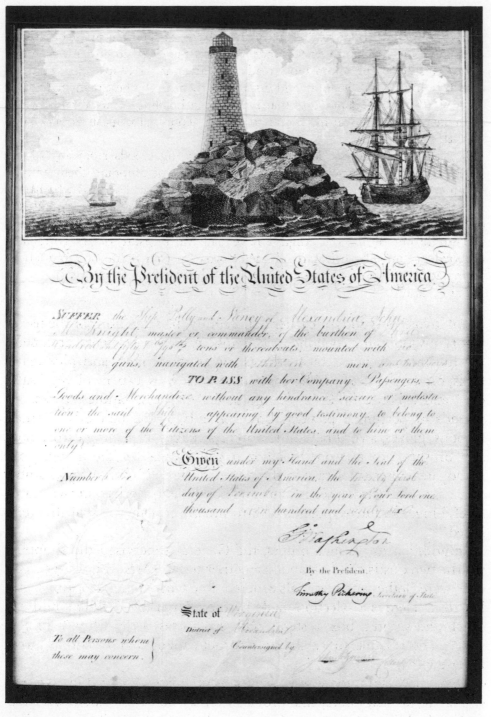

A Suffer to Pass of the ship *Polly and Nancy* of Alexandria; John McKnight, Master. Signed by George Washington. *(Courtesy Mount Vernon Ladies' Association)*

Five days ago I dropt a letter at Williamsburg, to take the first Conveyance to you, desiring Insurance on 50 Hhds Tobo pr. the Cary since then I have got 4 more Inspected and all on Float ready to deliver at the Ships side. You will therefore Insure that Quantity and dispose of them in the best manner for Our Interest. If Captn. Talman uses that Dispatch in Loading of his Vessell, which I am sure he now has in his power to do this Tobo. wl come to a very good market, I hope.

It is almost as much trouble and expense getting Goods from any of the Rivers round to Potomack as the Original Charges of Shipping them amount to, unless they are committed to the charge of very careful Captains who has an Interest in forwarding. I should be glad therefore if you would take the oppertunity of some Ship to that River of sending my Goods for the Future.

Your favour of the 6th Augt. I have had the pleasure of receiving, and acknowledge myself particularly obliged to you for your polite Congratulations on my Marriage, as I likewise am for your Dispatch of my Goods.

I am Gentn.[35]

An invoice of goods of earlier date sent by the same firm for the use of George Washington contained 194 items. Wearing garments, ornaments for the chimney place, busts, drugs, sugar, carpenter's and plowman's tools, candy, a case of pickles containing anchovies, capers, olives, "salid oyl" and a bottle of India mangoes; tea, harness, saddles, corks, six pounds of perfumed powder, three pounds of the best Scotch snuff, ribbons, gloves, sword belt, nine dozen packages of playing cards, paint and brushes, one and one-half dozen bell glasses for the garden; one mahogany closet stool case in the newest taste, with place for chamber pot, etc.; soap, garden seeds, nuts and condiments, locks and two dozen H&L hinges and three pounds of bird lime, were but a few of the items listed.

In addition to his own orders, the General supervised the shopping for the two Custis children and his mother-in-law, Mrs. Dandridge. Not only were clothes and materials ordered, fine ivory combs, stockings, etc., but toys. Here is a selection made by the Cary firm—a child's fiddle, a coach and six in a box, a stable with six horses, a toy whip, a filigree watch, a neat enameled watch box, a corner cupboard and a child's huzzit [housewife].

General Washington was a Virginia gentleman who lived in a fashion similar to his neighbors; like orders, we may be sure, went from Alexandria, and like articles were bought and received into its homes. Perhaps the system was not always so direct, for the average townsman doubtless relied more upon local merchants as agents. Washington followed this course at various times, but until the American Revolution he rather steadfastly depended upon Robert Cary & Company of London.

With the growth of trade and population came the necessity for expansion of the town, and we see the Assembly approving the petition of the trustees and sundry inhabitants of the town of Alexandria in 1762, "Praying that an Act may pass to enlarge the Bounds of the said Town."[36] All lots save those in the marsh were then built upon.

On May 9, 1763, the trustees proceeded to sell the new lots, which had been added by act of Assembly. The town property was enhancing in value and for that reason the lots were sold with a twelve-month credit, hoping to increase the sale value. Forty-six lots were disposed of, among the purchasers being George Johnston, Robert Adam, Francis Lee, John Dalton, John Carlyle, and George Washington, who at thirty-one years of age became a *bona fide* citizen of Alexandria. The town which he had honored returned the compliment four years later when the city fathers meeting on December 16, 1766, "proceeded to elect as Trustee in the room of George Johnston, decd, and have unanimously chosen George Washington, Esq., as Trustee for the town aforesaid."[37]

Fifteen years after the laying out of the town, at a session of the House of Burgesses, November 5, 1764, in the fifth year of the reign of George III it was "Resolved, That it is the Opinion of this Committee that the Petition of divers Proprietors of Lots, and other Inhabitants of the Town of Alexandria, in the County of Fairfax, praying that so much of the Act of Assembly for establishing the said Town as obliges the Purchasers of Lots therein to build and improve the same in a limited Time, may be repealed, and the Purchasers left at Liberty to build thereon when convenient to them, is reasonable."[38] George Washington found it convenient to build a house on one of his lots in 1769; the other was not built upon until almost thirty years later.

The prodigious development of the new port was accompanied by a growing civic pride and the demand for better public buildings. A story-and-a-half brick town hall was erected in 1759 by funds raised by lottery, tickets selling at ten shillings each, the trustees making themselves responsible for a sum adequate for the purpose. At the trustees' meeting of April 1767, John Dalton and John Carlyle produced an account of moving the courthouse amounting to £52 7s. 5½d.; while William Ramsay presented his account for a "scheme of a lottery to build a Church and Market house" in the amount of £11 12s.[39] The new town house with its clerk's office and assembly room stood on the northeast corner of the

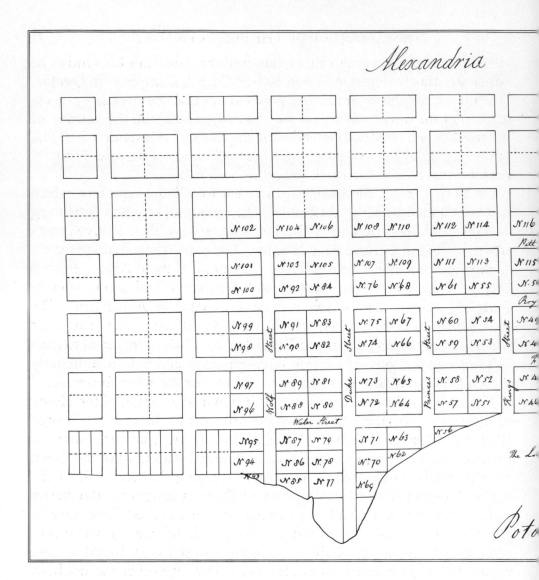

square; nearby on Cameron Street stood the Fairfax Court House, which town promotion had brought to Alexandria. The church and market did not materialize so early.

EARLY EDUCATION

Space in the lower floor of the town hall was provided for a grammar school soon after the completion of this building in 1760. Seven years later the town fathers found that the schoolhouse was so misused that repairs were urgent and minutes for the meeting of February 2, 1767,

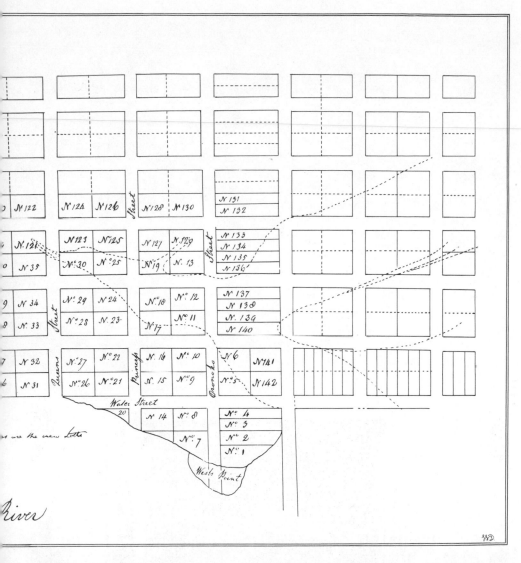

The addition to the town in 1763 and 1767. (Library of Congress)

record how they considered it necessary to put it in better condition, "also to make some additions in order to make the upper room usefull not only for meeting of the Trustees but for such other purposes as may be thought necessary." Apparently a separate entrance for the school-room dates from this time; other improvements included the raising of the roof for greater utility upstairs. The trustees further resolved: "As it appears to us that the House has been very much injured by the negligence of the School Masters it is now determined that each Master give security to repair any injury that the House may sustain during the time they have

Corner mantel at 211½ Prince Street in the house built about 1786 by William Hickman. The builder was trying to cram into a given space every motif in the *Builder's Handbook:* Greek entablature at the top of the pediment, crowded center panel, broken pediment, and the top of the pediment jammed into the cap fretwork. The whole is very amusing but interesting and altogether charming.

it." Robert Adam and Thomas Fleming were appointed overseers of
the property for a term of twelve months.

A grammar school reputed to have been supported by public funds was
in existence at Belhaven in 1739, just ten years before Alexandria was
founded. Presumably the Alexandria school of 1760 was put into operation under identical conditions and it may be that special classes beyond
the mere rudiments of education were conducted for children whose
families could pay extra tuition. Such a plan would closely approximate
the tutorial arrangement prevailing on outlying plantations. For or-
phaned children and the very poor who had to earn while they learned,
provision was usually made for a little schooling within the framework
of the apprenticeship system, and church wardens were charged with
responsibility for placing orphans with individuals to learn a useful
occupation. At a court held March 18, 1770, "James Gameron, five years
old the last of this month and Sarah Gameron three years old" were
bound out "to William Wren who is to learn them to read and write, and
the said James the trade of a shoe maker."[40]

After the Revolution, the town's educational system centered in the
Alexandria academy, which stood on the east side of Washington Street
between Wolfe and Wilkes, where now stands the present Washington
Public School. The old Marsteller house, acquired by the public school
system in 1882, when the present school building was erected, has by
many been confused with the old academy building. The Alexandria
academy was a one-story brick structure. Its cornerstone was laid September 7, 1785, by the Alexandria Lodge of Freemasons, Robert Adam, Esquire, Worshipful Master of the Lodge. Mrs. Powell, in her *History of
Old Alexandria,* states that after the stone was laid "a gratuity was distributed among the workmen." The school was incorporated in 1786 by act of
the Virginia Assembly and the trustees were to be chosen by those gentlemen who had contributed five or more dollars for the use of the academy,
thirteen fit and able men to serve beginning in 1788. In the meantime,
Washington, Dr. Brown, and twelve other generous public-spirited citizens were appointed by law as trustees until the annual elections should
begin. The letter asking Washington to serve is extant.

General Washington, always a believer and a patron of learning, contributed for many years prior to his death, £50 annually toward a free
department for poor students. In his will he left one thousand dollars
or "20 shares of stock which I hold in the Bank of Alexandria, towards
the support of a free school established at and annexed to the said

A Mantel in the home of the late Miss Saidee M. Field, 316 Duke Street, in the Adam-McIntyre manner. The house was built prior to 1795, at which time a trust to secure William Stoggett of Carnelsford, County Cornwall, England for £253.16.9 is cited. Note the large brick in the worn hearth and bit of original pine flooring. The fireback has been rebuilt.

Academy, for the purpose of educating such orphans or children of such poor and indigent persons as are unable to accomplish it with their own means, and who in the judgment of the trustees of the said Seminary are best entitled to the benefit of this donation."

By 1791 the school established by his bounty was caring for thirteen boy and seven girl pupils. One graduate, John Weylie, wrote to thank the General for his benevolence. This same young man later became tutor for the children of Dr. David Stuart. In January 1800, following Washington's death the month previous, the Alexandria council voted to provide a suit of mourning for each of the poor scholars educated at his expense that they might join in the memorial exercises scheduled for February 22.

George Steptoe Washington and Lawrence Augustine, sons of the General's deceased brother, Samuel, were both sent to the academy. They were boarded by Washington with one of the trustees, Samuel Hansen, who frequently reported to their uncle on their interests and behavior. In 1789, Hansen wrote to the General recommending for George one Cleon Moore as teacher of the violin at £12 per year.

These gentlemen were not as circumspect when students as was Lorenzo Lewis, who was cited in 1819 for "general deportment and propriety of conduct." Young Lewis was the son of Nelly Custis and Lawrence Lewis, the former Mrs. Washington's granddaughter and the General's ward, the latter the General's nephew. Robert E. Lee perchance might be included in this Washington family circle, by virtue of his subsequent marriage to the daughter of George Washington Parke Custis, brother of Nelly. Lee attended the academy from about 1820 until 1824, and was remembered by his teachers as an exemplary scholar.

Education for the opposite sex was not overlooked. Through the interest and encouragement of Washington, Mrs. Eliza Harriot O'Conner opened an academy for young ladies as early as 1788. Quaintly worded announcements appearing in local gazettes early in the nineteenth century reveal an ever-increasing number of girls' schools.

Female scholars clad in blue worsted dresses, black aprons, muslin handkerchiefs, leather shoes and colored hose, capes, blue lined straw bonnets, sporting crimson ribbons, studied the exotic subjects of "Painting in inks and colors on 'tiffany.' Embroidered landscapes both plain and fanciful in chenile, gold and silver, wrought maps in 'ditto'—printed work in Tambour and needlework—made fringe and netting."

Alexandrians were not without their lighter side. There were plays in town at least as early as 1768, for on September 20 of that year George Washington took Mrs. Washington and the Custis children to Alexandria to see "The Inconstant, or, Way to Win." They remained overnight and the next day attended the theatre again to see "The Tragedy of Douglas." The cost of the two entertainments was given as £3 12s. 6d.

In 1789 the *Virginia Journal and Alexandria Advertiser* announced the presentation of the "Tragedy of Jane Shore, with the musical farce of the Virgin Unmasked." Mr. McGrath opened the Alexandria Theatre for four seasons beginning in 1791. On November 6 he presented Garrick's comedy, "The Lying Valet" and on November 19, 1793, the American comedy, "The Contrast: or, the True Born Yankee." The theatre doors opened at six, and the curtain was raised promptly at half-past six—or so the announcement read, and it continued, "no money to be received by the Door-Keepers."

In 1797, Thomas Wade West, Manager of "The Virginia and South Carolina Comedians Companies" and Margaret, his wife, came to Alexandria for the purpose of erecting a theatre. A lot on the north side of Cameron Street, fronting thereon fifty-four feet, was purchased on July 8, 1797, from Thomas and Sarah Porter, the ground rental of which was 108 silver dollars yearly.

The patrons of this enterprise, some twenty-nine of the first citizens of Alexandria—among them Edmund I. Lee, William Herbert, Josiah Watson, Ludwell Lee, Elisha Cullen Dick, Joseph Riddle and Jonah Thompson—agreed with one another to contribute the sum of two hundred dollars each to be laid out and expended for the erection of a theatre upon the aforesaid piece of ground. The subscribers had free tickets of admission to every performance with the exception of benefits and charities. This was to continue in effect for one season after reimbursement at six per cent interest. Thomas Wade West agreed to furnish all the decorations, scenery and furniture to the value of £500. This was the New Theatre as shown on the early maps of the town.

Cockfights and horse racing, too, were popular, the latter attended by women and children. But in 1816 the council forbade these activities taking place within the town limits, and ruled that "every person who shall trim, heel, or pit any cock so fought and every owner of such cock consenting thereto and every person who shall bet on such a match or main shall severally forfeit and pay for every offense the sum of twenty dollars."[41] Since horse racing could not be easily secreted in cellars and

Doorway of the supposed Jockey Club of which Washington and Dulany were stewards. (814 Franklin Street)

walled gardens, no such drastic penalties accompanied that pertinent part of the act. Blooded horses were imported by John Carlyle as early as 1762. Alexandria races attracted the best horses in the Old Dominion. Famous Maryland and Tidewater stables participated in the Jockey Club races. George Washington was steward of the Alexandria Jockey Club. The gazettes were full of notices concerning the races and frequently gave pedigrees of certain horses advertised for sale or stud.

After the races, especially those of the Jockey Club, there was sure to be an Assembly Ball at one of the larger taverns, followed by a fine supper. In Gadsby's time the Jockey Club used his tavern as headquarters. After dining, the members were frequently entertained by "The Players" or "Jugglers and Tumblers." Maryland neighbors as well as nearby Virginians turned out for these festivities.

Mantel in the home of the late Mr. and Mrs. Norman H. Davis, 804 Prince Street. Late 18th and early 19th Century reeded carving, typical of the Federal House. The decoration is achieved by the returns around the pilasters, the reeded trim and diamond motif in the center panel

Fox hunting was indulged in frequently by Alexandria gentlemen who went often to Mount Vernon, Belvoir and to other estates near Alexandria for the sport.

Fairs and circuses from time to time filled the town with excitement. Feats of horsemanship, vaulting and dancing were performed every Fair Day during the visitation of Messrs. Pepin and Breschard in April 1810. The doors opened at half-past three and the performance commenced at half-past four; beginning with a Grand Military Manoeuvre by eight persons well mounted, and ending with the admired "Scene of the Domestic Horse" (by the famous Conqueror) who brought chairs and baskets when commanded, and the "Ladies Fireworks," composed by Mr. Condit.

Of course, there was much wining and dining out, followed by cards rendered more spicy when played for stakes. Taverns and oyster houses furnished recreation for those less affluent. Fields and streams furnished rare sport for fishermen; the successful fisherman or hunter could always dispose of his excess catch at the market. Fish fries were common entertainment.

DOMESTIC ECONOMY AND A NEW MONEY CROP

As the population grew, the markets were abundantly supplied. Great vessels packed with ice for sale in the town tied up at the wharves; open spaces devoted to gardens and outbuildings gave way to dwelling houses, and the town became more compact. Twelve or more servants were necessary for the maintenance of large establishments, varying in number according to the size of the family and the house. There was generally a butler, who acted as major-domo, a cook and kitchenmaid, body servants or valets for the head of the house and the young gentlemen, a ladies' maid, chambermaid, nurse and nursemaids, a coachman, stable boy, gardener, yard boy and laundress.

During the first twenty years of the city's development, an entire block might contain not more than four homes. Each of these units functioned as a miniature and self-supporting estate, surrounded by flower and vegetable gardens and the usual outbuildings—necessaries, kitchen, dairy, ice house, smokehouse, fowl house, servant quarters and stable. The following advertisement appearing as late as 1828 illustrates the traditional layout:

TO LET

An elegant two story Brick House, with kitchen, wash house, bath house, stable and carriage houses, an elegant garden, and a well of excellent water, a pump in the middle or centre of the square, a cistern for wash water and every convenience, equalled by few and exceeded by none of its size in Alexandria and suited only to a genteel family.

It stands on Prince Street. It will be let for one or more years as best suits the tenant and possession given at once.

Apply to ROBERT BROCKETT

In spring the gardens were prepared, the herring salted and packed. In summer great quantities of preserves, jellies, and pickles were put up for the long winter. At the first frost the smokehouses were filled with hams and great sides of bacon. Game was plentiful, and during the season venison, duck, partridge, wild turkey, and woodcock appeared in market and graced the tables of the well-to-do. With tea from China and India, coffee from Brazil, oil and condiments from Spain, sugar and fruits from the West Indies, Alexandrians fared sumptuously.

By 1770 Alexandria's tobacco trade had largely given way to wheat, and the local shipping merchants were finding their supplies farther and farther west in the valley of the Shenandoah. George Washington was one of the first planters on the upper Potomac to change his money crop from tobacco to wheat. He enlarged his mill and took advantage of the latest mechanical advances of his time. However successful he became as a wheat farmer, he never escaped the trials and grief caused by those middlemen, his agents. In 1767 he wrote a nine-page letter roundly berating Carlyle and Adam for the destruction of his bags and for delay in paying him for his wheat.

A list of merchants and factors doing business in Alexandria in 1775 emphasizes the transition from tobacco to wheat. Of twenty-one firms enumerated, fourteen were purchasers of wheat:

1. Hooe and Harrison—*wheat* purchasers.
2. Steward and Hubard—*wheat* purchasers.
3. Fitzgerald and Reis—*wheat* purchasers.

4. Harper and Hartshorne—*wheat* purchasers.

5. John Allison—*wheat* purchaser.

6. William Sadler—*wheat* purchaser.

7. Robert Adam and Co.—*wheat* purchasers.

8. Henby and Calder—*wheat* purchasers.

9. William Hayburne—*wheat* purchaser.

10. James Kirk—*wheat* purchaser.

11. George Gilpin—*wheat* purchaser, inspector of flour.

12. Thomas Kilpatrick—*wheat* purchaser, inspector of flour.

13. McCawlay and Mayes—import British goods which they sell wholesale.

14. William Wilson—seller of British goods who buys tobacco.

15. John Locke—seller of British goods who buys tobacco.

16. John Muir—seller of British goods who buys tobacco.

17. Brown and Finley—they import goods from Philadelphia and purchase tobacco and *wheat.*

18. Josiah Watson—he imports goods from Philadelphia and purchases tobacco and *wheat.*

19. Robert Dove and Co.—distillers.

20. Carlyle and Dalton—import Rum and Sugar.

21. Andrew Wales—brewer.[42]

It is said that Virginia wheat was the best to be procured and all Europe was a market for Alexandria flour. It was not long before the great wagons that had formerly carried wheat from Tidewater to Philadelphia and the Delaware found the Potomac port as good a market and a shorter journey. Numerous bakehouses appeared and Alexandria packed and shipped large quantities of bread and crackers along with flour to Europe and the Indies.

Alexandria had been a port of entry since 1779 and time was when the Potomac from mouth to port was so crowded with vessels that navigation was difficult. The early gazettes constantly referred to the crowded condition of the river. The water front seethed with activity. One finds the notice in a newspaper of 1786 of the arrival from St. Petersburg, Russia, of the ship *Hunter* of Alexandria. She was advertised to ply her trade between these two places. This ship was built, owned, and sailed by an Alexandrian, and was but one of many claiming Alexandria as home port. Far corners of the earth were united in this ancient harbor for a hundred years or more. "Commerce and Shipping" columns in the local journals were as well read then as are our "classifieds" today. Ships from China lay beside ships from Spain; flags from Holland, Jamaica, Portugal, Germany, France and Russia flaunted their gay colors. Private as well as public wharves were built. Large and rich shipping firms were numerous.

Great warehouses of brick lined the river front. A kinsman of President Washington wrote him in 1792 that the "port of Alexandria has seldom less than 20 square-rigged vessels in it and often many more. The streets are crowded with wagons and the people all seem busy."[43]

Sloops, brigs, barques and schooners unloaded osnaburgs, wild boars, moreens, brocades and damasks, bombazines, Russian and Belgian linens, Scottish wools, French and Italian silk, caster hats, morocco leather slippers, pipes of Madeira wine, casks of rum and port from Spain, spices, fruits, and muscovado sugar from the West Indies, chests of Hyson tea from China, neat sofas, bureaus, sideboards, harpsichords and spinets from London, along with other things "too tedious to mention."

By 1816 decline in the importance of the port had set in, but no less than 992 vessels entered and cleared the customs that year. This number did not include the "vast number of inland packets, coal traders, lumber vessells, wood dº, grain dº, etc." Of these 992 vessels, 195 were foreign —ships, brigs, schooners, sloops—while coastwise entrances and clearances reached 797. On January 22, 1817, the account of vessels in the port of Alexandria stood:

Ships	9
Barques	1
Brigs	11
Schooners	30
Sloops	15
Total	66

These figures do not include a number of small craft in the port or the steamboats *Washington* and *Camdon*.

AFTERMATH OF REVOLUTION

Participants in the Revolution made more impress upon Alexandria's history than the war itself. The town was divided in its sentiments. Many of the Scottish people remained loyal in their sympathies to the mother country. Old Lord Fairfax, a Tory of Tories, became incensed with young Washington, whom he had practically brought up, and 'tis said, refused ever to see or speak to him again. His heir, Parson Bryan Fairfax,

An early cartoon representing John Bull collecting indemnity from Alexandrians during the War of 1812. By Wm. Charles. *(Library of Congress)*

of Mount Eagle, afterward Eighth Lord, remained on the friendliest terms with the household at Mount Vernon, while holding the strongest of Loyalist convictions. Tradition has it that Washington personally saved him from molestation by the American troops.

The Alexandria Committee of Safety obtained and outfitted fifteen vessels for the protection of the town and the Potomac. On two occasions the people became much excited and badly frightened. Rumor was rife in 1775 that Governor Dunmore had dispatched an expedition of warships up the Potomac to "lay waste the towns and the country, capture Mrs. Washington, and burn Mount Vernon."[44] Martha Washington remained calm, and though finally persuaded by Colonel Mason to leave home, she stayed away one night only.

The second scare is revealed in a letter from the General's manager, Lund Washington, written in January 1776. "Alexandria is much alarmed and indeed the whole neighborhood," he wrote. "The women and children are leaving the town and stowing themselves in every hut they can find, out of reach of the enemy's cannon. Every wagon, cart and pack horse they can get is employed. The militia are all up, but not in arms, for indeed they have none, or at least very few."[45]

Mantel in the house of the late Mrs. Davidson Maigne, 220 South Royal Street, dates about 1800 and is a good example of the period, showing grace and restraint. Attention is drawn to the center panel in an interesting way

La Fayette, De Kalb, Rochambeau, John Paul Jones, and "Light Horse Harry" Lee, were in and out of Alexandria many times. On May 4, 1781, the Commander in Chief of the Continental Army recorded in his diary: "A letter from the Marq^s de la Fayette, dated at Alexandria on the 23rd, mentioned his having commenced his march that day for Fredericksburg"—that desertion had ceased, and that his detachment was in good spirits.[46] High morale and grand strategy brought victory for the Continental cause that October. Something like thirty-odd officers of the Revolution lived in or near Alexandria, or came to live here after the war. Sixteen of them became members of the Society of the Cincinnati, of which Washington was President General.

The Peace of 1783 revived strangulated commerce and construction. The harbor came to life. The brickmason and the carpenter took up their tools. Wheat and tobacco rolled in to fill again the empty warehouses. The citizens were gay and indulged themselves in festivities, as witness an old letter written from Alexandria on February 13, 1787:

Last Evening there was an elegant Ball in this Town, being the anniversary of General Washington's birth. No less than fifty Ladies elegantly dressed graced the Ball Room, tho the mud in our intolerable Streets was up to the Knees in Shoes (rather Boots) & Stockings.

Mr. Jenckes attended—says the Ball was agreeable for one so numerous. He has formed considerable acquaintances with the ladies, who are very agreeable but in general they talk rather too broad Irish for him.[47]

Brissot de Warville, who visited America in 1788, was impressed by the possibilities of Alexandria:

. . . where thirty or forty years ago there were only one or two houses, is now indeed smaller than Baltimore, but plans to surpass her. She is already quite as irregular in construction and as muddy. But there is more luxury evident at Alexandria, if a miserable luxury; you see servants in silk stockings, and their masters in boots.

At the end of the war the people of Alexandria imagined that the natural advantages of their situation, the salubrity of the air, the depth of the river channel and the safety of the harbour which can accomodate the largest ships and permit them to anchor close to the wharves, must unite with the richness of the back country to make their town the center of a large commerce. In consequence they are building on all sides, they have set up superb wharves and raised vast warehouses.

At the moment the expected commerce languishes. This is attributed to the heavy taxes. Whatever may be the cause many citizens are emigrating or planning to emigrate. Some ships of Alexandria are now trading regularly with the West Indies and at New Orleans.[48]

It was not long after the Revolution that the seat of the new federal

Classical Revival in mantel and doorway

government was selected near Alexandria. In fact, one old story has it that Alexandria was chosen as the site, and the patriot Washington was twitted with the advantages that would accrue to him, with such vast holdings of land so near the new capital. The tales go on that Washington waxed very angry and replied that never, if he could help it, should a public building be put south of the Potomac.

Be this as it may, the Virginia Assembly ceded to the federal government on December 3, 1789, a generous slice of Fairfax County to be incorporated with the State of Maryland's larger portion into a district for the federal capital, ten miles square. The Congress of the United States was pleased to accept this, and later an additional act of Congress of March 3, 1791, amended and repealed a part of the first act, naming Alexandria part of the ceded territory. And so for the next fifty-six years we have no longer Alexandria in Virginia, but Alexandria in the District of Columbia.

The Federal City (afterward Washington) which did not officially become the nation's capital until 1800, was an undrained marsh in 1790. Travelers visiting Alexandria about that time described it as having "upwards of three hundred houses," many "handsomely built."[49] In 1795 Thomas Twining passed through Alexandria and commented: "What struck me most was the vast number of houses which I saw building . . . the hammer and the trowel were at work everywhere, a cheering sight."[50] The Duc de la Rochefoucauld in the following year stated: "Alexandria is beyond all comparison the handsomest town in Virginia and indeed is among the finest in the United States."[51] That same year, 1796, Isaac Weld remarked, "Alexandria is one of the neatest towns in the United States. The houses are mostly of brick."[52]

Virginians were largely their own architects. Thomas Jefferson designed Monticello, the University of Virginia, and the Capitol at Richmond; George Mason built Gunston Hall; and George Washington directed the transformation of Mount Vernon from a simple villa into the famous mansion it is. Alexandria "Undertakers," or contractors, did the work—James Patterson in 1758 and Going Lamphire from 1773 onward for a number of years. One Mr. Sanders, was called in about roof troubles and afterwards dismissed. John Carlyle was the great gentleman architect and builder of Alexandria. He built his own fine house, he took over Christ Church in 1773 when James Parsons failed to complete his contract, and he also superintended the erection of the Presbyterian meetinghouse.

James Wren, Gentleman, is remembered as the designer of Christ Church in 1767. Thomas Fleming is referred to as a ship's carpenter and "one who is inclined to serve the Town." A story goes that George Coryell built a gate in Philadelphia which so pleased the first President that he persuaded him to move to Alexandria. True or not, the local *Gazette* carried Coryell's advertisements of building materials and he is known to have built a number of houses. Robert Brockett was building in 1785 the Presbyterian Manse. Benjamin Hallowell, William Fowle, and William Yeaton at a later time proved themselves able architects.

The designs of Alexandria houses derived from the Old Country, and follow the type of eighteenth century architecture found in the British Isles, especially Scotland. The general floor plans of Alexandria's homes are similar. With the *Builder's Companion and Workman's General Assistant,* it was well-nigh impossible to go wrong. This series of pamphlets, reprinted in 1762 by William Pain of London, offered the purest and best of classical designs. The Scottish founders adapted them to their needs, with the result that Alexandria differs from other Colonial towns in Virginia, as Scotland differs from England. The spiritual and physical variations are keenly sensed.

The interior trim of Alexandria's houses is simple and severe compared to the plantation houses lining the Virginia rivers; to the elaborate carving of the fine eighteenth century Charleston homes it seems plain and austere. Nonetheless, there is a substantial dignity about these houses that produces an atmosphere of calm, gracious peace not unlike the interiors of meetinghouses. Even the little brick-and-frame cottages partake of this same feeling and are remarkable for the charm of their inviting and harmonious rooms. The simple overmantels, chair rails, wide and low six-paneled doors hung on the proverbial H&L hinges, well proportioned rooms and large, hospitable fireplaces, all done in miniature, form interiors rare in scale, surprising in elegance, perfect in balance.

For the better part of ten years after the Revolution, buildings continued going up as rapidly as bricks could be made and artisans found to put them together. As the town grew, the gaps along the streets were filled. Alexandria assumed the character, not of Williamsburg or Annapolis, but rather of Philadelphia or some Old World town. By 1795 it wore an air of stability as row after row of fine brick buildings went up. Alexandria houses were city dwellings and homes of merchants. Comfortable and inviting they were, too, with a wealth of detail in finish

Varied were the designs and never were the twain alike

and appearance. Doorways and cornices for the outside; arches, mantels and paneling within. Very sad it is to relate how much of this has found its way into the museums of the country, and sadder still to tell how much has been wantonly destroyed. The New York Metropolitan Museum of Art houses one of the great rooms from Alexandria; the St. Louis Museum another; and some interior woodwork has found its way to Williamsburg.

Conceived and built as a trading center, by 1796, almost without exception, the first floor of every building was used as a place of business while the upper floors served as the family dwelling. This accounts for the more elaborate woodwork found on second floors. The Mutual Assurance Society archives reveal many instances of a store, countinghouse, office or shop located in a wing or attached building; likewise warehouses on the premises as well as along the water front.

ARTISANS AND TRADESMEN

Alexandrians owned and operated shipyards, sail lofts, ropewalks, lumber yards, brick kilns; print and apothecary shops; manufactories of harness, saddles, boots, shoes, mattresses, and cloth. And of course there were the taverns and hotels, inns and oyster houses, markets, stables, ferries, and fish wharves (where millions of herring were packed for export). Its citizens maintained churches, schools, academies, banks, fire companies, counting houses, and newspapers. They supported ministers, lawyers, doctors, dentists, oculists, cabinetmakers, artists, musicians, actors, merchants and a town militia. Mention has already been made of the important building professions—to the activities of house and ship carpenters, and the "undertakers," or contractors of the day.

Among the tradesmen and artisans of the town were watchmakers and clockmakers, jewelers, goldsmiths, coppersmiths, gunsmiths, blacksmiths, and ironmongers; confectioners, bakers and brewers; hatters, and wigmakers. Cottom & Stewart was a firm of publishers and vendors of the latest in literature. Joshua Delacour was a bookbinder who carried on his business in all its branches, not only supplying ladies with bandboxes, trunks, pasteboard stays and stomachers, but he also papered rooms in the neatest fashion. Books and stationery were imported by Joshua Merryman, who also advertised blotting paper, quills, ink powder, inkpots, sealing wax and wafers—in fact, all the adjuncts of polite correspondence.

Margaret Greetner set great store by her newly imported mangle, by which "silk, linen and cotton stockings, and other articles were smoothed and glossed in the most expeditious manner." She took in washing at "moderate terms" and apparently was the eighteenth century counterpart of our modern laundry. Joseph Delarue was her competitor in the dry-cleaning field, offering his services to ladies and gentlemen of the town and adjacent country as a scourer of silks, chintzes, and woolen clothes. Coachmaking was carried on by E. P. Taylor and Charles Jones. Unfortunately, records relating to Alexandria's early artisans are pathetically scanty or altogether lacking.

Alexandria in its heyday boasted as fine silver as could be found in the colony, and while there is a quantity of English silver thereabouts, much was made by her own craftsmen. It exists today in families who, while cherishing it for generations, have used it commonly for a century or more.

A partial list of silversmiths includes some nineteen or twenty names, for the earliest of whom there is any record, we must thank "the General,"

The Federal Period interpreted in iron

for it is in his ledgers that these first five names are found, noting some work done for Mount Vernon, usually of a repair nature. Salt spoons and ladles evidently saw hard service, or were kept so spick and span they had to go to the silversmith for frequent mending. In 1773 the Washington silver chest was the richer for a punch ladle made by William Dowdney. While this was in the making, one Edward Sandford was restoring a salt and mending a punch ladle. He also repaired Mrs. Washington's watch and made her a silver seal. The salt spoons were in the hands of one Charles Turner in 1775; and Mrs. Washington had a gold locket from one Philip Dawe. The punch ladle was out of order again in 1781 and had a new handle made by "Mr. Kanat."

About this time the Adam family of silversmiths began to attract attention. The first of that name in Alexandria was James Adam (1755-1798). He was working in Alexandria as early as 1771, and he who has an original Adam piece is either one of an ancient family in the town or a fortunate collector. The work of his son, John Adam (1780-1843), is more frequently found, and of the best type. The Adam grandson, William W.

(1817-1877), followed the trade of his progenitors, turning out good work certainly but in the Victorian idiom.

Charles Burnett, working in Alexandria in 1793, and probably as early as 1785, produced sauceboats, urns, tea sets, tankards, and so on. His flatware is usually distinguished by a shell motif, and gadroon edges finish and decorate many of his pieces. His work is very similar to his Philadelphia contemporaries.

Adam Lynn (1775-1836) was born in Alexandria, of Alexandria parents, the son of Colonel Adam Lynn, a Revolutionary officer and a member of the Society of the Cincinnati. He inherited property from his father, two lots of land on King and St. Asaph Streets. At the age of twenty-five, in 1800, he advertised himself as:

ADAM LYNN

Jeweler, Silver and Goldsmith, Silver Tea sets may be had to any pattern at short notice, warranted to equal any in America.

It is noted that in 1801 he "respectfully informs the public that he has commenced the clock and watchmaking business, in addition to that of jewelry. He has laid in a large assortment of the best materials in that line and is determined to give general satisfaction." Lynn's work is delicate and fine. Strangely, very little remains but what there is is satisfactory. He frequently decorated his flatware with a refined etching or gravure, his hollow ware with reeding. To the jewelry business Lynn combined another. In 1810 his advertisement read:

New Hardware Store
Adam Lynn & Co.

Have received by the Ship "Dumphries" from Liverpool, via Baltimore A Large and General Assortment . . . which they now offer for sale at their store corner King and Royal Streets—late occupied by Peter Sherron.

Lynn held several offices in the Masonic lodge and served for years as vestryman of St. Paul's Church. He had the added distinction of being drawn by M. de St. Memin.

A few spoons and ladles survive Mordecai Miller, 1790; John Duffey, 1793; George Duffey (1845-1880); James Ganet (1820-1830); William Cohen, 1833; Benjamin Barton, 1833; R. C. Acton, 1840; William A. Williams (1787-1846). The last-named craftsmen made the famous silver cup presented by the "grateful City Council" to the lovely Mrs. Lawrason for entertaining La Fayette in her home. John Pittman is listed

Top: Creamer, sugar and bowl by Charles Burnett. *Center:* Sauceboat and sugar urn by Charles Burnett, creamer by I. Adam. Owned by Mrs. John Howard Joynt. *Bottom:* Service by I. Adam. Owned by the Misses Snowden.

in a deed in 1801 as a goldsmith and silversmith, while the census for
1790 gives the names of Thomas Bird, William Galt, John Piper and
John Lawrason. In addition, from other deeds and advertisements, the
names of John Short (1784); James Galt (1801); Josiah Coryton, "late
of this town" (1801) are gleaned as watchmakers and clockmakers.

Slate roofing seems to have made its initial appearance around 1800.
In 1805 Joseph Riddle's dwelling house was "covered in copper" and
John Janney's warehouse in slate, and at least one building in "composi-
tion." At this date an insurance plat shows a tinsmith and coppersmith's
shop. The early roofs were covered in wood (*i.e.,* wooden shingles).

DECLINE AND RESURGENCE

With the death of George Washington in 1799, which emphasized the
close of the eighteenth century, the city whose prosperity seemed in some
mystic fashion to have developed and grown with him began a decline.

In 1803 came yellow fever, leaving desolation and mourning in its
wake. An English traveler wrote in 1807:

> Alexandria was about eight years ago a very flourishing place, but the losses
> sustained from the capture of American vessels by the French in the West Indies,
> occasioned many failures. In the year 1803, the yellow fever, which broke out
> there for the first time, carried off a number of its inhabitants. These shocks have
> so deeply affected the mercantile interest, that the town has but two or three
> ships in the trade with Great Britain; and there is little prospect of its ever at-
> taining to its former prosperity.[53]

Alexandria was further subjected to plagues. Cholera broke out in
1832, and people dropped dead in the streets while the population
shuddered. Illness, death, and burial was the fearsome sequence of only
a few hours. There was a Board of Health and a Quarantine Officer, but
ignorance of sanitation laws and preventive medicine resulted in appalling epidemics brought in by visiting vessels.

Fire, too, ravaged the town. There were two major conflagrations in
the early nineteenth century, one in 1810 and another in 1824, in each of
which at least fifty buildings were consumed. The fire in the latter year

all but demolished the west side of Fairfax Street between King and Prince Streets. George Washington is credited with having founded the first fire company and giving to the city what was then the finest of modern hand pumpers—a magnificent affair of red paint, brass trimmings, and leather buckets. A law of the town made it mandatory for each householder or proprietor of a dwelling or storehouse to furnish leather buckets of at least two-and-one-half-gallon capacity at "his or her expense"—in quantity equal to the stories of his house; no proprietor was expected, however, to provide more than three buckets. The buckets were numbered and lettered with the names of the owners, whose duty it was to send or carry them to any place where a fire broke out, or to "throw them into the street so that they may be taken there."[54]

The fire companies at the first alarm, in scarlet shirts, turned out on shortest notice, at a dead run on "shanks' mare." Woe betide the member who was late, for he was fined right heavily. Pumping by hand to put out a fire was a laborious affair and slackers were not tolerated. Even with the best of will and the most earnest of pumpers, the fires got out of hand and took a terrible toll of the early buildings. While insides were gutted, the walls often remained to contain again an interior of beauty and dignity.

Alexandria suffered more from the War of 1812 than from the Revolution. Before Washington fell to the British in 1814, Alexandria was forced to capitulate and had to pay a high indemnity for physical protection. This disaster, coupled with the failure of the canal which was to open up the vast Ohio country, all but wrecked the best financial hopes and plans of the city.

The opening of the Potomac River for navigation, to connect with the Ohio, was a project close to General Washington's heart. He had entertained this dream from the time of his first western venture in 1754. He calculated, plotted, and surveyed distances, and from 1770 onward his mind was set upon the accomplishment. In July of that year he was in correspondence with Thomas Johnson, to whom he wrote: "Till now I have not been able to enquire into the sentiments of any of the Gentlemen of this side in respect to the Scheme of opening inland navigation of the Potomac by private subscription."[55] Washington's trips to the Ohio, in October 1770 and again in September 1784—on both occasions accompanied by Dr. Craik—while in the interest of his western land holdings were also to forward this canal business.

All of this resulted in the founding of the Potomac Navigation Com-

pany in 1785, and Alexandria subscribed heavily to the bond issue. By
1829 the first steam locomotive was operating in America and the coming
of the steam engine was followed by the collapse of the canal project.
Thousands of local dollars were thus lost. When the deflation was complete, financial stagnation followed, from which Alexandria never entirely recovered. During these trying 1830s and 1840s many of her
younger men departed for the west hoping to better their fortunes.

Alexandrians did not take kindly to federal jurisdiction of their affairs, and within half a century from 1800—on February 3, 1846—a petition was presented from the citizens of the county and town of
Alexandria to the Virginia General Assembly, stating that they had
pending before Congress an application for recession to the Commonwealth of Virginia. They asked the Assembly for a law to accept them
back into the fold should their request be granted. By act of Congress,
dated July 9, 1846, it was provided that: "With the assent of the people
of the County and Town of Alexandria, that portion of the territory of
the District of Columbia ceded to the United States by the State of Virginia . . . receded and forever relinquished to the State of Virginia . . ."[56]

Virginia welcomed the recession as a mother would welcome home a
maltreated and divorced daughter. Alexandria County (later Arlington
County) and the City of Alexandria were accepted on March 13, 1847,
just two years short of the latter's centenary.

Fourteen years later the first blood of dreadful civil war was spilled
in Alexandria and the city found itself a pawn to arbitrament by the
sword. When General Robert E. Lee accepted the command of Confederate forces, a host of Alexandrians followed him into battle. To the
citizenry with Southern sympathies, war meant bitter severance once again
from Virginia. For the duration of the Civil War, Alexandria, under
federal jurisdiction again, became the capital of that part of the state
(West Virginia) which refused to secede with the Richmond government. To the old city came a governor and legislature with Northern
sympathies, making welcome any federal forces camping on the outskirts
of town. Old prints show the Union flag in the hands of marching
soldiers on King Street, and camps and cantonments, beginning at the
"Round House," extending for miles.

Even so, the best and noblest donned the gray, and Alexandria's own
marched out to become part of the 17th Virginia Infantry, C.S.A., upon
the bloody battlefields of the South.

With the close of the Civil War, prosperity departed. Fewer and fewer ships came to anchor in the Potomac port, until finally nothing remained to show the important part that Alexandria played for a century in the sea commerce of the world save rotted piles that once supported wharves, and a few grimy, scarred old warehouses whose collapsing roofs and loose bricks threatened the very life of the pedestrian.

Other wars have come and gone and each has had a conspicuous effect upon the town. The tragic era of 1861-65, binding our great nation into an indissoluble union, began likewise the process of cementation which steadfastly links Alexandria to the District of Columbia by bands that are basically nonpolitical (maybe stronger for that same reason). Paradoxically, Alexandria is a free city—part of Virginia, though not characteristic of the State; allied to the District, but no part of it.

Alexandria's cultural heritage has appealed for many reasons to Washington officialdom, and many persons prominent in national affairs have crossed the river to settle and to restore the gracious old homes of bygone days. George Washington's Alexandria is a city at once assured and self-conscious. Confident in its background, its venerable traditions, and its associations with the great in the country's development, Alexandria ponders its destiny.

All faithful sons and daughters, whether native or adopted, fondly hope that this bicentennial year of the city's existence may bring closer to fulfillment the famous toast voiced by La Fayette in 1824: "The City of Alexandria: May her prosperity and happiness more and more realize the fondest wishes of our venerated Washington!"

Adam Lynn, Silversmith. (By Saint Mèmin)

L'ENVOI

Where is the great seaport that was Alexandria? Where are the ships that plied their trade to the four corners of the earth, built, outfitted, loaded from this port, officered and manned by the men of this town? Where the great shipyards down whose ways slipped vessels of any magnitude; the ropewalks where black slaves trod the weary miles twisting the hemp to lift the sails made in Alexandria sail lofts? Where the great docks, wharves and warehouses that lined the water front?

Only phantom vessels, locked in the eternal secrets of the deep, float at anchor and crowd the harbor with a pale tracery of masts and rigging. Only the voices of sailors long silent float ashore on the breezes in a polyglot of languages, while ghostly laughter and oaths of those held in taverns by rum and sugar at three pence ha'penny disturbs the sobriety of the water front.

Gone are the shipyards. Upon ways destroyed by rot will rise no more the skeleton ribs of sloop nor barque nor brig.

Silent are the sail lofts. Long ago the last workman at day's end put down the canvas and the thread.

Empty are the ropewalks of docile slave and pungent hemp.

Cold are the bake ovens—crumbled the last biscuit . . .

The worn and polished cobbles are destitute of coach and four, of chariot and chair. Nor does the mail arrive by stage.

No more will hoops and wigs add allure to the progress of beauty —nor peruke nor smallclothes invest the beau with grandeur.

The factor and the sea captains have departed. The weary clerk has put up the last shutter; empty stools and blunted quills abandoned. Only the ledgers remain, free of blot and blemish to attest the skill and patience of the forgotten scribe.

An autumn moon lights the old town, turning to silver the tiny waves lapping the old sea wall, shimmering on the panes of dormer windows, silhouetting the high brick façades against the white night, outlining trim and cornice. Lighted transoms dimly reveal the white paneled doorways . . . Let us enter . . .

PART TWO

The Presence of George Washington 1749-1799

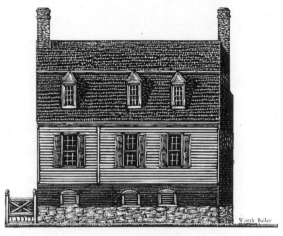

Chapter 1
William Ramsay: Romulus of Alexandria*

Some two hundred years ago a sturdy-bottomed little sailing ship riding at anchor in the port of Dumfries in Scotland, and bound for the port of Dumfries in Virginia, was boarded by a young Scotsman. No *parvenu* voyager he, but a young man of settled background and promising future, educated for his calling and going out to take his place in one of the Scottish firms trading in Virginia.

Our adventurer belonged to the Ramsay family of the noble house of Dalhousie, which goes back into Scottish history of the thirteenth century. King Edward I, in July 1298, spent the night at Dalhousie on his way to battle with William Wallace; and in 1400 Sir Alexander Ramsay defended the walls of Dalhousie against Henry IV. In 1633 William, Second Lord Ramsay, was created First Earl of Dalhousie. This young adventurer bore the name of the Second Lord, William. He was born in 1716 in Kirkendbrightshire in the Galloway district of Scotland, and he was destined to play no small part in his own particular sphere. He brought the integrity and industry of his native land to the new world shores, and was one of that band of Scotsmen of whom President Madison said, "Their commercial edicts served the colony as substantial legislation for many years."[1] These traits, added to vision, wisdom, sound morality and a tender nature, formed the character of the future first citizen of Alexandria.

---

*Historic Ramsay House, once the home of Alexandria's first mayor and oldest building standing in the city, miraculously escaped destruction by fire in 1942. Later threatened by the "wheels of progress," it was saved by heroic efforts of Alexandria antiquarians who persuaded the city fathers to purchase the structure as a gesture to the 1949 anniversary. As this book goes to press an active campaign is under way by Alexandria historical societies to raise funds for restoration.

The year 1744 found William Ramsay settled in business with John Carlyle, trading under the name of Carlyle & Ramsay in the village of Belle Haven. This little settlement lay on the banks of the upper Potomac behind the Great Hunting Creek warehouse.

Ramsay early sensed that the large harbor of Belle Haven with its deep water and fine approach was a better situation for a town than many then being agitated before the Burgesses. Forming friendships with Colonel Fairfax, Lawrence Washington, George Mason, George Johnston, and other large planters, he impressed them with the importance of this situation as a site of great promise for a city and a port.[2]

When this dream became an accomplished fact it was a natural conclusion that William Ramsay was one of the seven men chosen by the Virginia Assembly for the purpose of laying out the town at Hunting Creek warehouse.[3]

His faith in Alexandria was supported by his pocketbook. At the first auction of lots on July 13, 1749, he bought lots Nos. 46 and 47; and he never lost an opportunity to invest his hard and dangerously earned money in the soil of his begotten city.

At the outbreak of the French and Indian War he was appointed (on George Washington's recommendation) Commissary in 1756. Many letters dealing with commissary affairs, and more interesting, the movement of troops, written from Rays Town are among the Washington papers.

His partnership with Carlyle was followed by one with John Dixon which was dissolved in 1757, when Dixon returned to England and his native Whitehaven. Ramsay incurred a large debt by buying Dixon's interests. He wrote to Washington in July 1757, saying he had been extremely unfortunate in all his affairs, and asking for a loan of £250, saying, "I have made application to the monied ones—My L^d Fx, Mr Speaker, Mr Corbin, Mr Cary and many others with^t success wch I put to the Acco^t of my perverse fortune, not to the want of ability to serve me." These gentlemen were among the richest and most influential men in the colony, but George, a young colonel of militia, scraped up £80 in August and another £70 in September, to lend his good friend and mentor.

William Ramsay had given Washington some sound advice in September 1756, when the young Colonel was somewhat upset by criticism of militia officers and not too happy in his official duties. Ramsay wrote, ". . . Know sir, that Ev'ry Gent^n in an exalted Station raises envy & Ev'ry person takes the Liberty of judging or rather determining (with judging) from appearances (or information) without weighing circumstances, or the proper causes, on wch their judgem^t ought to be founded. . . . Upon the whole, S^r, triumph in your innocency, your disinterestedness, your unwearied Application & Zeal for your country's good, determine you to continue in its service at a time there may be the greatest call for you, & when probably some signal Day may mark you the bravest (as hitherto you have been) of persons . . ."[4]

Ramsay served Alexandria some thirty-six years as a public servant. He was town overseer, census taker, postmaster, member of the Committee of Safety, colonel of the militia regiment, adjuster of weights and seals with John Carlyle at Hunting Creek warehouse in 1754, town trustee, mayor, and did his duty as gentleman justice for many years, beginning that service prior to the settlement of Alexandria. Tradition has it that he was the most beloved citizen of Alexandria, which is certainly confirmed. In 1761 he was elected by his fellow townsmen their first and only Lord Mayor. The enthusiastic inhabitants decorated him with a golden chain bearing a medal. "Upon one side was represented the infant state of Alexandria and its commodious harbour, with these words in the legend, '*Alexandria Translate et Renate Auspice Deo,*' and in the exerque, '*Condita Reg^o Geo. II. An. Dom. 1649.*' The reverse has this inscription: '*Dig^{mo} Dom^{no} Guilielmo Ramsay. Romulo Alexandriae Urbisque Patri, Consuli Primo. Bene Merenti. An. Dom. 1761.*' "[5]

The election and investment over, the *Maryland Gazette* tells us, "the Lord Mayor and Common Council preceded by officers of State Sword and Mace bearers and accompanied by many gentlemen of the town and county, wearing blue sashes under crosses, made a grand procession . . . with drums, trumpets and a band of music, colors flying." The shipping in the harbor displayed "flags and banners while guns fired during the afternoon." A "very elegant entertainment was prepared at the Coffee House," where the new Lord Mayor and his entourage sat down to a sumptuous repast. This was followed by a ball given by the Scottish gentlemen "at which a numerous and brilliant company of ladies danced." Ceremonies ended with fireworks, bonfires, and "other demonstrations." Perhaps this enthusiasm may be somewhat explained by the fact that this celebration took place on St. Andrew's Day.[6]

In 1765 Ramsay went back to Scotland, whether to see again his family or on business is not revealed. But that he had a most remarkable reception cannot be questioned. Dumfries and Kirkendbright conferred extraordinary honor upon him. Yellowed by age, two pieces of engraved parchment are treasured by his descendants. These towns each made him a "Burgess," the most signal distinction to be conferred upon a visitor.

Besides the original lots which William Ramsay purchased on July 13, 1749 (Nos. 46 and 47 for forty-six *pistoles*), he later purchased lot No. 34. Augustine Washington forfeited his lots, Nos. 64 and 65, for neglecting to build within the required time, and Ramsay bought this property. When William Seawell, the peruke-maker, lost his holdings for indebtedness, Ramsay also acquired lot No. 61. He owned the Royal George, a tavern of importance, and had numbers of slaves and indentured workmen. In 1749 he paid taxes on seven blacks and seven whites. In 1782 he owned twenty-one blacks, four horses and a coach. His will, dated the month before his death, enumerated seven slaves by name, specifying special considerations for two, *viz:* "that they may be better cloathed both in Winter and Summer than is common for slaves, and that they be particularly taken good care of as a reward for their long and faithful services."

William Ramsay married Ann McCarty, daughter of Dennis McCarty Sr. and his wife Sarah Ball, who was a kinswoman of George Washington and sister of Mrs. George Johnston. Ann McCarty Ramsay was one of those women of the day who by the laws of the land lost their property and identity with marriage. Yet, when this retiring, gentle person was called upon to raise funds in Alexandria and Fairfax County, no modern matron working for bond drive or Red Cross ever did a more successful work. Thomas Jefferson, as Governor of Virginia, in a letter from Richmond written on August 4, 1780, to General Edward Stevens, attached a list of "female Contributions, in aid of the War, Probably in 1780." Among the thirteen ladies who gave their watch chains, diamond drops and rings is the name of "Mrs. Anne Ramsay (for Fairfax), one halfjoe, three guineas, three pistareens, one bit. Do. for do. paper money, bundle No. 1, twenty thousand dollars, No. 2, twenty-seven thousand dollars, No. 3, fifteen thousand dollars, No. 4, thirteen thousand five hundred and eighteen dollars and one third.'"[7]

This excellent wife took her Presbyterian husband into the Established Church and we find Washington crediting him with £33 for pew No. 20 in Alexandria (Christ) Church in January 1773. But the Presbyterian citadel of learning was the choice over William and Mary College when time came for the eldest son, William Jr., to prepare for a professional career. The strict discipline of Old Nassau was more to the liking of

Scottish conservatism than the laxness reported among students and faculty at the Williamsburg institution. At Princeton young William studied medicine under Dr. Benjamin Rush. In 1775, after joining the General in winter headquarters at Cambridge, Mrs. Washington wrote the family that she had seen young Ramsay as she passed through Princeton and that "he was very well but did not talk of comeing home soon."[8] Maybe this was a woman's subtle way of breaking the news of young William's plans to follow the Continental cause wherever it might lead. As surgeon in the army, he served throughout the Revolutionary War.

Following the custom, the elder William Ramsay placed his second son in trade with the firm of Jennifer & Hooe in Dumfries. From Alexandria, on December 5, 1774, he sent young Dennis, then a lad of eighteen years, the following letter brimming with sound parental advice and Scottish business acumen:

Dear Dennis

Tho' you have been but a short time from us, I cannot help informing you that we are all well—But as a Parent, I must say more but I hope you are so well grounded in the principals I would inculcate, that it need only put you in mind of the duties we owe to the supreme Being & our fellow Men—your first duty my dear Son, is to your God, do not by any means neglect your duty in paying your adorations & supplications to him for a blessing on your endeavors, & your gratefull acknowledgements for every benefit and money you receive, which you & I every day experience—Your next duty is to your Parents, who, I hope you will pay that respect to, you always have done, & continue to listen to their advice with proper attention, because you must be assured, it flows from the parental and affectionate regard they have for you and your welfare here & hereafter. Your next duty is to your fellow Men, more especialy to your employer, his interest demands your justice, your diligence and utmost attention to his business and interest, your secrets & his relating to your affairs you must religiously keep, mind his business only, do not intermedle with that of other peoples, and avoid entering into any dispute with them: you may gain much observation & society, but nothing by disputetation. Let your intimates be few and those well chosen, for the formation of youth depends on the companions they chuse, therefore in this be very cautious. I will not say any more to you on this head but hope that you will conduct yourself as hitherto you have done & shun even the Appearance of evil. When yᵒ lodge by yourself be cautious in securing your Windows and doors, and if you cou'd, as probably you may, get some agreeable young fellow to sleep with you if not always, very often; he wou'd be company to you, and made your time less lonesome, but your own prudence will suggest to you these things better than I can —When your Bed and Chest comes down, I will send Anthony down to you, he can make your fire, clean your Shoes, fetch you water &c . . . As I mentioned

Bill of Lading to William Ramsay at Bellehaven, dated 1751. *(Ramsay Papers)*

to you, that what you now get from your industry shall be your own, besides, I will help you all that I can 'till you are of age, please God to bless me & you with the sight of that day, I will strain every nerve to set you forward in the World, your behavior I hope will entitle you to it, and give your Mother and me the highest pleasure we can hope for here, that is, your doing well—If you want a Waistcoat and Breeches you may get them in town yourself. Mr. Hooe says that he will immediately send you some Rum & Sugar on their Acco[t] to dispose off in the Wholesale way, that you may take your choice out of it to retain on your own Account—Be cautious and do not trust. I do not know my dear Dennis anything I can say more to you at this time. I expect to hear from you next Post and that you will be particular with regard to your situation &c. Your Mother gives her blessing to y°, all your sisters,

I am, my dear Dennis, your most Affectionate Father,

WM RAMSAY[9]

When war came, Denny Ramsay, like his brother, threw his lot with the cause of liberty and served with distinction in the army, reaching the rank of colonel.

Dennis Ramsay closely followed in the footsteps of his father. Both served as mayor of the town and it was the official duty of both to address General Washington upon commemorative occasions—William in 1781 after Yorktown, and Dennis in 1789 when the General paused in Alexandria on his way to be inaugurated as President of the new republic. Both father and son were Freemasons and members of the Sun Fire Company.

After the death of Martha Washington's little daughter, Patsy Custis, her empty heart sought solace in association with the young daughters of her friends. The girls of Alexandria kept the carriage wheels rolling to

Mount Vernon, where they were joyfully received, and where they were
nearly always numerous enough to make a gay evening. The young ladies
from the houses of Carlyle, Dalton and Ramsay were near neighbors in
Alexandria and frequenters of Mount Vernon, as were the Misses Craik,
Herbert, Fitzhugh, Lee, and Fendall, whose presence brightened the
mansion house with girlish laughter and confidences. At these gatherings
none was held in more affection than the young daughter of William and
Ann McCarty Ramsay. Where could a more charming letter be found
than this written by the hand of Martha Washington one hundred and
seventy-four years ago, within the sounds of the guns of Bunker Hill, to
Mistress Betty Ramsay:

Cambridge
December the 30th 1775

Dear Miss

I now set down to tell you that I arrived hear safe, and our party all well—we
were fortunate in our time of setting out as the weather proved fine all the time
we were on the road—I did not reach Phila^d till the tuesday after I left home,
we were so attended and the gentlemen so kind, that I am lade under obligations
to them that I shall not for get soon. I dont dout but you have seen the Figuer
our arrival made in the Philadelphia paper—and I left it in as great pomp as if
I had been a very great some body.

I have waited some days to collect something to tell, but allass there is nothing
but what you will find in the papers—every person seems to be chearfull and
happy hear—some days we hear a number of Cannon and shells from Boston
and Bunkers Hill, but it does not seem to surprise any one but me; I confess I
shuder everytime I hear the sound of a gun—I have been to dinner with two of
the Generals, Lee & Putnam and I just took a look at pore Boston—& Charlestown—from prospect Hill Charlestown has only a few chimneys standing in it,
there seems to be a number of very fine Buildings in Boston but God knows how
long they will stand; they are pulling up all the warfs for fire wood—to me that
never see any thing of war, the preparations are very terable indead, but I
endevor to keep my fears to my self as well as I can.

Your Friends Mr Harrison & Henly are boath very well, and I think they are
fatter than they were when they came to the Camp—and Capt. Baylor is a lusty
man to what he was when you see him. The girls may rest satisfied on Mr. Har-
risons account for he seems two fond of his country to give his heart to any but
one of his Virginia Friends, there are but two Young Laidis in Cambridge, and
a very great number of Gentlemen so you may guess how much is made of
them—but neither of them is pritty I think.

This is a beautyfull Country, and we had a very pleasant journey through
New england, and had the pleasure to find the G[eneral] very well—we came
within the month from home to the Camp.

I see your Brother at princeton he was very well but did not talk of comeing
home soon.

Plese to give my love and good wishes to your mamma & grand mamma, Mr. Ramsay and Family, my compliments to all enquiring Freinds, the good gentlemen that came with me up to Baltimore, and Mrs. Herbert—in which the general and Mr. and Mrs. Custis join, please to remember us to Mr. and Mrs. McCarty and Family.

I am Dear miss your most affectionate Friend and Well &C

MARTHA WASHINGTON.[10]

Ramsay did not wait for death to close his eyes ere he provided for his children. As early as 1777, and probably before, he divided his original purchase of lots Nos. 46 and 47 among his eight children. There is a much-worn old plat still in the hands of his descendants showing this division; on file at Fairfax Court House there is a deed to his youngest son, Dennis, for that part of his lot No. 47 fronting on Fairfax and King Streets, "Beginning at the S.W. corner of said lot extending north up Fairfax 90 feet more or less to Ramsay's Alley, then east down said alley 75 feet more or less, then South 90 feet to King Street, and then West with King 75 feet to the beginning with all houses warehouses Buildings, etc."

To his eldest son and namesake he gave his dwelling house and lot lying to the north of the alley. As the custom of primogeniture prevailed it was but natural that William Jr. fell heir to the dwelling house of his father. At the time of this gift in December 1784, William reserved to himself an "absolute right and title to take away as much earth or dirt from said ground even up to my Dwelling House, if necessary without prejudice to the said House to be applied towards filling up my wharf and Peers until they are finished . . ."[11] After the death of his father, William Jr., bachelor, "farm let" to his brother, the married Dennis, for the full term of ten years from the 10th day of May last [1785], "the rent to be fixed by Robert McCrea, John Allison, or any other person whom they shall choose—the lot lying and being on the north side of King Street and the east side of Fairfax, beginning upon Fairfax Street ten feet south of the south end of the Kitchen, which stands upon the said street belonging to William Ramsay, then running east sixty-six feet parallel to King, then north parallel with Fairfax twenty-five feet, then with a line parallel to King West twenty-two feet, including a Brick Smoke House, then with a line parallel to Fairfax north to a four-foot alley lately laid out in the said lott by William Ramsay, Esq., deceased, then East with the line of the alley 84 feet, then south to Ramsays Alley then West parallel to King until it reaches Fairfax Street, then with Fairfax and binding there upon to the beginning and all Buildings, Houses, Yards, Gardens,

Stables, to the said premises belonging or in any wise pertaining. Furthermore Dennis Ramsay may erect upon the premises a Kitchen in such part as will be most convenient, and at the expiration of the lease Dennis Ramsay has Liberty to remove the same from the premises."[12] Ten years later, on July 6, 1795, William Ramsay Jr. sold this property to Guy Atkinson. This gentleman owned the property until his death in 1835 and requested in his will, probated July 14 of that year, that his children reside "in my present mansion."

This is the house standing today at 113 North Fairfax Street,* and unless other research at a later day denies the assumption that this brick mansion was the last home of the Romulus of Alexandria, it is so declared.

The little white frame clapboard house with the Dutch roof, standing on the northeast corner of King and Fairfax Streets was certainly the property of William Ramsay—probably his office or kitchen, and later occupied by the descendants of his son, Dennis, after additions and improvements. The architect who is restoring this ancient and quaint house thinks that it is far older than the town of Alexandria, and that it is not now established upon the original foundation, but has been moved over from another location. It is interesting to think that it might have been part of Carlyle & Ramsay's original office in Belle Haven in 1744.

On February 12, 1795, George Washington was at Mount Vernon happily engaged in planning his garden and planting his shrubs when he "Received an Invitation to the Funeral of Willm. Ramsay, Esqr., of Alexandria, the oldest Inhabitt. of the Town; and went up. Walked in a procession as a free mason, Mr. Ramsay in his life being one, and now buried with the ceremonies and honors due to one."[13]

A few days later the town's newspaper carried the following tribute:

MEMORIAL

On the 10th, instand departed this Life, in the 69th year of his age, WILLIAM RAMSAY, Esq., a Gentleman generally esteemed for the humane and generous sentiments of his heart, as well as for his uprightness and integrity, throughout a long and active life.

This Gentleman first proposed and promoted the establishment of the town of Alexandria, and was its first inhabitant. He was consoled on the verge of life, with the reflection of having acted his part well, and of having reared and leaving to represent him a numerous and amiable family, in possession of as much happiness as generally falls to the lot of humanity. Thus he met the lingering,

*Owner: Miss Frona Matthews.

but certain approach of death with a composure and resignation of mind very remarkable and truly exemplary.

His remains were interred on the 12th, in the Episcopal Church Yard, and attended by a very numerous and respectable company, preceeded by the Brotherhood of Free Masons in procession with the solemnities usual on such occasions.[14]

Within less than two months, Washington, still at work upon his garden, grafting cherry trees, was interrupted to go to Alexandria to "attend the Funeral of Mrs. Ramsay who died (after a lingering illness) on Friday last . . . Dined at Mr. Muir's and after the funer[l] obseques were ended, returned home."[15] Again was spread upon the sheets of the town paper an obituary:

MEMORIAL

On Saturday last departed this life, Mrs. ANN RAMSAY, relect of the late WM. RAMSAY, Esq., in the 55th years of her age.

The amiable character of this lady, exemplified in her conduct as a wife, a mother, and a neighbour, as it procured her through life the general esteem and affection of all who knew her, will render her loss long regretted not only by her nearer relations, but by the inhabitants of this town, and neighbourhood of every rank and description, to whom her benevolence and humanity displayed in numberless good offices, and her agreeable deportment have heretofore been a social blessing and comfort.

On Monday her remains were interred with every mark of respect, contiguous to the grave of her late deceased husband.[16]

The General had seen the "Romulus of Alexandria" to the grave. Fourteen years later the latter's son served as honorary pallbearer for the Father of His Country at Mount Vernon, on that fateful December 18, 1799.

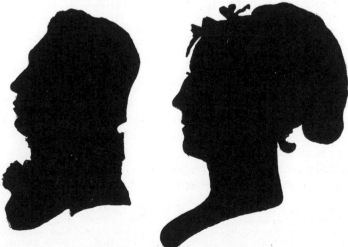

Mr. and Mrs. Dennis Ramsay

Chapter 2
John Carlyle and His House*

In an ancient will book at Fairfax Court House is the inventory of a gentleman's estate—household fabrics, mahogany and walnut furniture, family pictures, maps, prints, books, silverware, glassware, chinaware, and all manner of utensils, and drawers of "Trumpery!" More personal items imply a rich wardrobe and a man who doubtless cut a figure in society, for the list of apparel is long, containing, "1 scarlet cloth jacket with broad gold lace," "1 crimson velvet jacket with broad gold lace," "1 pair scarlet breaches with gold knee bands," "1 silver tobacco box," "1 tortoise shell ditto with silver top," "2 pair silver shoe buckles and 1 pair gold studds," "24 silver large coat buttons and 1 stock buckle," "1 box with 4 wiggs," etc.[1]

Another entry in a more ancient tome reads:

At a court held for the County of Fairfax, 19th March, 1754. Present John Colvill, Geo. Wm. Fairfax, John West, William Ramsay and Thomas Colvill, Gentlemen Justices.

Mr. John Carlyle produced a commission from the Honorable the Governor under the seal of the Colony appointing him Commissary of provisions and stores for an expedition intended to the River Ohio pursuant to which he took the oaths according to Law, repeated and subscribed to the Test . . . Lieutenant Colº George Washington, Lieutenant John West Jr. and James Townes pursuant to their military commissions from the Honorable the Governor took the oaths according to Law and subscribed to the Test.[2]

---

*Like nearby Ramsay House, the home of John Carlyle has also been threatened by business interests and was in danger of demolition just before the outbreak of World War II. It was saved by Mr. Lloyd L. Scheffer who acquired the property from the Wagar estate and continues to maintain the residence as a historic house museum. Entrance to the Carlyle Home is through the lobby of the Wagar apartments at 123 North Fairfax Street.

John Carlyle's Alexandria Mansion

Military echoes are not lacking from the inventory of his possessions. Is it possible that "1 Blue cloth coat with vellam holes"[3] related to his military service as major of Virginia militia? Was this perchance the coat worn by Major Carlyle in 1755 when the Redcoats of His Britannic Majesty's forces and the Virginia Militia fought under General Edward Braddock and met defeat at Great Meadows at the hands of the French and Indians? Major Carlyle was quartermaster in those days, with the mission of scouring the countryside for horses and forage. Objects of military use more easily picked out of the list taken by his executors include a spyglass, guns, pistols, swords, saddles, saddlebags, holsters, a powder horn and "2 spontoons." It is a local tradition that a store of these latter antique weapons were left behind in Alexandria by Brad-

Mantel in the dining room

dock's direction and that they constituted part of the equipment of the town watchmen until the outbreak of the War Between the States.

John Carlyle was a Scotsman of gentle birth, of the Limkilns branch of Carlyles of Torthorwald Castle. He left his home in Dumfrieshire for Dumfries in Virginia at the age of twenty to enter one of the Scottish shipping firms in that town in the year 1740. Foreseeing the end of that port, he moved to the village of Belle Haven, and with John Dalton set

John Carlyle's shell and silver snuffbox. Listed and described in the inventory of his estate

up in the mercantile and shipping business by 1744. This firm, under the name of Carlyle & Dalton, was destined to become the most important one in the new port, and John Carlyle the leading citizen. He was one of the influential men in Fairfax County who agitated for a town at Belle Haven, at the Hunting Creek warehouse. He was selected by the assembly as one of the incorporators of the town of Alexandria, and as one of the first trustees. Active in the town from the beginning, he helped build the courthouse and market place. He was the town's first "Overseer." In 1755 he was ordered to build a warehouse at Point Lumley, a hundred feet long, twenty feet wide, with thirteen-foot pitch, as well as to build roads and clear streets.

Carlyle bought the third lot put up for auction on July 13, 1749, No. 41, paying thirty *pistoles*. As the auction continued, he purchased another lot adjoining the first for sixteen *pistoles*. Upon his two lots he erected in 1752 the greatest private house in Alexandria for two or more decades, and furnished it with the best his ships could carry.

The Carlyle house stands high above the river and so strong and thick are the foundations that tradition has it they were early fortifications against the Indians. The house of stone is oblong, being almost as long again as it is wide and is believed originally to have had connecting

Portrait of John Carlyle's mother, Rachel Carlyle, which hung always above her son's bed

wings. Two-and-a-half stories high, large twin chimneys rise out of the hipped roof and three dormer windows break the front and back. Double galleries stretch across the river end, and before modern buildings obstructed the view, the river could be viewed for miles in each direction.

Inside, a large hall divides the house. A stairway that has neither the appearance nor character of so old a house, and is doubtless an "improvement," winds up to the second floor. Four rooms open into this hall —fine rooms, too—but the blue or drawing room is the gem, architecturally and historically. This is paneled from floor to ceiling. There are three windows with low window seats and heavy paneled blinds which become a part of the jambs when closed. Over the doorways are elaborate pediments, with broken arches. The chair rail is carved in a fret pattern and the dog-eared fireplace mold in the familiar egg-and-dart design. In the overmantel, double dog-eared molding outlines the center panel and two flat fluted pilasters reach from mantelshelf to the heavy modillioned cornice which is carved in alternating modillions and rosettes. The room is sixteen by eighteen feet, painted a light slate blue with white or cream trim. On the second floor five comfortable bedchambers open upon a narrow hall.

To this home Carlyle brought his first wife, Sarah Fairfax, whom he married in 1748. She was the daughter of Colonel William Fairfax of Belvoir, sister of Ann Fairfax Washington and George William Fairfax. After her death in 1761, when Carlyle married Sybil West, he named their only son for his well loved brother-in-law, George William Fairfax. When his will was opened, it was by the side of Sarah he wished to be buried: "As to my Body, I desire it may be interred under the Tombstone in the enclosed ground in the Presbyterian Yard near where my first wife and children are interred."[4]

This house was the social and political center of Alexandria. Such men as Charles Carroll, Aaron Burr, John Paul Jones, John Marshall, Thomas Jefferson, George Mason, George Washington, and the two Fairfaxes are but a few of those who gathered here for good food, good wine, and better talk. Any visitor of importance was entertained at "coffee"; the house was often filled with music, and "balls" were common.

The "Congress of Alexandria" met here Monday, April 14, 1755, and on the following Tuesday and Wednesday, when with Braddock and the five colonial governors plans were made for concerted action against the French and Indians. Here that famous letter, still in existence, was

Mantel in the music room. Probably a later "improvement"

written, urging upon the British government the necessity of taxing the colonies. This letter set into movement a chain of events disastrous to the mother country. It resulted in the loathed Stamp Act and led ultimately to the Revolution of 1775.

Carlyle was appointed collector of His Majesty's customs on the South Potomac in 1758, succeeding his father-in-law, William Fairfax. In 1762 he was importing race horses into the colony. These were imported, "just as they imported Madeira wine and other luxuries." One of the early Maryland gazettes of July 29, 1762 carries the following advertisement:

Imported by Carlyle & Dalton in the ship *Christian*, Captain Stanly, and for sale, three horses [Thorne's Starling: Smith's Hero, and Leary's Old England] and three mares [the other two being the Rock-mares Nos. 1 and 2] of full blood, viz: A *ch. m.* with a star and two white heels behind, eight years old: Got by Wilson's Chestnut Arabian: her dam by Slipby, brother to Snap's dam; and out of Menil [sic] the dam of Trunnion. Menil was got by Partner: out of Sampson's-Sister, which was got by Greyhound: her grandam by Curwen's Bay Barb: her g. grandam by Ld. D'Arcy's Arabian: her dam by Whiteshirt: out of a famous mare of Ld. Montagu's.

JOHN CARLYLE[5]

Alexandria, Va., July 1762.

In 1772 Carlyle took over the incomplete work on Christ Church and carried it to completion. In 1773 he bought pew No. 19. In 1774 he built the Presbyterian meetinghouse. In between times he was hunting at Belvoir and Mount Vernon, dancing at Alexandria assemblies, sitting as town trustee and gentleman justice, journeying to England and back, laying out and planting his garden, taking part in long, hot arguments with his family and neighbors in the ever-widening breach between the colonies and the mother country, breeding race horses, and joining in the frolics of the Jockey Club. Heir to a title old and honorable as it was, he ardently espoused the cause of the colonies. Too ill for active military service, he nevertheless served as a member of the Committee of Safety until his death in 1780, at the age of sixty.

John Carlyle divided his lands, named after the Scottish family holdings, Limkiln, Bridekirk, Torthorwald Taken, between his two grandsons, Carlyle Fairfax Whiting and John Carlyle Herbert. To his daughter, Sarah Herbert, he left thirty feet on Fairfax Street and one hundred feet on Cameron Street, to include his dryware house. The mansion and all other property were for a brief period the property of his only son.

In his will he expressed the utmost concern for the education of this boy, George William Carlyle, and urged his executors to spare no expense and to send him to the best schools. Alas, for the plans of men! The lad, fired by the talk of father and friends, was serving in Lee's Legion in 1781, and ere John Carlyle was moldering in his grave this boy of seventeen years, spirited, brave, heir to large estates, great fortune and honorable name, and to the title of Lord Carlyle, was dead at Eutaw Springs, led by that boy hardly older than himself "Light Horse Harry" Lee.

Enough of serious and sad history; let us in lighter vein go once more into the lovely paneled blue room where not only weighty conferences occurred, but where, in lace and satin, noble figures threw aside the cares of state and trod a measure to the tinkling of the spinet; where games of cards were indulged in and the *pistoles* changed hands. Let us go into the dining room with its fine Adam mantel and its mahogany doors, and visualize again the terrapin and the canvasback, the Madeira and Port so abundantly provided from that great kitchen below, and the most famous wine cellar of its day in Alexandria. Let us stroll in the still lovely garden where the aroma of box and honeysuckle mingle, and turn our thoughts once more to the inmates of this fine, old house. Built in the days when Virginia was a man's world, when men who wore satin, velvet and damask were masters of the art of fighting, riding, drinking, eating, and wooing. When a man knew what he wanted, and got it by God's help and his own tenacity, enjoying himself right lustily in the getting. Perchance Major John Carlyle, clad in Saxon green laced with silver, will be wandering up and down his box-bordered paths with his first love, Sarah Fairfax, watching the moon light up the rigging of Carlyle & Dalton's great ships at anchor just at the foot of the garden.

Chapter 3
The Married Houses*

When the new town of Alexandria was laid out, John Dalton purchased, on July 13, 1749, the first lot put up for sale (No. 36) for the sum of nineteen *pistoles*. The lot faced the Potomac River and was bounded by Water (now Lee) Street, Fairfax Street and lot No. 37. When the latter lot, which lay on Cameron and Fairfax, was put up later in the day, it was purchased by Dalton for sixteen *pistoles*.

Within three years Dalton had finished a small frame-and-brick cottage, neatly paneled, in which he is purported to have lived and died. The house faced on Cameron Street, standing about the middle of lot No. 37, with an extensive garden running the depth of the premises to the river, surrounded by outbuildings, orchards, wells, and so on, as was the custom of the times. His will mentioned the fact that he lived on this lot and left to his daughter, Jenny Dalton (later Mrs. Thomas Herbert), his new brick building on the corner of Fairfax and Cameron. His will further stated that the house must be finished out of his estate. To his daughter, Catherine (later Mrs. William Bird), he left the remainder of the lot which included his dwelling and another house on that same lot, at the time occupied by John Page.

On February 27, 1750, John Dalton succeeded Richard Osborn as a trustee of the town. His appointment was the first after the original selection of trustees by the assembly in Williamsburg.

John Dalton was a partner of John Carlyle in the firm of Carlyle & Dalton, which for many years acted as agent for the Mount Vernon produce. He was a pew owner with George Washington at Christ

---

*209-211 North Fairfax Street. Owner: Mrs. Herbert E. Marshburn.

The old Clapboard House on the John Dalton property and believed to have been his original house. *(Courtesy of Mr. Frank McCarthy)*

Church, which he served as vestryman. With his wife and daughter, he was a frequent visitor at Mount Vernon and a later chronicler has asserted that he barely missed becoming the General's father-in-law. A fox-hunter and horse-lover, in a company of Alexandria gentlemen or alone, he hunted with Washington and bred his mares to the blooded Mount Vernon stud.

On January 12, 1769, Washington went up to Alexandria to "ye Monthly Ball." He lodged with Captain Dalton and the next day being very bad he was "confined there till afternoon by rain."[1] Sometimes when attending court he "lodged at Captn. Dalton's."[2]

John Dalton's bequest to his daughter, Catherine, included the home place. On April 24, 1793, Catherine and her husband, William Bird, sold to Jonah Thompson and David Findley for £1,500 (about $7,500) the property described as being in Fairfax Street, 60 feet to the north of Cameron, and extending north upon Fairfax Street 119 feet 3 inches to the line of Herbert, Potts and Wilson, thence East parallel to Cameron to cross Water and Union Streets into the Potomac River, thence with a line parallel to Fairfax south 119 feet 3 inches, and included houses,

Jonah Thompson's House purchased from John Dalton's daughter, Catherine Bird

buildings, streets, lanes, alleys, and so on. But the Birds reserved the right
to the "use and occupation of the dwelling House now occupied" and the
kitchen and garden, until the "1st day of October next" and also reserved
unto Lanty Crowe the house "demised unto him to the end of his term,
he paying the annual rent thereof unto the said Jonah Thompson and
David Findley."[3] Findley died within the year and Jonah Thompson
bought from Amelia Findley, the mother and heir of David Findley,
equal and undivided portion of the already described lot and paid her
the sum of £500 12s.

Jonah Thompson was an important citizen of Alexandria. He was a
shipping merchant, banker and large property owner. He married Margaret Peyton and they had three sons, Israel, William Edward, and James;
a daughter, Mary Ann, married a Mr. Popham, and another daughter,
Eugenia, married a Mr. Morgan.

In 1809 Jonah Thompson mortgaged this property to the Bank of
Alexandria for $13,500, which he paid within four years. In May 1850,
the heirs of Jonah Thompson sold to Benjamin Hallowell for $4,600 a
lot beginning at the south side of the alley which divided the block,
running south 43 feet 7 inches. Benjamin Hallowell, in turn, sold to
James S. Hallowell for nine thousand dollars in April 1854, and from
James S. Hallowell and his wife the property passed through various
hands until it became St. Mary's Academy.

The Jonah Thompson house, part of it at least already built in 1793, is
one of the most interesting houses to be found anywhere. It is unusually
large and has two handsome arched stone entrances. One, although
similar, obviously was added, as the line of demarcation is plainly visible
between the bricks.

The house has been sadly abused with no thought given its architectural merits and much of the woodwork has been removed. The stair is
perhaps the finest in Alexandria, with spindles and risers carved in a
more elaborate fashion than was the practice of the thrifty Scotsmen of
Alexandria. At the rear of this large house, separated only by a narrow
area, stands another house, facing the long garden and originally the
river. The front of this house boasts the loveliest bit of Georgian
architecture left in the old seaport. A pure Adam loggia, executed in
stone, runs across the garden façade. While arches are now filled in and
clothes hung to dry flap on the gallery, the outline is so chaste in its classic
form that nothing can destroy the illusion of beauty.

No search of records reveals how or why these two houses stand back

The Adam Loggia. Originally open between column and pilaster

to back. Whether Jonah Thompson built the first for his bank or business offices, or whether his family outgrew the house and he needed more room is not known. The two are treated as one house in all the documentary evidence, and one's curiosity, interest, and imagination are excited by the twin or married houses. One story has it that Jonah Thompson built the rear or twin house for his eldest son so that the two families might be together but with separate ménages.

Captain John Dalton forged a link between Mount Vernon, his family, and his posterity that was stronger than he knew. It was his granddaughter who was so deeply distressed at the ruin and desolation of the home of Washington that she fired her daughter's imagination with an idea that saved the spot for the nation. This great-granddaughter of John Dalton was Ann Pamela Cunningham, whose name will ever be indissolubly connected with Mount Vernon. In 1853 she formed the Mount Vernon Ladies' Association, and as its first regent stirred the women of America with her ardor and directed the entire campaign until adequate funds were collected. In 1859 John Augustine Washington sold the Mount Vernon estate to Miss Cunningham for two hundred thousand dollars—after the Virginia Legislature and the federal government had both refused to acquire it.

This sale was negotiated by the Alexandria banker, John W. Burke, who was appointed executor and guardian of John Augustine Washington's estate after he was killed during the Civil War while on active duty as a member of General Robert E. Lee's staff.

When the war broke out, Alexandria was occupied by Union troops. The Union authorities knew of the sale of Mount Vernon and repeated but futile efforts were made to find the securities. Mr. Burke's home was searched no less than three times. The funds were never found in their hiding place of the soiled-clothes basket. There they reposed until Mrs. Burke (*née* Trist, great-granddaughter of Thomas Jefferson) and Mrs. Upton Herbert (*née* Tracy), both Philadelphia-born ladies, sewed the bonds in their petticoats and with high heads carried them through the Union lines to Washington and delivered them to George W. Riggs, who held them for the duration of the war, when he returned them to Alexandria—and Mr. Burke.

An interesting sequel to the story occurred only a short time ago when the last of John Augustine Washington's children died. Mr. Taylor Burke, grandson of John W. Burke, and president of the Burke & Herbert Bank, administered the estate of the late Mrs. Eleanor Washington Howard, and distributed her estate, composed of the remainder of that purchase price, among her heirs.[4]

Chapter 4

The Fairfaxes of Belvoir and Alexandria

Of the families in Virginia closely associated with George Washington, none bore so intimate a relation as that of Fairfax.

William Fairfax, founder of the Virginia branch of the family, was born in 1691 in Towlston in Yorkshire, England, the son of the Honorable Henry Fairfax, Sheriff of Yorkshire, and grandson of the Fourth Lord Fairfax. Educated as a member of the governing classes, he began his career in the navy, later entering the colonial service. Before he was twenty-six he had acted as chief justice of the Bahamas and Governor of the Isle of Providence. Prior to 1717 he married Sarah Walker of Nassau, daughter of Colonel Walker, by whom he had four children, George William, Thomas, Anne, and Sarah. In 1729, Colonel Fairfax was appointed Collector of the Port of Salem, Massachusetts, and removed to that colony. In 1731 his wife died, and very shortly afterward he married Deborah, widow of Francis Clarke and daughter of Colonel Bartholomew Gedney of Salem, by whom he had three children, Bryan, William Henry, and Hannah.

In 1734 Fairfax came to Virginia as agent for his first cousin, Thomas, Sixth Lord Fairfax (who, by direct inheritance from a royal grant of

Charles II, had come into possession of some five million acres of Virginia land lying between the Rappahannock and the Potomac, and extending from Chesapeake Bay to the foothills of the Blue Ridge Mountains, known to Virginians as the Northern Neck) ; and to serve as Collector of Customs for the South Potomac. Fairfax first went to Westmoreland, where he was associated with the Washington and Lee families. Next he moved to King George, and lived at Falmouth. By 1741 he was representing Prince William County in the House of Burgesses. Colonel Fairfax was elevated to "His Majesty's Council of State" three years later. Becoming President of the Council in 1744, he continued in that office until his death.

About this time William Fairfax completed his dwelling house, Belvoir, situated on a high bluff overlooking the Potomac River, halfway between Mount Vernon and Gunston Hall. It was described by Washington in an advertisement as having "four convenient rooms and a wide Hall on the first floor." In one of these "convenient rooms," more than two hundred years ago on July 19, 1743, Anne, eldest daughter of Colonel Fairfax was married to Lawrence Washington of Mount Vernon.

A few years after his marriage, Lawrence (to whom George Washington owed his start in life) took his impecunious young half-brother into his home at Mount Vernon, whereupon the in-laws became intimately concerned with George's future. Young George was wise enough to realize that the way of advancement led through this important family and he never lost an opportunity to cultivate the President of the Council. Colonel Fairfax became a benefactor of the young man's fortunes, an inspiration to his ambition, and was truly and wholeheartedly attached through his affections to the gangling youth. To the end of his life Fairfax signed his letters to George, "Y^r very affect^e & Assur^d Friend."

In 1747 George William Fairfax, the Colonel's eldest son, returned home from England, where he had received his education, with the promise from Lord Fairfax of falling heir to his father's agency of the Northern Neck.

The fifteen-year-old George took a great liking to young Fairfax, and despite a difference in age, a friendship began which was destined to last throughout their lives. A letter from George William Fairfax to Lawrence Washington stated, "George has been with us, and says he will be steady and thankfully follow your advice as his best friend. I gave him his brother's letter to deliver with a caution not to show his."[1] Doubtless this was the occasion when George was seriously considering the navy.

Lawrence had served under Admiral Vernon, William Fairfax was trained for the navy, and Lord Fairfax was in Virginia to add either persuasion or influence as needed. Mary Washington was set in her determination that George should not become a sailor. Thus it was decided that surveying or engineering was the best outlook for the young man's future career, and Mount Vernon and Belvoir the seat of his further learning. Lord Fairfax would employ the embryo engineer as soon as he had sufficient instruction to be useful. The pupil was adept, the instructors efficient, and we see young Washington setting out with his new friend, George William, in March of 1748, upon his first surveying mission in the employment of Thomas, Sixth Lord Fairfax.

On his return from this mission, serious, sober young Fairfax (he was twenty-three at the time) offered himself as a burgess for Frederick County and was duly elected. He followed his father to Williamsburg, where he found attractions more absorbing than lawmaking. After "several opportunities of visiting Miss Cary" he fell a victim to the wiles and graces of the belle of the season. *The Virginia Gazette* for December 1748 carried this bit of social news: "Married on the 17th inst., George William Fairfax, Esqr., eldest son of the Honorable William Fairfax of His Majesty's Council to Sarah, eldest daughter of Colonel Wilson Cary of Ceelys."

Of all the colonial belles whose shades furnish theme for pæan and lighten the pages of history, none is more colorful than Sally Cary. This girl, only seventeen, with head of red-brown hair, great intelligent eyes shaded by long, thick lashes, long rounded throat and beautifully modelled hands, arms and shoulders, had an intellect which far surpassed her husband's.

When not at Williamsburg attending the assembly, the young Fairfaxes resided at Belvoir, where Sally acted as hostess for her widowed father-in-law or the bachelor Lord from Greenway Court. This house, after the Palace at Williamsburg, was the center of the social and political life of Virginia. The Fairfaxes were of ancient, noble lineage, with ample fortune, representing the very best in Old World culture. William Fairfax, as President of the Council, was second only in importance to the royal governor, serving as head of the state during the absences of His Excellency. Naturally, his home was the gathering place for men of eminence in the colony, as well as visitors of state.

Belvoir was a rendezvous for neighborhood gaiety. Overflowing with the young people of the family, more were attracted. George Washing-

Colonel George William Fairfax

ton was a daily visitor—Sally, but two years older than himself, filled him with delight. At Belvoir he met with the heads of government and gleaned from these meetings knowledge and inspiration to carry him through ordeals never experienced by his preceptors. Here, too, the feminine contacts smoothed the rough edges; George learned to turn the music for young ladies performing upon the harpsichord, to rescue times without number skeins of silk and balls of wool as well as lacy bits of

Mrs. George William Fairfax. (Sally Cary)

linen continually dropped by fair hands; he was taught the latest dance step from London and learned the most elegant of court bows. In those days the turn of a wrist and the flip of a lace ruffle were not considered inconsequential. It was here he acquired that never-failing interest in the "newest taste and the latest fashion."

Under this hospitable roof in early and formative years, associated with the cavaliers in daily intercourse, Washington developed an ease of manner and a dignity of deportment that became him well. In the library of this home he became familiar with the best in literature, his love of beauty was aroused, his knowledge of homemaking and gardening acquired, for this household wielded a highly civilizing influence, and awakened George Washington to the charms of culture and refinement. To appreciate the influence of this family upon Washington, it is only necessary to recall how brief was his schooling, how limited his prospects, how poor his pocket when, at the age of fifteen, he came to make his home at Mount Vernon.

At Belvoir and at Mount Vernon, George Washington first learned of the new port to be built at Hunting Creek warehouse. Long and often the talk was concerned with the progress being made before the assembly by Lawrence Washington and the two Colonels Fairfax. The latter gentlemen, being engineers, were both familiar with the construction of the towns in Great Britain and on the Continent. To Belvoir came Colonel Carlyle and Colonel Ramsay, as well as other gentlemen from Dumfries and the county, occupied with the same interest, who hoped to better their fortunes by the shipping trade which they expected the new town to attract, and willing to gamble time and money upon the erection of dwellings, warehouses, and docks.

These men were all purchasers of lots at the first auction on July 13, 1749, and at once began carrying out the mandate of the assembly, *i.e.,* to build within two years or forfeit their holdings.

Within six years the town, so neatly built, so strategically situated, was "honoured with 5 Governors in Consultation; a happy presage I hope, [wrote George Washington to William Fairfax at Williamsburg] not only of the success of this Expedition, but for our little Town; for surely such honours must have arisen from the Commodious and pleasant situation of this place the best constitutional qualitys for Popularity and increase of a (now) flourishing Trade."[2]

That Sally Fairfax was in residence in Alexandria and evidently in her own house taking part in the festivities arranged for General Braddock at the Carlyle house, dancing at the assembly balls, attending reviews, is indicated by a communication from her friend, young Washington:

Fort Cumberland
May 14,1755

Dear Madam:
I have at last with great pains and difficulty discovered the Reason why Mrs. Wardrope is a greater favorite of Gen¹ Braddocks than Mrs. Fairfax; and met with more respect at the late review in Alexandria.

The cause I shall communicate, after rallying you for neglecting the means that introduced her to his favour which . . . to say truth were in [?] a present of delicious Cake, and potted Woodcocks; that wrought such wonders [?] upon the Heart of the General as upon those of the gentlemen that they became instant Admirers, not only the charms but the Politeness of this Fair Lady.[3]

After his father's death on September 3, 1757, George William Fairfax came a step nearer the title of Lord Fairfax. He went on a very curious mission to England to refute in person a rumor that he was a black man, and to show any doubting relations the hue of his skin was exactly the same as theirs. This was especially strange, for William Fairfax had taken Sarah Walker Fairfax, his wife and mother of George William, to England in 1717, and certainly they must have met representatives of the family on that visit. Nevertheless, it is to Sally that the knowledge of this peculiar circumstance is due. In 1802, writing to her nephew in Virginia in reference to an inheritance of her husband's she says, "He [Henry Fairfax, William Fairfax's older brother] would have left it to your uncle William Henry Fairfax [George William Fairfax's younger half-brother] from an impression that my husband's Mother was a black woman, if my Fairfax had not come over to see his Uncle and convinced him he was not a negroe's son."[4]

While in England on this or other equally private affairs relating to his inheritance, George William wrote his wife from London on December 12, 1757:

Dear Sally:
I am sorry to say I have not succeeded and that it is uncertain whether I shall. But be as it may, I find it was necessary to be here, and I should not have excused myself if I had not. Mr. Fairfax went down to Leeds Castle yesterday and left me to push my own way, and then to follow to spend my Xmas and to prepare for his embarking with me in March. Therefore I beseech you'll employ Old Tom, or get some person to put the garden in good order, and call upon Mr. Carlyle for his assistance in getting other necessary things done about the house in order to receive so fine a gentleman. And I must further recommend, and desire that you'll endeavor to provide the best provision for his nice stomach, altho I suppose he will spend chief of his time with his brother.
However to make his and other company more agreeable I shall endeavour to engage a butler to go over with me at least for one year.
My Dear, I have often wished for your company to enjoy the amusements of this Metropolis, for I can with truth say, they are not much so to me in my present situation and that I now and then go to a play only to kill time. But I please myself with my country visits imagining the time there will pass more agreeable.
Permit me Sally to advise a steady and constant application to those things

directed for your welfare, which may afford me the greatest satisfaction upon my arrival.

Your affect. and loving husband

Go. Wm. Fairfax[5]

Back in America within the year, at a court held for Fairfax County on August 19, 1758, George William Fairfax "presents a commission from his honor the Governor appointing me Lt. Colonel of Militia" of the county and at the same court he took the oaths according to law as a vestryman for Truro Parish.[6] In 1760 he went back to England again and remained nearly two years. On this occasion Sally accompanied him.

All the while, George William Fairfax was occupied with his English inheritance, he was gradually losing interest in his Virginia life. Although he is credited with being loyal to the colonial cause (certainly he never failed in loyalty to his colonial friends) it is more than possible that the friction between the two countries swayed him somewhat in his determination to quit Virginia for the more settled state of the Old Country.

On a June afternoon in 1773, George William and Sally set out from Belvoir to Mount Vernon for the last time to take leave of George and Martha Washington. Dr. Craik arrived in time to meet them and say goodbye. The next day, June 9, in the afternoon, Martha and George went to Belvoir to see these old and devoted friends "take shipping."[7] As the breeze lifted the sails and the sturdy little ship faded out of sight down the Potomac, it carried the Fairfaxes away from Belvoir forever.

Until his own affairs became too involved, Washington supervised George Fairfax's Virginia interests. In August 1774, a year after the master's departure from Virginia, the contents of Belvoir house were sold. Washington himself bought many things—the sideboard, card tables, and other things. Other Fairfax furnishings came to Alexandria; Dr. Craik became the possessor of a Wilton carpet which Washington bought for him.

George and Sally Fairfax settled in Bath in a red-brown sandstone house at 11 Lansdown Crescent, where they became a part of the gay parties taking the waters at the Pump Room and attending assembly balls in the fashion of Jane Austen's most aristocratic characters. Friendly letters went back and forth between Bath and Mount Vernon. After the Revolution, Fairfax wrote to Washington: "I glory in being called an American," regretted his inability to contribute to the "glorious cause of Liberty" and offered his "best thanks for all your exertions . . . to . . . the End of the Great work . . ."[8]

Washington replied from New York on July 10, 1783: "Your house at Belvoir I am sorry to add is no more, but mine (which is enlarged since you saw it) is most sincerely and heartily at your Service till you could rebuild it" and expressed his pleasure at George William's approbation of his Revolutionary actions.[9]

Fairfax, after becoming involved in lawsuit after lawsuit and dissension with his relatives, died in 1787 before inheriting his title. Sally lived on at Bath for twenty-five years after her husband's death. The damp English climate crippled her joints with rheumatism, but did not distort her slender, erect figure, and she maintained her beauty to the end. A year before his death, Washington penned his last letter to Sally, his affection for her undiminished, and his pride in Alexandria growing:

Mount Vernon, 16 May, 1798

My dear Madam,

Five and twenty years have nearly passed away, since I have considered myself as the permanent resident at this place, or have been in a situation to indulge myself in a familiar intercourse with my friends by letter or otherwise.

During this period, so many important events have occurred, and such changes in men and things have taken place, as the compass of a letter would give you but an inadequate idea of. None of which events, however, nor all of them together, have been able to eradicate from my mind the recollection of those happy moments, the happiest of my life, which I have enjoyed in your company.

Worn out in a manner by the toils of my past labor, I am again seated under my Vine and Fig-tree, and wish I could add, that there were none to make us afraid; but those, whom we have been accustomed to call our good friends and allies, are endeavoring, if not to make us afraid, yet to despoil us of our property, and are provoking us to Acts of self-defence, which may lead to war. What will be the result of such measures, time, that faithful expositor of all things, must disclose. My wish is to spend the remainder of my days, which cannot be many, in Rural amusements, free from the cares from which public responsibility is never exempt.

Before the war, and even while it existed, although I was eight years from home at one stretch (except the en passant visits made to it on my march to and from the siege of Yorktown) I made considerable additions to my dwelling-house, and alterations in my offices and gardens; but the dilapidation occasioned by time, and those neglects, which are coextensive with the absence of Proprietors, have occupied as much of my time the last twelve months in repairing them, as at any former period in the same space;—and it is matter of sore regret, when I cast my eyes towards Belvoir, which I often do, to reflect, the former Inhabitants of it, with whom I lived in such harmony and friendship no longer reside there; and that the ruins can only be viewed as the memento of former pleasures; and permit me to add, that I have wondered often, (your nearest relatives being in this Country), and that you should not prefer spending the evening of your life among them, rather than close the sublunary scenes in a foreign country, numerous as your acquaintances may be, and sincere, the friendships you may have formed.

A century hence, if this country keeps united (and it is surely its policy and interest to do it), will produce a city—though not as large as London—yet of a magnitude inferior to few others in Europe, on the banks of the Potomack, where one is now establishing for the permanent seat of Government of the United States (between Alexandria & Georgetown, on the Maryland side of the River) a situation not excelled, for commanding prospect, good water, salubrious air, and safe harbour, by any in the world; & where elegant buildings are erecting & in forwardness for the reception of Congress in the year 1800.

Alexandria, within the last seven years (since the establishment of the General Government), has increased in buildings, in population, in the improvement of its streets by well-executed pavements, and in the extension of its wharves, in a manner of which you can have very little idea. This shew of prosperity, you will readily conceive, is owing to its commerce. The extension of that trade is occasioned, in a great degree, by opening of the Inland navigation of the Potomac River, now cleared to Fort Cumberland, upwards of two hundred miles, and by a similar attempt to accomplish the like up the Shenandoah, one hundred and eighty miles more. In a word, if this country can steer clear of European politics, stand firm on its bottom, and be wise and temperate in its government, it bids fair to be one of the greatest and happiest nations in the world.

Knowing that Mrs. Washington is about to give an account of the changes, which have happened in the neighborhood and in our own family, I shall not trouble you with a repetition of them.

I am

G⁰ WASHINGTON[10]

Chapter 5
The George William Fairfax House*

The 200 block of Prince Street is probably the finest left in Old Alexandria, in that it has suffered less change. No less than seven brick eighteenth century town dwellings remain in almost pristine condition. A small and fine Classical Revival building, and Mordecai Miller's "double three storied wooden buildings" make for diversity, while the old textile mill, later Green's furniture manufactory, adds the practical Scottish note to the locality.

On the north side of the street, on lot No. 57, separated today from Lee Street on the east by garden and the former Old Dominion Bank Building, and flanked by John Harper's gift to his daughter Elizabeth on the west, stands a three-storied dormer windowed town dwelling, battered by time and the elements. It stands after nearly two hundred years,

*207 Prince Street. Owners: Colonel and Mrs. Charles B. Moore.

a silent sentinel—the Fairfaxes' contribution to the erection of the town at Hunting Creek warehouse.

The house was originally nearly square. The wing, added after the main structure was built, was standing in 1782 at which time the house is described as it stands today. Due to the loss of one deed, that of father to son, it can be questioned whether the house was built by William Fairfax before 1752 or by George William, to whom it was deeded at that time. Like most old houses occupied by a succession of owners, much damage has been done to these old walls. The brick is worn and soft; paint is necessary to preserve them. The front door and stairway were changed a hundred and fifty years ago, as well as mantels and much of the trim and woodwork. The chimneys and dormers were blown down in 1927 and replaced in 1929. When the house was renovated at that time and the plaster removed from the drawing-room walls, wooden blocks or stobs were exposed in the bricks, indicating paneled walls.

The house has had some fourteen owners, each with his own idea of "improvements." The occupants of the house for the first hundred years are interesting as having been the founders and builders of the old trading port. Let us begin with the original purchaser of lots Nos. 56 and 57 and learn a little of the early inmates of the premises identified in Alexandria today as the Fairfax or the George William Fairfax house.

William Fairfax and his son, Colonel George William Fairfax, both purchased lots at the first auction held on July 13, 1749. The former had purchased the lots numbered 56 and 57 for thirty-five *pistoles,* while the latter had acquired two others across the street, lying south and designated Nos. 62 and 63 on the plat of the town. At the meeting of the trustees held the following day, it was ordered that deeds be made for September 20, 1749, for all lots disposed of. George William Fairfax retained his property until March 1750, when he sold the lots to Willoughby Newton, Gent., for £41 18s. 6d. Newton conveyed them, on November 10, 1752, to George Johnston for £44.

Lot No. 58, adjoining Colonel Fairfax's purchases on the west, was early the property of Colonel Champe, but the fact that it soon passed to Fairfax ownership can be established by two references in the minutes of the trustees.

On May 30, 1763, it was "ordered that Robert Adam Gentⁿ be overseer of the Main street [now Fairfax] from the upper part of Mrs. Chews Lott to the lower part of her Lotts and that he make so much of the said Main street dry and fitt for traveling for Waggon & foot people by the

Entrance hall and stair detail

first of Septem^r Next or pay for his failure twenty Shillings to the Trustees for the use of the Town . . . And that Wm Ramsay Gent. in like manner and under the same penalty put the said main street in order from the upper part of his own lott to the lower part thereof together with half the next street and that William Ramsay continue his district down to Col George Fairfaxes lott . . . And that John Carlyle in like manner and under the same penalty put the main Street in order from the corner of Mr. Fairfaxes Lott to the lower corner of the said Fairfax's Lott and one half of the adjacent street."[1]

On December 16, 1766, it was resolved that, "Whereas deeds were granted by William Ramsay and John Pagan two of the trustees of the town of Alexandria bearing date of the 28th day of March Anno Domini 1752 to the Hon Geo Wm Fairfax Esqr for two Lotts of Land in the said Town No. 56 & 57, on the motion of Geo Wm Fairfax Esqr it appears to us the above mentioned Trustees that No. 56 should have been included in Lott No. 57 as one lott liable to the Conditions of improvement by act of Assembly—and that he never having had a deed in his name or his fathers for Lott No 58 It is now ordered that one Deed of Conveyance be made out to the said Geo Wm Fairfax his Heirs and Assigns and that Mr Wm Ramsay and Mr John Carlyle be appointed and are hereby authorized to make good the said deed of Conveyance for these Lotts being improved agreeable to the Act of Assembly for constituting and erecting the said Town."[2]

That deed, bearing date of January 30, 1767, cited that on March 1, 1753, lots Nos. 56 and 57 were conveyed to George William Fairfax, Esq., and that as lot No. 56 was only part of a lot it should be holden as parcel of the lot numbered 57 and that the purchaser hold the same without being compelled to make any improvements other than what was by law required on one whole and entire lot.

In 1771, when Fairfax by reason of prospective inheritances of land and titles, was contemplating removal to England he turned to Robert Adam, a successful businessman, for assistance in disposing of his Alexandria property. Court records reveal that George William Fairfax and Sarah, his wife, sold on November 25, 1771, to Robert Adam, lots Nos. 56 and 57 with all "Houses, buildings, orchards, ways, waters, water courses" for £350 current money of Virginia.[3]

The transaction deed was witnessed by George Washington, Anthony Ramsay, and James Adam, and it is interesting that the entry for that day in Washington's diary reads: "went a hunting in the morning with Jacky

Custis. Returned about 12 o'clock and found Colo. Fairfax and Lady here, Mrs. Fanny Ballendine and her neices, Miss Sally Fairfax, and Mr. R. Adam, Mr. Jas. Adam, and Mr. Anthy. Ramsay, all of who went away in the afternoon, when Miss Scott came."[4] This deed was recorded at Fairfax Court on September 23, 1772, with another deed from John Carlyle and George William Fairfax, executors of the estate of William Fairfax, to convey lot No. 58 with all houses, building, etc., to Robert Adam for £125. Up to this time only one house stood on lots 56 and 57.

It may well be that Adam acted only as agent for George William Fairfax, or that he assured title to the property for cash advanced. Within the month he had sold half of the lots to Andrew Wales, a brewer, for £331 17s. 6d., nearly as much as he paid for the entire property. The other portion he sold to John Hough, Gentleman, of Loudoun County, Virginia.

Robert Adam was quite the man of affairs in Alexandria. Born in Kilbride, Scotland, in 1731, the son of the Reverend John Adam and wife (née Janet Campbell), he came to Maryland at about twenty years of age and was in Alexandria before 1758, associating himself with that merchant prince of the town, John Carlyle, as early as 1760. The firm of Carlyle & Adam acted as agents for Mount Vernon as well as Belvoir, handling the wheat and tobacco from these plantations. Washington was close to both men until he was outraged by treatment accorded his wheat and bags, though he afterward did Adam the honor of dining with him.

Following Colonel William Fairfax's death, Robert Adam succeeded to his place as a town trustee. In 1782, with others from Alexandria, he was active in founding the Masonic lodge. At the opening of the lodge in 1783, he was elected and served as its first Worshipful Master, along with Robert McCrea as Senior Warden, Elisha C. Dick as Junior Warden, William Herbert as Secretary, and William Ramsay as Treasurer. The year 1785 saw the erection of the Alexandria academy and Robert Adam laying the cornerstone.

Like Adam before him John Hough had only a passing interest in the property of George William Fairfax. He disposed of two small lots, one to Benjamin Shreve, a hatter, and one to George Gilpin, the colonel-to-be. He sold the remainder of lots Nos. 56, 57 and 58, fronting on Prince Street to John Harper, a sea captain of Philadelphia, in June 1773 for the munificent sum of £780, with all and every improvement and all houses, buildings, and so on.

The small parlor, restored. A blending of old and new

It is possible that Harper occupied George William Fairfax's house, but it is certain that he let it to Colonel William Lyle of Prince Georges County, Maryland, in 1782—probably before—and also as late as 1789, when Lyle returned to Maryland. Tax records show that Lyle was renting from Harper on Prince Street during this time. In 1782 he was taxed for "2 whites, 13 blacks, 2 horses, and 12 cattle."[5] He is mentioned several times in Washington's diaries as being at Mount Vernon, and at least once Washington came to Alexandria and dined with Colonel Lyle.

For a time Colonel Lyle was associated with Colonel John Fitzgerald in the shipping trade under the firm name of Lyle & Fitzgerald. During the Revolution he served on the Alexandria Committee of Safety. From 1783 until his departure to Maryland, Lyle was an active member of the Sun Fire Company. He owned considerable property in Alexandria. At one time he determined to build a dwelling house on part of lot No. 57 on the corner of Prince and Water [now Lee] Streets, which he had purchased from John Harper, but he sold the lot without fulfilling his intentions.

When peace came in 1783, Captain John Harper, whose real-estate plans had been deferred by hostilities, began the division of his Fairfax property into building lots. At amazing speed and increasing prices he

The front room: The excellent Adam mantel from the Jonah Thompson House
is an improvement to replace a later one with a Latrobe stove

sold off what had formerly been gardens and orchards, and as soon as
George William Fairfax's house was vacated by Colonel Lyle, Harper
disposed of it to William Hodgson of Whitehaven, England, in 1790.
Now our story of the Hodgson tenure must leave Alexandria to combine
for a brief moment with the great house of Lee.

Among the famous sons of the sire of Stratford Hall (Westmore-
land County, Virginia), Thomas Lee, and his wife Hannah Ludwell, was
William Lee, who was born in 1739. He went to England about 1766 as
a Virginia merchant selling tobacco and acting as London agent for his
Virginia clients. In London in 1769, William Lee married his cousin,
Hannah Phillipi Ludwell (daughter of Philip Ludwell and Frances
Grymes of Green Spring).

William Lee took an active interest in politics and was elected as an
alderman of London in 1774. This did not prevent him from doing all in
his power to aid the American colonists. We find him going to Paris in
April 1777 as commercial agent for the Continental Congress and working with his brother, Arthur Lee, on various diplomatic missions. While
serving at The Hague he was ordered to the courts of Berlin and Vienna,
but his services were thought to be so valuable it was decided to leave him

200 block of Prince Street. The Old Dominion Bank and the houses of George

in Holland. Arthur Lee was sent on to Berlin in his place, but later William Lee was appointed to the Austrian capital.

The four children of William and Hannah Phillipi Lee were born abroad. The first child, William Ludwell (1775-1803) was born in London; Portia (1777-1840) either in London or at The Hague; Brutus (1778-1779) at The Hague; and Cornelia (1780-1815) at Brussels. William Lee remained abroad until 1783, when he returned to his plantation, Green Spring, near Williamsburg. Peace had not then been concluded and he had such difficulty in obtaining passage for himself and family to Virginia that he was forced to purchase a ship for the voyage. The Lees set sail from Ostend on June 30, arriving home September 25.[6]

While living in London William Lee was thrown into contact with William Hodgson, formerly of Whitehaven. This gentleman was an "active friend" of America, a "fire-eating radical," and a member of "The Honest Whigs," a supper club of which Benjamin Franklin was a member, and the "presiding genius." Hodgson, also a member of the Royal Society, then composed of the intellectuals of the day—the premier scientific society of the English world—rendered valuable aid to the American commissioners in Paris by correspondence with Franklin in which he passed on much useful information.

An enthusiastically outspoken recalcitrant, Hodgson was not content with his contribution to the American cause, but took up the cudgels for the French, and was promptly launched into very hot water. Two years in Newgate prison followed his hearty toast "The French Republic," and the epithet he applied to His Majesty, George III, of "German Hogbutcher."[7] After this experience, it is not surprising that Hodgson removed himself beyond the seas. He turns up at dinner at Mount Vernon in June 1788. Two years later we find him buying a house and lot for £1,650 from John Harper on Prince Street. The evidence is that he was already in this house as a tenant. Here he set up in the dry-goods business, using the first floor for his store and countinghouse, and the upper part as his dwelling.

What could be more natural than Mr. Hodgson looking up his friends, the Lees, on his arrival in Virginia? His old friend, William, had died. Portia, now an orphan, was a young lady of handsome estate. Mr. Hodgson was dining rather frequently at Mount Vernon in 1798, and the General was writing of him always as "Mr. Hodgden."[8] Twice he was in company with Portia, the last time appearing in a diary entry of June 1799 with his wife at dinner. Mrs. Hodgson was, of course, the former

Miss Portia Lee. Sometime this same year he brought her to his dry-goods store and dwelling house on Prince Street. Built some forty-odd years before, this house was doubtless in need of numerous repairs.

The Hodgsons resided for upward of twenty-five years in the old town house of the Fairfaxes. They were the parents of eight children, so many that Hodgson found it necessary to give over to his family the lower floor of the house that he had been using as his store and counting-house and to confine his activities to his warehouse and wharf on Union and Prince. About this time the house seems to have undergone many changes. A new front entrance was added, the stairway changed, a fashionable arch and reeded mantels appeared. In other words, the house was "done over" in the newest taste and latest fashion.

In 1816 Hodgson was forced to sell his house due to his inability to meet a trust placed on the property in 1807. It was purchased in 1816 by John Gardner Ladd, senior partner of John Gardner Ladd & Company. Ladd appears to have come to Alexandria from Providence, Rhode Island, late in the eighteenth century. He is mentioned in Washington's diary as dining at Mount Vernon on February 1, 1798. A little glimpse into his private affairs is revealed by an old customs house record for the year 1817. Under the entry for Thursday, January 2, we discover that the ship *America,* Captain Luckett in command, sailed for the West Indies and that "John G. Ladd, Esq., of the house of J.G.L. & Co. goes out in this ship, with a view of benefitting his health." His will, bearing date of February 18, 1819, and leaving to his wife, Sarah, for her life "the entire use and emoluments of my dwelling house and lotts on Prince and Water Streets (formerly the property of William Hodgson)," seems to indicate that this wish was not realized. The home remained in the Ladd family for the better part of thirty-five years.

To Alexandrians of later days, 207 Prince Street was known for many years as the home of the Honorable Lewis MacKenzie. This house had the first bathroom and tub in Alexandria. A niece of MacKenzie has stated that her childhood had no more enthralling experience than leaning out of the third story window and watching the water pour into Prince Street from a hole in the wall. It was hit or miss with the pedestrians below! MacKenzie also had the first heated halls in Alexandria, and nearly burned up the house in consequence. He simply bricked up a small chimney in a corner of the hall and installed wood stoves. Despite the hazard, the warm halls were a great luxury in those days, for before the advent of central heating all Virginians regarded halls in the wintertime as places to pass through as quickly as possible.

Lewis MacKenzie, who owned the Fairfax house until 1891, was one of the eight children of Captain James MacKenzie, mariner. The unique wedding of his father and mother had been reported by the *Times and Alexandria Advertiser* almost a century earlier (1798). Its nautical motif arrests our attention and carries us to the wharves of Alexandria in the time of George Washington:

We have to record an event of unusual interest which took place in our harbor yesterday, on board the good ship "Lexington" which lay in the stream opposite the town.

The "Lexington," dressed in her gayest rig, was loaded with a full cargo of tobacco, in hogsheads, and only awaited the arrival of her commander, Capt. James MacKenzie, before proceeding on her voyage to Holland. The wind was fair, and the sun shone brightly. The jolly tars had donned their holiday garb, and as the first officer walked the deck and looked anxiously towards the town, it was evident that an unusual event was about to occur.

The shipping in port showed the flags of all nations, and on the British man-of-war, which lay close to the "Lexington," could be seen the bright uniforms of the marines marshalled by their officers.

Precisely at ten o'clock several boats put off from Conway's wharf, and on rounding under the stern of the "Lexington," the rolling of the frigate's drums could be heard as the crew manned the yards. A gay company passed up the gangway, led by the commander of the "Lexington" who was accompanied by Miss Margaret Steel and a clergyman from Maryland.

On the order of the officer on board the frigate, the marines came to "present arms" in handsome style. It was then that Capt. MacKenzie received his bride, the fine band of the frigate discoursing its sweetest music as the guests departed. The order to "weigh anchor" was then given, and the gallant captain, accompanied by his youthful bride, "squared away" for his port of destination, with many good wishes for his safe return.

Gadsby's Tavern doorway comes home after four decades in the Metropolitan Museum of Art, New York, as Alexandria celebrates its 200th anniversary

Chapter 6
John Gadsby and His Famous Tavern*

When Alexandria was one of the three largest seaports in America, a busy city of shipping merchants, a rendezvous for travelers, soldiers, and people of note, it was from necessity a city of taverns and hotels.

Many are the tales, handed down from the late eighteenth and early nineteenth century travelers, and from the advertisements of the journals of that time, that, put together, form a very complete picture of this early American hostelry.

The most famous tavern in Alexandria, perhaps in America, are the buildings on the corner of Cameron and Royal Streets, generally known and spoken of today as Gadsby's Tavern. Built in 1752, the smaller of these buildings was known for fifty years or more as the City Tavern, and sometimes as the Coffee House. John Wise built the large brick addition adjoining the City Tavern in 1792. On February 20, 1793, the *Alexandria Gazette* carried the following announcement of Mr. Wise's City Tavern:

---

*Gadsby's Tavern is controlled today by the Gadsby's Tavern Board, Inc., under the auspices of the American Legion. The patriotic organizations of Alexandria have joined in the restoration of this building. In 1932 the Alexandria Chapter of the Colonial Dames of America, the Alexandria Chapters of the Daughters of the American Revolution and the Washington Society, restored the first floor, which included the famous dining rooms of the City Hotel.

Due to the untiring efforts of the late Mrs. C. A. S. Sinclair, State Regent of the Virginia D.A.R., and Mrs. Robert M. Reese, one of the most worthwhile restorations in Virginia was completed in the fall of 1940 in the replacement of the woodwork in the ballroom. Happily, the floor is original. The inventory called for a coal grate, and in the attic the original grate, of Adam design, was found.

In 1937-38, the Alexandria Association made a careful restoration of the roof, cornice and dormers, enabling other much needed work to go forward and before this book goes to press the original doorway in which Washington stood to receive his last official tribute in Alexandria will have been brought back from the Metropolitan Museum of Art (where it has been for four decades) to its rightful location. This patriotic restoration of the doorway by the Alexandria Association has been made possible by the past president and Honorary President of the Association, Colonel Charles B. Moore, U.S.A., Ret.

SIGN OF THE BUNCH OF GRAPES

The Subscriber informs the public in General that he has removed from the Old House where he has kept Tavern for four years past to his new elegant three story Brick House fronting the West end of the Market House which was built for a Tavern and has twenty commodious, well-furnished rooms in it, where he has laid in a large stock of good old liquors and hopes he will be able to give satisfaction to all who may please to favor him with their custom.

David Rankin Barbee says that the hotel was opened on February 11 with festivities commemorating the birthday of General Washington: "As the guests assembled they were amazed as well they might be, at the internal arrangements of the new Hostelry."[1]

In Wise's new hotel, Alexandria architecture reaches its highest expression. For its day and time it was the ultimate in comfort and elegance; more than that, it was in exquisite taste. A well known architectural historian has written of the ballroom, "One can sense that it was built as an Assembly room for Gentlefolk";[2] and gentlefolk used it for near a century.

When the Jockey Club races were run on November 6, 1793, we find the members dining at Wise's inn, "the dinner to be on the table at three o'clock."[3] For the better entertainment of the guests, "Mr. Card performed wonderful feats at the Tavern every evening during the races. Feats in cards, slack-wire, celebrated equilibrist, ground and lofty tumbling."[4]

And for the benefit of the ladies, November 6: "Information is hereby given that there will be a dancing assembly this evening at Mr. Wise's, to which are invited the ladies of Alexandria and its vicinity on both sides of the river. Tickets for the gentlemen, without which none can be admitted, may be had at the bar."[5] Out turned crimson velvet breeches, green damask coats laced with silver, or cinnamon damask with broad gold lace, while ladies in failles, lena gauzes, velvets, lace and ribbon took their places beside the dandies. Logs and coals glowed, candles burned, while the gossips sat against the wall and passed on the grace of this or that gallant and his lady. When the gentry came to the races, they remained for the dance!

High above the floor, attached to the wall, hung the musicians' gallery[6] and to the strains of fiddle, flute, and banjo, the quality of the neighborhood bowed and glided. Upon these boards skipped little satin slippers and many times the heavy tread of the first citizen of America, for this gentleman was ever fond of the dance. Here gathered the Masons from

The doorway from hall to ballroom stands invitingly open

Gunston Hall and Hollin Hall; the Lewises from Woodlawn; the Dulanys from Shuters Hill; the Lears from Wellington; the Ramsays, Herberts, Fairfaxes, Craiks, Browns, Roberdeaus, Lees, Fitzhughs, Diggeses, Custises, Swifts and many other of the town's Scottish gentry and their neighbors across the river.

In 1794 an Englishman, one John Gadsby, took over the tavern under a long lease. As fine as the tavern had been under Wise, it was to reach new heights of public entertainment. Running the two taverns as one, under the name of Gadsby's, he brought its culinary fame to such a state of perfection that the odors of his dinners linger in the memory and titillate the palate to this day.

There was always a fine stock of game, fish, oysters, terrapin, turkey and ham; Madeira, Port and brandy on hand for the traveler. Our own great Washington sat down to a very good dinner in his last days, if his adopted son, George Washington Parke Custis be correct, for on being assured of a plentiful supply of canvasback ducks about which he had just made inquiry, he gave the following order: "Very good, sir, give us some of them with a chaffing-dish, some hommony, and a bottle of good Madeira, and we shall not complain."[7]

The fame of the tavern went out through the country and from Boston to New Orleans the traveler bent his efforts to make Gadsby's. John Gadsby established his own coach line from Alexandria to Philadelphia, and it was necessary to be a guest in City Tavern or his associated inns to get seat or ticket. Then he inserted the following notice in the *Gazette:*

March 1st, 1796.—John Gadsby informs the Gentlemen of Alexandria that he has fitted up a large and convenient stable well provided with hay, oats, etc., and an attentive hostler, and those who may send their horses may depend on proper attention being paid to them on moderate terms.

This was very enticing to gentlemen traveling by horseback as well as those in the city not having private stables.

Such men as George Mason, Thomas Jefferson, Alexander Hamilton, George Clinton, Benjamin Franklin, Braddock, the Byrds, Grymeses, Fitzhughs, Lees and Washingtons are among those who came here. One fine old tale has it that in 1777, in the old tavern courtyard, John Paul Jones met two bewildered Frenchmen in a dreadful dilemma—strangers in a strange land, speaking a strange tongue, unable to make themselves understood and doubtless very cross. By his knowledge of French, our brave privateer was enabled to smooth the way for these gentlemen, none

Ballroom of Gadsby's Tavern, purchased and taken from Alexandria by the Metropolitan Museum of Art of New York, where it is now on exhibit

other than Baron de Kalb and the Marquis de la Fayette, and the tale goes on that this assistance was so gratefully received that a friendship lasting a lifetime resulted from the encounter. The two taverns housed and fed most of the important persons visiting the country from 1752 for the next hundred years.

The Fairfax Resolves were prepared here—those resolves that eventually grew into the Virginia Bill of Rights. In this tavern met the little convention called by General Washington to settle the import duties upon the Potomac River commerce which led in time to the convention in Philadelphia which prepared the Constitution of the United States.

In 1802 Gadsby entered into a new lease with Wise for fifteen years. In the indenture, reference is made to a three-story brick house and a two-story brick house, a brick kitchen and several wooden houses. Gadsby at this time was granted permission by Wise to erect at his own expense a brick stable one hundred feet long and twenty-seven feet wide and of a

In the ballroom the musicians played from the balcony suspended from the ceiling. This is the restored ballroom

suitable height. He was also given permission to erect at his own expense another brick house forty-five feet long and fifteen or sixteen feet wide and two stories high, finished in a neat and decent manner so as to be habitable, and he also agreed to extend a wall thirty feet long and of the same height. The annual rent was to be two thousand dollars, and Gadsby agreed to paint the three-story brick house and the two-story house outside and inside, and he had permission to remove what wooden buildings were necessary and to keep the remainder in good repair.

That Gadsby did not desire to keep the tavern so long is borne out seven years later when on November 13, 1809, John Wise, N. S. Wise, and R. I. Taylor leased the tavern to William Caton for three months and then for nine years for two thousand dollars a year, and stated the tavern was "formerly occupied by John Gadsby."[8] But the following year Caton had had enough and the *Alexandria Gazette,* on March 9, 1810, carried the following advertisement:

To the Public

The Subscriber has taken for a term of years that noted and eligible establishment known by the name of the City Hotel, and once occupied by Mr. Gadsby whose distinguished abilities as a Publican gave it an éclat which the subscriber hopes to preserve by his unremitting exertions. . . . James Brook.

Ballroom fireplace containing original grate before which the gentry were wont to stand on winter nights

In 1811 an Englishman traveling incognito, put up at the tavern, formerly Gadsby's, became ill, and after it was discovered that he belonged to the Masonic fraternity, he was nursed by the gentlemen of the Alexandria lodge. Making a happy recovery, the gentleman departed, and apparently that was the last of him. Four years passed. One day there arrived by ship an enormous packing box for the lodge. It contained twenty-five hundred pieces of cut glass, decanters of all sizes, and glasses for any liquor distilled. The bottom of each piece was engraved with the Masonic emblem and the initials and number of the lodge. The enclosed card read simply: "From an English Gentleman and Brother in appreciation for fraternal courtesies." One hundred and seventy-five pieces remain in the Masonic Museum today, after more than a hundred years of use, and excellent crystal it is.

One of the most romantic stories told of Gadsby's, a true one at that, is the mysterious tale of the Female Stranger. On a day in early autumn of 1816 a ship docked at the wharf in Alexandria, purported to have come from the West Indies. Down the ways came a striking couple. Luxuriously apparelled, they presented figures of great elegance. The handsome young "milord" was all tender solicitude for the fragile beauty clinging weakly to his arm in a state of collapse. Bystanders were considerably intrigued and greatly impressed by the distinguished strangers. Unquestionably they were rich, and certainly noble. It was indeed curious that such important people had no attendants, neither manservant nor maidservant, and the young lady sadly in need of assistance. Even while the sailors were busy with the great ropes and anchors the handsome stranger was making arrogant inquiries for the best tavern in the town and demanding a carriage for transporting the lady there with the least delay. First impressions were borne out, the gentleman was undoubtedly English, and he was a person of importance!

Naturally the strangers were directed to the best the town afforded, and to "Mr. Gadsby's City Hotel" the young people came looking for rooms. The gentleman evidently took mine host into his confidence and was provided with the most elegant accommodations. The young woman was put to bed and a physician ordered in attendance. She was truly very ill. Two of Alexandria's good Samaritans were informed of the pitiful little sick girl's condition and Mrs. John S. Wise and Mrs. James Stuart took their turns with the invalid. The husband proved himself devoted and fairly daft with anxiety, and 'twas said rarely left the bedside. The young woman grew rapidly worse. The skillful nursing, the constant

In the Coffee House. A fine mantel and panelled chimney breast

Doorway to Coffee House or City Tavern

The Coffee House or City Tavern which later was run as one with Gadsby's Tavern and City Hotel. Headquarters for Washington and the Alexandria Militia in 1754

and faithful attendance of the physicians were all useless, and after an illness of several weeks, the Female Stranger died. Thus she has been remembered in Alexandria, for a very curious thing had occurred. The doctors and volunteer nurses were asked to take an oath before ever they entered that sick chamber, and swore never to reveal aught that they heard, saw, or learned. That oath they kept. The young woman's name, her destination, her former habitation, have never been revealed, and her secrets lie buried with her.

Many are the stories that survive. Some say the husband decamped without paying his host, doctors, and nurses. Others that he had eloped with this girl of good family and destroyed her reputation, and so brought about her death. One story claims that he was a criminal and was seen in prison by a gentleman from Alexandria, and others far more romantic tell of his reappearance at stated intervals in Alexandria when he was observed prostrate upon the tomb. Whatever his own story, he placed the mortal remains of the little stranger in St. Paul's Cemetery and covered her with a table tomb which is inscribed with the equally mysterious inscription:

To the memory of a Female Stranger Whose mortal sufferings terminated On the fourteenth day of October, 1816.
This stone is erected by her disconsolate Husband in whose arms she sighed out her last breath, and who under God did his utmost to sooth the cold, dull hour of death.

How loved, how honor'd once avails thee not,
To whom related or by whom begot.
A heap of dust remains of thee
'Tis all thou are, and all the proud shall be.

In 1808 the celebrated actress, Anne Warren, known as the "ornament of the American stage," was acting at the new theatre, Liberty Hall, just across from the Tavern on Cameron Street. While stopping at Gadsby's she became ill and died. (Not all the Tavern's patrons were so afflicted.) It is said that her interment was the last in old Christ Church yard.

On October 16, 1824, La Fayette was entertained by the Alexandrians "amid the wildest popular demonstration of joy and affection,"[9] and again in February 1825, he returned to Alexandria and Gadsby's for a farewell entertainment by the Masonic lodge. The tavern at this time was run by a Mr. Claggett.

Washington's association alone is sufficient fame for Gadsby's. In the little tavern he recruited his first military command, when as colonel of Virginia Militia in 1754 he set out to protect the Virginia frontier from the French and Indians. Again in 1755, as aide to General Braddock, he established headquarters at the City Tavern. Here, prior to the Revolution, he celebrated the King's birthday anniversary balls, an institution subsequently replaced by festivities of his own birthnight anniversaries:

February 11th, 1799 [22nd, new style] went up to Alexandria to the celebration of my birthday. Many manoeuvres were performed by the Uniform Corps, and an elegant Ball and Supper at Night.[10]

At Gadsby's he was entertained right royally by proud and patriotic citizens on his way to New York to be inaugurated as President, and on his return to Mount Vernon and private life. Throughout his life he attended the assembly balls, and from the steps of the new building he gave his last military order and took his last military review.

John Gadsby left Alexandria for greater fields—his hotels in Baltimore and Washington were in time more important than the City Hotel. He had a positive talent for Presidents, and knew them all from Washington to Polk. On the least provocation, it was said, he could put on an entertainment that would furnish food for gossip for a week.

In 1836 Gadsby bought the Decatur house in Washington, and proceeded to entertain the élite of the town with the finest his kitchen and wine cellar could produce. President and Mrs. Polk often attended these functions. Again to quote Barbee: "The Chevalier Adolph Bacourt, Minister from France, attended one of these functions."[11] The gentleman was not very happy about it, and denouncing Gadsby, he wrote of him:

He is an old wretch who has made a fortune in the slave trade, which does not prevent Washington Society from rushing to his house, and I should make myself very unpopular if I refused to associate with this kind of people. This gentleman's house is the most beautiful in the city, and perfect in the distribution of the rooms; but what society, my God![12]

Gadsby died in the Decatur house in Washington in his seventy-fourth year, leaving his widow (a beautiful third wife!) to reign in this mansion some years after his death. He is buried in the Congressional Cemetery, surrounded by his children and grandchildren.

Chapter 7
The Michael Swope House*

There is an ancient house in Alexandria whose rusty rose brick façade and beautifully hand-carved eighteenth century doorway add ornament and distinction to the 200 block of Prince Street.

Not many years ago Mrs. Alexander Murray (the daughter of a former owner) who had spent her girlhood in this old house remarked to the author, "You know, the house has a ghost. There is a story that an American Revolutionary spy who was executed by the British haunts the place." Every proper old mansion should have a ghost—and what could be nicer than an American patriot—blue coat and cocked hat?

Time passed. Mrs. Murray's story remained to be written, when about 1930 General Dalton came into possession of 210 Prince Street. Hearing that his house had been broken into, he requested his friend, Mrs. Sheen, the wife of Colonel Sheen, to examine the house and have the lock repaired. Mrs. Sheen with her son, Gordon, and a Negro went to General Dalton's empty house to repair the door and to lock the mansion. While the Negro was working on the lock, he said, "I certainly does feel funny. There's something strange about this house. Let's hurry and get out o'

---

*210 Prince Street. Owners: Mr. and Mrs. Hugh B. Cox.

Doorway to Colonel Michael Swope's House

here." Whereupon Gordon Sheen pooh-poohed the idea, standing by the Negro to reassure him. Suddenly he saw (or said he saw) in the doorway at the end of the hall a soldier in Revolutionary uniform walking toward him. When the apparition reached the music room or library, it turned sharply to the right into the room and disappeared.

Some time after this Mrs. Sheen was showing General Dalton's house to friends who had been living abroad and wanted a home. The two ladies had been through the lower floors and started to the third story. At the top of the steps the visitor said, "I can't go farther. Something is pushing me back." Mrs. Sheen at once descended the stairs, thinking her friend ill. When they reached the first floor the lady from abroad said, "A force was pushing me backward. I am quite psychic, you know, and the ghost who inhabits this house would make it impossible for me to live here. I love the house and should like to own it, but I should not be permitted to do so."

At the second auction of lots held on July 14, 1749, Augustine Washington, brother of Lawrence Washington and half-brother of George, bought lots Nos. 64 and 65 for fifteen *pistoles*. At a meeting of the trustees on June 15, 1754, lots Nos. 64 and 65, the property of Augustine Washington, along with other lots were ordered to "be sold to the highest bidder at a Public Vendue, the several Proprietors thereof having failed to build thereon according to the directions of the Act of Assembly in that case made and provided and it is further ordered that the Clerk do give Public Notice that the sale of the said lotts will be at the Town aforesaid on the first day of August next."[1] In the minutes of the trustees for September 9, 1754, lots Nos. 64 and 65 were entered as sold to William Ramsay for 39½ *pistoles,* or £37 1s. 9d.

The next document in regard to these lots is an indenture made July 21, 1757, between William Ramsay, of the County of Fairfax and the Colony of Virginia, merchant, and Anne, his wife, of the one part, and John Dixon of the County of Cumberland in the Kingdom of England, merchant, of the other part, whereby William Ramsay in consideration of the sum of £810 7s. sterling money of Great Britain to him in hand paid by John Dixon releases, grants, confirms, etc. to John Dixon certain lands described fully (1,261 acres) and "also the following lotts or half acres of land situate lying and being in the town of Alexandria in the County of Fairfax to wit Lott number thirty-four, forty, forty-six, forty-seven, and the lotts number *sixty-four, sixty-five* [author's emphasis] as the same are numbered in the plan and survey of the said Town originally

The Great Room

made by John West Junr., as also the following Negro and mulatto slaves with their increase (to wit) Peter the joyner, Jacob, Sophia, Whitehaven, Moll, Sall, Peter, Imanuel, Winnifrid and her child, Zilla, Phillis, and Clarisa, all which said lands and tenements lotts of land and slaves are now in the actual possession of the said John Dixon by virtue of one indenture bearing date the day before the date of these presents and by force of the statute for transferring uses into possessions to have and to hold the said lands tenements and all and singular other premises with them and every of their appurtenances together with the aforesaid slaves unto the said John Dixon, his heirs and assigns forever,"[2] provided always that if William Ramsay shall pay or cause paid to John Dixon of the town of White Haven, England, the just sum of £810 7s. with interest at five per cent per annum on the first day of July next, he will again come into possession of this vast property.

In the following August, Dixon appointed Harry Piper of Alexandria his true and lawful attorney to collect and receive for him all sums of money or tobacco which might become due, "and furthermore for as much as I have taken a Deed of Mortgage from Mr. William Ramsay of the town of Alexandria in the Colony of Virginia, Merchant, for sundrie lotts or half acres of land in the town of Alexandria with ye houses, gardens and other improvements thereon, together with sundrie slaves as also one tract or parcel of land . . ."[3]

In 1757 by a letter of attorney, dated August 8, John Dixon, merchant, of the town of White Haven in the Kingdom of Great Britain, authorized and empowered his attorney, Harry Piper of Alexandria, to take all legal means of foreclosure to receive the sum of £810 from William Ramsay who had mortgaged certain part of lots Nos. 64 and 65 with sundry slaves to secure that amount.

John Dixon in turn sold this property to the Scottish firm of shipping merchants, Robert McCrea, Robert Mease, & John Boyd in 1774, and in 1778 Boyd released his part of the property to McCrea and Mease for the sum of £253, with all houses, alleys, profits, commodities, and so on.

That William Ramsay built at least a part of this house seems almost indisputable. First, Augustine Washington had forfeited the property by not complying with the law to build thereon, and it seems hardly possible that Ramsay should have owned the property from 1754 to 1757 without complying with this act of the assembly. Furthermore, in the appointment of Piper as Dixon's attorney on August 16, 1757, the property is referred to as consisting of houses, gardens, and other improvements thereon. Dixon disposed of the property in 1774 to McCrea, Mease & Boyd, and four years later Boyd released his part for £253, with all houses, alleys, and so on. Little construction was done in Alexandria from 1775 to 1783, for this was the period of the Revolutionary War and no capital was going begging in the colonies at this date. Besides this evidence, the house has every appearance of a colonial building and the woodwork is all mid-eighteenth century in design. William Ramsay was an original trustee, appointed by the assembly for laying out the town. For a time he was successful and prosperous, owning much property, until overtaken by great misfortunes and compound interest!

All of which brings us to Michael Swope of York, Pennsylvania, a worthy gentleman of ancient lineage, patriotic inclinations, and distinguished service. The family Bible attests the fact that he held many offices of trust—judge of the Orphans' Court; justice of the peace; member of the assembly; Colonel, First Battalion, First Brigade, Pennsylvania Flying Camp Regiment, being but some of them. He was captured at Fort Washington and kept a prisoner of war for a number of years, suffering great hardship and privation.

Stairway and kitchen at Colonel Michael Swope's

When the Revolutionary War was over, Colonel Swope's health was undermined and he found the severe Pennsylvania winters unbearable. With his wife and family he moved south to Alexandria, where he set up in the ship chandlery business with his sons. He purchased from Robert and Ann McCrea and Robert Mease the property already described as a residence in 1783. In a later deed of June 29, 1809, it is recited that Michael Swope erected a large three-story brick building on these premises in 1784.

This house at 210 Prince Street is a fitting memorial to this officer. The doorway to the dignified old town mansion is one of the best examples of Georgian woodwork in Alexandria, and remains, save for one small patch and a new fanlight, in its original state.

The back drawing room is splendidly proportioned. The paneled mantel flanked by fluted pilasters is in keeping with the other woodwork which is good throughout the house. Some of the best, a cupboard, was found on the third floor and brought down to replace one missing in the great room. Since it fitted perfectly, it is quite possible that it has only been returned to its original place. The rear wing of the house seems older and more worn than the front, giving the feeling of earlier construction.

During Colonel Swope's occupancy fine furniture filled these rooms. In the Alexandria clerk's office an inventory of Colonel Swope's possessions, taken in 1786, fills several pages of legal paper when copied in its entirety. Such things were listed as "one clock and case, one mahogany dining table and eight chairs, one spinnett, one large looking glass, four small ones, one dressing table, one desk and drawers, five beds with all their furniture and linen belonging to them and bedsteads, two Franklin stoves, one riding chair and harness, sundry china and Queensware, eight decanters, 75 pounds of pewter, sundry silver furniture, to wit, two cream pots, five tablespoons, six teaspoons, two soup laddles, one tankard, and also one Negro woman and her child named Jude."[4] These are but a few of the Colonel's possessions, scattered these many years among his descendants.

Michael Swope and his sons were successful in the thriving seaport of Alexandria, and when Adam Walter, the second son, was married he moved to Philadelphia, where he set up in the shipping business as a partner of his father. His father built for him a home at 31 Catherine Street and 'tis said that the architecture very much resembles the Prince Street house.

Michael Swope died in 1809, aged eighty-four years. The body of the old hero was taken by boat from the port of Alexandria to the port of Philadelphia where he was interred in the Swope family vault in Union Cemetery at Sixth and Federal Streets. About 1858, during the yellow fever epidemic, the city board of health issued orders to have this vault cleaned out. It is said that the metal casket containing the earthly remains of Michael Swope was then in good condition. Perhaps, after all, Colonel Swope is the ghost that haunts this old house and chooses its inmates.

Chapter 8

Dr. William Brown and His Dwelling*

Between George Mason's house, Gunston Hall, and Mount Vernon, on Highway 1, about seventeen miles south of Alexandria, stands the colonial church of Pohick. There is an old cemetery behind a brick wall, beginning at the very door of the church and rambling over an acre or so of the yard. Among the tombs is that of one man peculiarly and intimately connected with the town of Alexandria.

He was one of the forty-odd officers of the Revolution to go from here, one of the twelve or more charter members of the Society of the Cincinnati, prominent for his contribution to his profession, and remembered for his friendship and association with Washington. His tomb was not originally placed at Pohick. It stood for many years in the private graveyard at Preston, now the site of the Potomac railroad yards, and was removed when that vandal of our port, "Progress" claimed the site.

Let us trace the worn letters on the old stone:

In Memory of/William Brown, M.D./(Formerly Physician General to the Hospital of the United States)/who died on the 11th day of Jan'y 1792/in the 44th year of his age;/This Tablet is inscribed/by/his affectionate & afflicted widow/His zeal & fidelity as a Patriot/His patience, diligence & skill as a Physician/His benevolence, curtesy & integrity as a Man/Secured him/the applause of his country/the honor & emoluments of his Profession/the respect of

---

*212 South Fairfax Street. Owners: Honorable and Mrs. Howard R. Tolley.

the Wealthy/and/the veneration of the Poor/Let/the grateful witness of his virtues in domestic life/add/that as a Husband, Father & Master he was tender, instructive & humane/that he lived without guile/and died without reproach.

Dr. Brown's grandfather was Dr. Gustavus Brown who emigrated to Maryland in 1708 and in 1710 married Frances, the daughter of Colonel Gerard Fawke. Their son, Richard Brown, returned to England to prepare himself for the church. Richard's son, William, was born in Scotland in 1748; was educated at the University of Edinburgh, graduated in 1770, and came to America. This is Alexandria's Dr. Brown.

This young Scotsman, gentle born, learned, traveled, handsome, came to Virginia at the age of twenty-two. He began to explore the south side of the Potomac, and his path often led to Dumfries and to the homes of his relations there, the Reverend James Scott's family, at the rectory, and the Blackburns at Rippon Lodge. Sometimes the carriage was brought out, or the horses saddled, or even the barge manned, and off to Mount Vernon the family would go.

It was always pleasant at Mount Vernon for young people. Never the week went by but some of them gathered for dinner or to spend the night, and often both. When Washington returned from Alexandria, where he was attending court on May 19, 1772, he found his guests included Colonel Blackburn and lady, from Rippon Lodge, Miss Scott, Mrs. Blackburn's sister (both were daughters of James Scott, rector of the Church at Dumfries), Miss Brown and young Dr. Brown. "This company spent the night and went away the next morning."[1]

Whether this was the beginning or the culmination of the romance, none now can tell, but by 1774 Miss Scott was already Mrs. Brown, and the mother of two very small sons, William Jr. being born that year. The young family was doubtless residing in General Washington's town house, and for this there is the authority of the General himself. In a letter to his nephew, Bushrod, dated November 1788, he writes, "If you could accomodate yourself to my small house in Town (where Doctr. Brown formerly lived) you shall be very welcome to the use of it rent free."[2]

Previous to this, in 1785, Lund Washington's ledger reveals that he had received £40 from Dr. Brown on account of Gen[l] Washington for "Rent of House in Alexandria."[3] In the General's own account ledger he refers to Dr. Brown's rent as having been fixed by "M[r] L[d] Washington at £60 a year for My House," and the sum is cancelled due to advances made by Dr. Brown and for professional services.[4]

In July 1783, Dr. Brown purchased from John Mills the white clap-

Dr. William Brown's clapboard residence

board house that has been identified as his Alexandria home. He purchased twenty-six additional feet south on Fairfax Street adjoining his dwelling house, from Robert Townshend Hooe and Richard Harrison, merchants, on July 10, 1790. This property became his garden.

An Alexandria tradition and the Brown family belief is that the house was built by him prior to the Revolution. It is, indeed, very old and probably dates between 1757, when the property was mortgaged by William Ramsay to John Dixon of White Haven, England, and 1783, when the property was sold to Dr. William Brown by John Mills, for the sum of £280, indicating a substantial structure. There was at least one house on lot No. 65, and Dr. Brown's house is the only one standing on that lot today at all indicative of a pre-Revolutionary dwelling. If the house was not built by Ramsay, the probability is that it was built by Mills between 1777 and 1783, which is doubtful, as building during the Revolution was so difficult as to make it almost impossible.

The home of the young Browns was the gathering place for the élite of Alexandria and the countryside. The Washingtons dined and passed the evening frequently. The Blackburns came often from Rippon Lodge, the Brown cousins from Port Tobacco, and of course Dr. Craik from around the corner. Colonel Fitzgerald, Colonel Swope, and Colonel Lyles were all near neighbors.

The Doctor was a man of fine attainments. Active in the church, he served as vestryman at Christ Church; public spirited, he was the moving force in the founding of the Sun Fire Company; and the Alexandria academy was largely his idea. It was in great part due to his efforts that Washington was aroused to take an active part in this project, to contribute £50 annually, and at his death to will £1,000 to this institution.

At the outbreak of the war with England, Washington showed his confidence by appointing Dr. Brown Physician-General and Director of Hospitals of the Continental Army. He served throughout the Revolution. Brown wrote and published the first *American Pharmacopoeia* in 1778, "For the sake of expedition and accuracy in performing the Practice, and also to introduce a degree of uniformity therein throughout the several hospitals," the title pages read.

It was due to hardships suffered at Valley Forge that he died in 1792 at the age of forty-four years. The following notice appeared in the *Virginia Gazette and Alexandria Advertiser* for Thursday, January 19, 1792:

On Friday, last, after a tedious and excrutiating illness, the iron hand of relentless Death arrested and hurried that amiable citizen, DR. WILLIAM BROWN, to the World of Spirits, "from whence no Traveller returns!" All the love we bore him could not add one "supernumerary gasp." He long felt the approaches of vital dissolution—no vain laments—but sustained it with religious intrepidity, such as marks the dignity of a Christian Hero.

He felt the force of Republican Principles early in life, and stept forth, in the infancy of the American war, to oppose the British King.—How often have I heard him, with the ardour of a Patriot, expatiate on the firmness and virtues of a Hampden and a Sidney! Viewing with horror the piteous situation of our virtuous and wounded Soldiery—the derangement of the hospitals and medical department—he relinquished his domestic ease and lucrative employment, and

Hall and stairway in Dr. Brown's House

offered his services to the Continental Congress. They were accepted—How he conducted the interesting and important charge, the testimony of that respectable body and his grateful country have long declared. Having arranged and reformed the constitution of the army allocated to his care, and reduced the wild and extravagant practice to system and order, he left the service, and resumed his vocation in this Town; in which he discovered the most exemplary tenderness, and unusual depth of professional knowledge. He was sagacious by nature, inquisitive and comprehensive, improved by study, and refined by sentiment. He was equalled by few in the social and domestic virtues of politeness and benevolence. He was the accomplished Gentleman, and finished Scholar—the best of Husbands, and the best of Parents. The Poor and needy ever experienced the humanity of his tender and sympathetic soul. He was a man to hear "Afflick-tion's cry." The loss of so much charity, friendship and beneficence but claims the tributary tear; But, temper your grief, ye pensive Relatives, and afflicted Friends—

> "The toils of life and pangs of death are O'er;
> And care, and pain, and sickness are no more."

He is gone, we fondly hope, to chant anthems of praise to an approving God! Though the struggles of nature are agonizing and prevailing, yet disturb not his gentle shade by impassioned woe!—"The Lord gave, and the Lord hath taken away; Blessed be the name of the Lord."

There are not many reminders left of the good Doctor. In the Library of Congress a few bills rendered to Colonel John Fitzgerald for outfitting ships' medicine boxes and attending sick sailors; a letter from one Thomas Bond of Philadelphia written in April 1784 to Colonel Fitzgerald stating that his brother "goes to Virginia to study Physic under Dr. Brown." In the Virginia State Library is a tax report showing that for the year 1784 he owned eight slaves and one cattle, and that in 1789 the Doctor had three blacks and two horses. The minutes he wrote as clerk and treasurer of the Sun Fire Company are preserved and, of course, a few copies of his *Pharmacopoeia*.

The Dr. William Brown house stands today much as it stood during his lifetime. Architecturally and historically it is one of the most interest-ing in Alexandria. No great house, this modest home built of white clapboard over brick and sitting close to the ground, rises two and one-half stories, hiding behind its stout doorway some of the best and certainly the most original woodwork in the old town.

One enters a spacious hall, the wide board floors of which are worn with the passing of many years, and colored by use and time a deep amber. Running around the hall is paneled wainscoting in alternating vertical and horizontal panels. The stairway rises from about the middle of the hall in easy steps to the second floor, the spindles are rather primi-tive and the entire stairway has a provincial air. The white baluster rail is matched by a handrail and supported by half a matching newel post; wherever the cornice breaks, it turns against itself. An amusing feature, one found sometimes in old houses, is an inside window opening from the back drawing room into the hallway.

If the stair is simple, certainly the woodwork in the upstairs front room is most ambitious. Mantel, overmantel and matching cupboards cover one entire wall, the chimney end of the room. The mantel is flanked by

Dr. Brown's upstairs parlor

two fluted pilasters, reaching from floor to denticulated cornice. Above the shelf is a rectangular dog-eared panel, in each of the four ears of which is a rosette. Under the shelf, oblong panels carry out the same design, divided by a carved half urn. The shelf is supported by consoles and decorated by a fret that returns around the urn. The cupboards on each side of the mantel have, at the top, circular glass doors, surmounted by an arch and keystone. The bottom doors are wood paneled. The remainder of the woodwork is conventional, plain chair rail, baseboard and trim.

The kitchen with its Dutch oven in the great brick chimney; the large fireplace where the old crane still hangs sturdily enough to support Mrs. Brown's best dinner, are in an excellent state of preservation. One is intrigued by some very ancient and peculiar waterworks that formed a part of the sanitary equipment in the culinary department and which function to this day. There is a heavy hand-hewn stone sink and a copper caldron with its own firebox and ashpit. Formerly a large oaken bathtub stood in the back room off the kitchen and the water heated in the copper caldron was available to both rooms. An old brass spigot that served the bathtub remains.

At Dr. Brown's death the house passed to his widow. She left it in trust for her daughter, Sarah Maynadier, and the Maynadier grandchildren at her death in 1813. The house remained in the Maynadier family until April 26, 1842, when the property was purchased by James Green for seventeen hundred dollars. In 1940, the present owners, the Honorable and Mrs. H. R. Tolley, acquired the property.

Dr. Brown's home has fallen into sympathetic hands. Today Queen Anne chairs and piecrust tables grace the parlor. From the hall comes the vibrating tick-tock of a fine old clock. Logs blaze cheerfully in open fireplaces, the flames reflected in old and polished silver. The hall window frames Catherine Brown's garden, which is divided into three sections, one shut off from the other by wall or fence, making private living areas of each. Old trees, brick walks, ivy and flowering shrubs add their attractions. A tall brick smokehouse stands sentinel, all that remains of a number of outbuildings which clustered, village fashion, about the dwelling.

Dr. William Brown. From a miniature.
(Courtesy Mrs. Bessie Wilmarth Gahn)

Chapter 9
The Peruke Shop*

This house is completely surprising. Many years ago the owners put on a new pressed-brick front and changed the sash from the usual small lights to two single lights of large dimensions. The transition from this 1890 front to an eighteenth century interior in a perfect state of preservation, produces upon one crossing the threshold the sensation of walking straight through the looking glass. And whither does the looking glass lead? Right into the parlors of Mr. William Sewell!

The stairway rises on the far side of a fine arch in the entrance hall. Halfway up, it becomes obscured from view, leaving one gazing at a paneled ceiling, as it makes an abrupt about-face. The rooms on the second floor are quaint. Low-pitched, sloping ceilings, off-center mantels with odd panels and chimney closets and six-paneled doors with H&L hinges, are amusing as well as charming.

Two parlors on the ground floor, opening off the hall, are formal and elegant. Fine paneled chimney breasts dominate these rooms. Dentils and fret trim cornices and mantels. Chair rails, six-panel doors, wide board pine floors, and double doors opening flat against the walls, making the two rooms into one, are found here. In the front room the interesting feature is a Franklin stove set in the fireplace—quite the last word in comfort in the 1780s.

On July 14, 1749 the Reverend John Moncure bought lot No. 61 for £5 9s. On March 28, 1752, the deed for this property was filed at Fairfax Court House and described as lot No. 61, a half acre of land on Royal and Prince Streets, as surveyed and platted by John West. Two years

*405 Prince Street. Owners: The Moore Family.

later, June 15, 1754, the Reverend John Moncure, along with other gentlemen of prominence in the colony, lost his lot for having failed to comply with the directions of the assembly to build thereon within three years. The following September there took place an auction of these forfeited lots, and No. 61 passed to William Sewell for £5 7s. 6d.

At a court held at Fairfax, on April 18, 1759, with five gentlemen justices presiding; *to wit,* John Carlyle, John West Jun., John Hunter, Robert Adam, and William Bronaugh:

William Sewell brings into court his servant Elizabeth McNot for having a base born child. Ordered that she serve for the same one year and she agrees to serve her said master six months in consideration of his paying her fine.[1]

Thus out of the mist of one hundred and ninety years emerges again the dim figure of William Sewell. And who, pray, was William Sewell? Peruke-maker! So called in a deed of trust dated 1766, "William Sewell Peruke Maker," and Elizabeth, his wife. The same Elizabeth?

Nearly two hundred years have passed since William dressed a wig or powdered a head, but if these parlors were his shop, and certainly they were, all the gentry in the town waited his pleasure here. Visitors who came to Alexandria and took part in the balls testified to the elegance of the ladies' apparel (almost always) and a lady to be elegant must have a well dressed head. It was rare, too, to see a gentleman without his peruke. William must have had a very large business. One likes to think that Major Washington dealt with Sewell, and it is not difficult to imagine on ball evenings Mrs. Carlyle's maid rushing in, making a hasty curtsy and breathlessly demanding Madam's wig; or perhaps Mrs. Fairfax's maid presents Mrs. Fairfax's compliments and "Please, will Mr. Sewell come at two o'clock to dress Mistress Fairfax's hair?" Nor, is it difficult to picture William, when the shop day is over, with his apprentices bent over the fine net, meticulously crocheting, by candlelight, the white hair into a lofty creation that will, in about six months time, take a lady's breath away.

Alas! Alack! Peruke-making and hair-dressing were not all they ought to be. Poor William owed a lot of money. He was indebted with interest to John Carlyle and John Dalton for £42 15s. 7d.; William Ramsay for £83 14s. 4d.; John Muir for £23 7s. 9d.—all merchants of Alexandria. But that was not all; the Kingdom of Great Britain was concerned. He owed one Henry Ellison, of White Haven, merchant, £62 10s. 7d., and Joshua Pollard of Liverpool, shipmaster, £17. Poor

Mantel in home of William Sewell, perukemaker

William put up for security lot No. 61, with all buildings thereon, water rights, watercourses, etc., which led, eventually, to a sheriff's sale. By due process of law, and to satisfy and pay sundry mortgages, lot No. 61 fell to William Ramsay.

Ramsay sold a part of this lot on Prince and Royal Streets in 1785 to Colin McIver, and the property was described as bounded today: "Beginning 24 feet 6 inches west of Royal and running West on Prince 24 feet, 6 inches, thence 88 feet North to a six foot alley, etc., for £225, with all houses, buildings, streets, lanes, allies, profits, etc."

In 1795 Colin McIver's son, John, sold the property to a Philadelphia merchant named Crammond for £450 and Crammond agreed to give up the house and land within a stated time to anyone paying more, or to pay the difference.

After twenty-three years the property was bought by another merchant of Philadelphia, Thomas Asley, for $750.00, and within two years Mr. Asley sold it to John Gird of Alexandria, in the District of Columbia, for $1,300. In September 1819, John Gird had a note endorsed for $4,100 by Isaac Entwistle, and mortgaged some of his personal possessions which were listed as "one clock, one sideboard, two mahogany dining tables, two tea ditto, one pair card tables, one secretary, two bureaus, one writing desk, one dozen rush bottom chairs, one ditto with settee to match, one sofa, two looking glasses, carpets, brass andirons, two fenders, shovel, tongs, window curtains, three bedsteads and beds, chair, wash stand, chest, house linen, one set gilt tea china, four waiters, one half dozen silver teaspoons, one set plated castors, sundry glass and earthen ware, kitchen furniture, etc."[2]

Six years later this debt was not cleared up and John Gird secured the debt with his house and lot. Thus ended Gird's tenure and the property passed on through other hands for twenty-four years to the Miller family; thence to Isaac Rudd, until the Moore family purchased the house about 1892.

Chapter 10
Historic Christ Church

Earliest parish records shed little light upon the spiritual life of the infant settlement of Alexandria. First mention of services held in the town turns up in the old Truro Parish vestry book, under date of June 4, 1753, when it was "ordered that the Rev. Mr. Charles Green do preach every third Sunday."[1] Later entries in 1754 and 1756 respectively for "building the desk at Alexandria"[2] and "to have seats made for the Church at Alexandria"[3] are puzzling since no mention occurs for any levies or appropriations for building or repairing. The inference would seem that some individual had provided a meeting place for services, though local tradition is firmly entrenched that a Chapel of Ease stood on Pitt Street near Princess.

Fairfax Parish emerged in 1765 as a daughter of the mother parish of Truro. Whatever previous arrangements for church attendance were provided for in Alexandria, an increasing population now demanded a more appropriate and commodious place of worship. James Wren, gentleman, designed the church and a contract to build it was originally let to one James Parsons in 1767 for the sum of £600. For some reason, Parsons failed to fulfill his contract and in 1772 the vestry appropriated an additional £220 and gave Colonel John Carlyle the task of finishing the building.

Wren proved himself an able architect and Carlyle a great builder. No cathedral in Europe conveys greater serenity than this little church. Cherished by Alexandrians for one hundred and seventy-seven years, the ancient interior expresses all the spiritual and sacred qualities of man. The reredos is centered upon a Palladian window, included as an element of the design. The window is flanked by the tablets for which James Wren was paid eight pounds "to write" the Lord's Prayer, the Creed, and the Golden Rule. Fluted pilasters frame the windows and the tablets. A hexagonal wine-glass pulpit rising on its slender stem is surmounted by a hexagonal canopy. The pews, originally square, were divided in 1817. The balcony was added much later, but is in perfect harmony with the earlier woodwork. The brick tower and interesting "pepper pot" steeple were built in 1818.

In an old deed at Fairfax Court House, dated 1774, between John Alexander of Stafford County, gentleman, of the one part, and Charles Broadwater and Henry Gunnell, church wardens, of the other part, Alexander, for and in consideration of the sum of one penny, current money, gave to the parish:

All that piece or parcell of Land situate lying and Being near the Town of Alexandria in the parish of Fairfax aforesaid where the new Church built by James Parsons stands, containing one Acre, Beginning at a locust post in a north west Corner from the northwest corner of the Church standing on the said Land and at the Distance of Twenty three and one half feet from the said Corner thence South Seventy eight Degrees East and parallel to the north wall of the Church, Twelve poles and Sixteen and a Quarter links, thence South 19 deg. W. 12 poles and 16 and 1/4 links, thence N. 75 deg. W. 12 poles and 16 and 1/4 links, thence N. 12 deg. E. 12 poles and 16 and 1/4 links to the Beginning to have and to hold the aforesaid piece or parcell of Land with all and Singular its Appurtenances unto them the said Charles Broadwater and Henry Gunnell and their successors Church Wardens of the said Parish of Fairfax forever, to and for the use and Benefit of the said Parish, and the said John Alexander for himself his Heirs Executors and Administrators the aforesaid piece or parcell of Land against the right, Title interest, claim and Demand of him the said John Alexander and his Heirs, and of any person claiming or to claim by from or under him the said John Alexander or his Heirs, to them the said Charles

Christ Church where both Washington and Lee worshipped

Broadwater and Henry Gunnell and their Successors Church wardens of the said parish of Fairfax, to and for the use of the said Parish of Fairfax, will warrent and for ever Defend by these Presents.

In Testimony whereof he the said John Alexander hath hereunto set his hand and affixed his Seal the Day and year aforesaid.

John Alexander [Seal]

Signed, Sealed and Delivered in presence of I. Kirk, David Henley, Rd. Harrison, Rob. H. Harrison.

Received this 10 day of October 1774 of the within named Charles Broadwater and Henry Gunnell Church Wardens of Fairfax parish the Consideration Money in the within Deed.

John Alexander

Witness I. Kirk, David Henley, Rd. Harrison, Rob. H. Harrison.
At a Court held for the County of Fairfax 20th March 1775 This deed and Receipt was proved by the oath of David Henley, James Kirk and Robert Hanson Harrison to be the Act and Deed of John Alexander and ordered to be recorded.

Test   P. WAGONER, Cl. Ct.

As early as 1762, General Washington was chosen vestryman for Truro Parish and at the first election held in March 1765, for the newly created Fairfax Parish (including Alexandria) he was elected to that office. This development stemmed from the terms of an act of the Virginia Assembly which set the boundaries in such a way that Mount Vernon lay within the new parish. As repealed and revised four months later, legislation returned Mount Vernon to Truro. Technically, then, Washington was vestryman-elect in the new parish for less than three months, yet his association with the Alexandria church was always close. Even before the new church (later to be known as Christ) was finished and delivered to the vestry, he had purchased pew No. 15, for which he paid £36 10s., thought to be the highest price paid for any pew.

Pohick Church in Truro Parish was completed about the same time as Christ Church in Alexandria. It was Washington's home church until after the Revolution, when it was practically abandoned by the Episcopal congregation. The General's habitual attendance at Christ Church apparently dates from about April 1785, when he bound himself to pay an annual pew rent of "five pounds, Virginia money."[4]

An anecdote told in Alexandria of how a group of girls tried to save the silver marker from the Washington pew during the War Between the States is worth repeating. The town was under Union jurisdiction. A group of half-grown girls of whom the leaders were Molly Gregory (Mrs. Robert Powell) and Connie [Constance] Lee (Mrs. George E. Peterkin, wife of Bishop Peterkin) banded together to help the Confederate cause in any way they could. One of their ideas was to go to Christ Church and remove the silver plate marking Washington's pew and take it home for safekeeping. No one was taken into their confidence. In very short order the Yankee provost marshal arrived at Cassius Lee's house and demanded the return the plate. Of course, Lee knew nothing whatever of the removal, but he summoned his children, lined them up,

The Holy Interior of the old church

and demanded if any of them had any knowledge of the plate. There was silence for some time. The provost marshal became threatening before admission was made that the removal of the plate was not a theft, but had been taken for safekeeping. The plate was returned to the church. The next day it disappeared and nothing has ever been known of it since.

Interesting and distinguished men have occupied the pulpit of Christ Church, beginning with the Reverend Townsend Dade, rector (1765 to 1778); and including such men as David Griffith (1780-1789), Bryan Fairfax (1790-1792), and Thomas Davis (1792-1802). The last named officiated at General Washington's funeral. But in the second year of Davis' ministry, President Washington had received the following solicitation:

Alexandria. 22^d Feby 1793

Sir

The Episcopal Congregation of this Town and Neighborhood, being extremely pleased with the induction of that Respectable Character and accomplished Preacher, Mr. Davis, wish to compleat their satisfaction by the acquisition of an Organ.

As no one can be more desirous of obtaining it than myself, I have been requested to undertake the Collection of Subscriptions; and I have been instructed to leave a place at the head of my Paper for a Name which has always been foremost in every undertaking both of private and public munificence.

I think it necessary to mention my being only an Agent in this business, that, should there be any impropriety in the present application, no more than a due share of it may be imparted to me. I may have been mislead by the Opinions of others, and seduced by my own Eagerness to accomplish a favorite purpose, but I beg of you Sir, to be persuaded that no Earthly consideration should tempt me to violate, wittingly, those Sentiments of perfect respect with which I am

                                    Sir
Docket: From   Your most obliged & obedient Servant
    Col⁰ Samˡ Hanson   Sm Hansen of Samˡ
    22ᵈ Feb. 1793⁵

The letter was long in passage, but it elicited the desired result the following April. The President entirely approved this measure and affixed his name to the paper, regretful at the same time that public subscriptions of all sorts limited the size of his contribution.

This instrument, now preserved in the Smithsonian Institution, has had an engaging history. Built in England in 1700, it was first used in the colonial church at Port Royal and from thence was acquired for Alexandria. After considerable service at Christ Church, it went to the Episcopal church at Shepherdstown, West Virginia, and about the middle of the nineteenth century passed to St. Thomas Episcopal Church at Hancock, Maryland. It was presented to the Smithsonian by the vestry of the latter church in 1907.

Christ Church is proud of its association with the Reverend William Meade, afterward the Virginia bishop of beloved memory. His pastorate was short, from 1811 to 1813, but his fame as preacher, gentleman, and scholar forecast his later attainments. The Reverend Charles B. Danna was another nineteenth century divine who faithfully served the congregation. Dr. Danna occupied the pulpit from 1834 to 1860, when he left to take a church at Port Gibson in Mississippi. He later removed to Natchez, Mississippi, in 1866 to be rector of Trinity Church. He was a trusted friend of Mrs. George Washington Parke Custis and Mrs. Robert E. Lee, and he baptized the children at Arlington House. It was during his pastorate that Robert E. Lee was confirmed on July 17, 1853, by Bishop Johns. When word was received in Alexandria of Dr. Danna's death, in 1873, Christ Church was draped in mourning.

There is an odd and sad sequel to Dr. Danna's pastorate in Natchez. Some years ago there occurred an astounding and mysterious death in

The open door marks Robert E. Lee's pew. Here he came for spiritual guidance

Natchez, Mississippi. A very prominent woman whose father had represented his country at a foreign court was found in her own home brutally murdered. Suspicion at once fell upon her nearest neighbors, a man and a woman, eccentric characters, who shared the same house. They were arrested and tried for murder. Their house immediately attained notoriety as "Goat Castle" and was so known over the United States from the manner in which the inmates lived. The strange fashion in which dogs, goats, chickens, or any animal on the place was made welcome in the drawing room was very queer and gave cause for the name.

The murdered woman had objected to the presence of her neighbors' pets on her place, especially the goats, which were prying and curious, as well as other tame animals which belonged by right in the barnyard, but preferred the drawing room. Ill feeling sprang up, quarrels, lawsuits, all the dreadful sequel of a neighbors' feud. At the trial circumstantial evidence piled up and up. It was not enough for conviction. The inmates of "Goat Castle" were acquitted. Even so, black distrust was their portion from many of their fellow townsmen.

Some people from Alexandria were making the Natchez pilgrimage

and came unwarned upon "Goat Castle." Lovely strains of music could
be heard, coming from an old piano, sometimes improvised, sometimes
a bit of Bach, Mozart, Chopin, played with much feeling. As the strangers approached the house they were shocked at the dilapidation—sash
missing in the windows, doors off hinges, boards decayed and missing
from the house and porch. Embarrassed, they hesitated to enter when to
the door came a man, the musician. Speaking in a quiet voice, he asked
them in. Upon the piano a large hen was standing, perfectly at ease. The
deterioration of the interior was more pronounced than that of the outside—springs bursting through upholstery, beds unmade and without
linen, neither carpets upon the floors nor curtains at the windows. Animals wandered in and out at will. Yet upon the walls hung some portraits
and the furniture had been good. There were many books. The man was
obviously cultivated in his speech and manner. The host collected the
stipend for entering the place and proceeded to show the tourists the
house, which was interesting, and his inventions, which were not; a collection of senseless, pitiful, useless things.

Upstairs, and downstairs, into this room and that they were taken to
be shown an "invention." Each room was more squalid than the last.
Finally the end in sight, escape near at hand, the gentleman said, "I'll
show you something," and took the Alexandrians into a room opening
off the hall. There was a large mahogany bookcase, sealed by a court
order, which the host opened at will, carefully replacing what he took out
after it had been examined. One of the strangers, flipping the pages of
an old book, saw the signature of Robert E. Lee, Alexandria, Virginia.
Startled, she asked where the book had come from. "It was my father's,"
was the simple reply. "That is my father," pointing to an old oil portrait
of a clergyman. "He lived in Alexandria. He was rector of Christ
Church."

Not long after this a Negro, arrested in the West, but formerly employed in Natchez, was purported to have confessed to the murder for
which these people had been tried and acquitted.

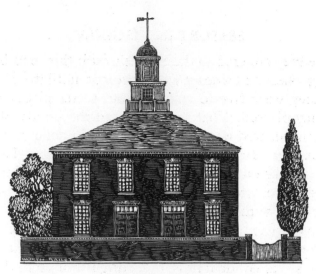

Chapter 11

The Presbyterian Meetinghouse*

One does not associate religious intolerance with America; nevertheless, the Act of Toleration which permitted religious freedom of worship was not signed until 1760. French Presbyterians were seeking refuge in the New World as early as 1562. The Church of England was the official form of worship in Virginia from 1607 until after the Revolution. Prior to 1760 worship not of the Established Church was done secretly and behind closed doors, generally in the fastness of a citizen's private home or place of business, though from time to time one finds permission given to preach. For example, in 1699, Francis Makemie was granted permission from the colonial authorities to preach Presbyterianism at Pocomoke and Onancock on the Eastern Shore of Virginia. Francis Doughton preached in Virginia as early as 1650-59, and is considered the father of British Presbyterianism in the middle colonies, having begun his work as early as 1643.

, Here in the little town of Alexandria, the population was largely composed of Scottish agents, shipping merchants, and sea captains, sincere followers of Dr. John Knox. Outwardly they conformed to the Episcopal Church, punctually attending services, by compulsion or otherwise. At

---

*In 1928 the church was restored as a shrine and the cemetery put in order by a group of persons, many of whom were descendants of the original society members. In 1940 the Alexandria Association replaced the missing pulpit with one, which while not a replica, conveys the spirit if not the pattern of that destroyed. Ecclesiastical settlement has vested the property in the name of the Second Presbyterian Church of Alexandria.

Before this book goes to press the Old Presbyterian Meetinghouse will have opened its doors again for regular services.

the same time they adhered to the Scottish faith they had brought with them, meeting where and when it was expedient, until the day came when unmolested they were free to emerge from secret places and publicly worship as they pleased. That they practiced the liberty of conscience, which they won the hard way, is proclaimed in an announcement carried in *The Columbian Mirror and Alexandria Gazette* of November 28, 1793: "At 12 o'clock on Friday the 30th instant a charity Sermon will be preached in the Presbyterian Church, by the Rev. James Muir, for the benefit of the Poor without respect to country or sect."

Major John Carlyle, after completing Christ Church in 1772 for his Church of England friends, undertook the direction of the Presbyterian meetinghouse, so-called, doubtless, to distinguish it from the Church of England. According to a report written in 1794 by the pastor, Dr. James Muir, "No church was yet built . . . to accommodate them in worship [*i.e.*, in 1772]. It was determined to build one; Mr. Richard Arrell and his wife, Eleanor, presented the Society with a lot of ground . . . the members of the Society came forward with generous subscriptions and loans; some assistance was afforded by their brethren of other denominations; they were thus enabled to erect and cover in a brick building sixty feet long and fifty feet broad."[1] This was partially completed by 1774. Not until after the Revolution was the church plastered and finished off.

The first minister of the congregation, the Rev. William Thom, was ordained in Pennsylvania in 1772 and called to Alexandria. But in one year the "Little Minister" was dead of a pestilential fever. Further steps to improve the House and organize the Society were interrupted, according to Dr. Muir's report, by the war which commenced between Great Britain and the colonies.

In 1780 the Rev. Isaac Stockton Keith was invited to remain with the Society during the winter. He remained nine years. The "Contract for the erection of the manse was let in July, 1787, to Mr. Robert Brockett."[2] In March 1789, Dr. Muir was called to the pastorate and remained until his death, serving for thirty-one years. Dr. Muir was a trustee of the Alexandria academy. As president of the board of trustees, he rendered to Washington satisfactory accounting on how his donations were being applied and what good was being accomplished, after a rather sharp letter of inquiry. As chaplain of the Masonic lodge, he assisted Dr. Dick with the Masonic ceremonies at the funeral of George Washington on December 18, 1799. Ten days later the *Gazette* carried the following notice: "The walking being bad to the Episcopal Church the funeral service for

George Washington will be preached at the Presbyterian Meeting House tomorrow at 11 o'clock." This was a memorial service, one of a countless number held throughout the length and breadth of the land. The Rev. James Muir's "Funeral Sermon on the Death of George Washington" was widely circulated in its day by means of a printed broadside.

When Dr. Muir died on August 8, 1820, he was held in such great affection and respect that it was decided to bury him under the pulpit and to erect a suitable monument to his memory. The committee appointed for this purpose was working at least five years and submitted reports again and again on the cost of altering the pulpit for the memorial. The last mention of the subject in the Committee Book reads: "Mr. Mark reports that the bannisters of the Cupola have been taken away as ordered at last meeting . . . Rev'd E. Harrison, Mr. Jno. Adam & Mr. Jos. B. Ladd are appointed a Committee to make all necessary arrangements for procuring and erecting a suitable monument to the memory of the late Dr. Muir."[3]

An old table gravestone with its inscribed eulogy formerly marked the spot where Dr. Muir was buried under the pulpit. It was removed to the burying ground to the lot beside the tombs of his wife and children after the restoration of the church building following the fire of 1835. A mural tablet under the gallery on the north wall now bears eloquent testimony to his beloved memory.

Dr. Muir's widow was allowed to continue on in the manse where she conducted a school for several years. Near the end of her life she moved from the manse with expressions of gratitude, and her daughters took up and continued the school for some years after her death. These ladies might have stepped out of the pages of Barrie's *Quality Street* so gentle and so inadequately equipped were they to battle with cold dollars and cents and naughty children. Eleven years after the good doctor's death, this announcement in the *Gazette* shows Dr. Harrison and Mr. Hallowell giving a helping hand:

Female Board School (The Misses Muir)

Tendering to the public their grateful acknowledgements for the liberal patronage hitherto received, take this method of giving notice that their school will re-commence, on Monday next the 5th of September. The course of instruction will be as heretofore, and very similar to that of all other respectable Female Seminaries in the District.

The higher classes besides being examined twice a week by the Rev. Mr. Harrison, will have also the privileges of attending the lectures of Mr. Hallowell on Astronomy and Chemistry. And in addition to all the ordinary branches of a solid education, they are prepared to teach and do teach, the more ornamental ones of Music, Drawing, Painting, and French.

Terms of boarding and tuition, as usual, moderate.[4]

On a hot Sunday afternoon in July 1835, during an electrical storm, the meetinghouse was struck by lightning. On that day the pastor, Dr. Harrison, had been invited to Georgetown to preach, and the usual Sunday afternoon services were postponed. Imagine his horror upon returning to discover the "severe and Awful calamity which had befallen the church and congregation." In the session book of the meetinghouse, we find this vivid description:

It has pleased God in his inscrutably mysterious yet wise and adorable providence to permit that on this day consecrated to holy rest, and to public services of devout worship in his earthly sanctuary, their venerable Church Edifice—for so many years, the place of hallowed devotion for their fathers and themselves, should be totally consumed by the lightening of Heaven.

This melancholly event took place about a quarter before three o'clock in the afternoon—a few minutes previously to the time ordinarily set apart for the ringing of the bell for the exercises of Public Worship. It was just at the close of a refreshing shower of rain, attended as is usual at this season of the year, with peals of thunder and flashes of vivid lightening. The Electric fluid seems to have been attracted by the spire of the Steeple, which—running up from the centre of a four-sided roof rising in the form of a pyramid—was rapidly conducted by means of a large quantity of iron used for the security of the timbers, to the shingles and other combustible materials of three of the corners of the building, almost directly under the eave. There entirely inaccesible for some minutes to any efforts which could be made use of for the purpose of quenching it, and continually fed by the qualities of the matter with which its work of desolation, with a rapidity which was truly awful and appalling. In a space of time too brief almost to be deemed credible by such as were not witnesses of the sublime and fearful spectacle, the entire roof exhibited to the immense multitude gathered around to mingle their sympathies and tender their assistance, nothing but one mighty map of living fire—curling in rapid and terrific volumes around the still suspended tho tottering steeple; and smiling at every effort towards extinction, save that of Him—that Dread and Aweful Being, by whom the flame had been enkindled. A period of two hours had not elapsed from the commencement of the conflagration, before the whole edifice except the walls, was involved in one shapeless mass of smoking ruin, presenting a scene, as desolating and repulsive to the common citizen, as it was tearful and heart-rending to the church and congregation. Our holy and beautiful house where our fathers praised the Lord—to use the language of the Prophet,—was thus burned up with fire; and all our pleasant things laid waste.

With the exception of the lamps, a venerable clock in front of the Gallery

The old Presbyterian Meetinghouse showing the new tower

opposite, the pulpit, the books and cushions, a part of the windows, the Stoves, a large proportion of the pipes of a Splendid Organ which was split open with an axe for that purpose, and some of the plank broken from the pews—all was destroyed; and but for the real and practical sympathy of many of our esteemed citizens in braving dangers of no common magnitude, a like destruction had been the fate of these also.

The house had been standing for more than 63 years—the steeple and galleries had been built somewhat later—and except the Episcopal church on Washington Street, generally known by the name of "Christ's Church"—was the oldest of all the ten places of religious worship in town. For many years its bell was the only Church-going signal within the limits of the corporation; and owing to this circumstance, connected with its peculiarly clear and inviting tones, the destruction of it—which was caused by its fall from so lofty an eminence—seemed the occasion of regrets to the public at large, more immediately expressed than for the edifice itself. To the congregation, no loss besides the house, was more deeply deplored than that of the large and richly toned Organ. Not only because of its superior worth as an Instrument of Music, the difficulty of replacing it by another, and the sacred uses to which it was applied, but equally because it had been presented by a few venerated and much esteemed individuals, most of whom are now sleeping in the dust.

For several years, there had been an Insurance effected on the building to the amount of five thousand dollars—two thousand five hundred on each of the Offices in town. But it so happened in providence, that one of these Policies, which had expired about four or five months previous, had never been renewed; —so that with the exception of twenty-five hundred dollars, the loss to the congregation was total.

Yet there was one circumstance which ought to be recorded with emotions of adoring gratitude. The calamity took place at a time when on ordinary occasions, some individuals would have been in the house—as it was so near the hour of the afternoon's service,—and had that been the case now, there is much reason to fear, that it would have been attended, if not with loss of life, at any rate with serious injury to not a few. But it had been so ordered by Infinite Wisdom no doubt, that, for the first Sabbath in more than two years, the Church was closed during the whole of that day—the Pastor having been providentially called away to supply the pulpit of a sick brother in the neighboring city of Georgetown. So that no individual was in the house, and no serious injury occurred to any individual during the progress of the fire—and thus, while there is much to produce sadness and to call for deep humiliation before God, the Session would feel, that there is still something to awaken emotions of gratitude and praise; and that however severely the loss may be felt, yet it has not been unattended with significant expressions of kindness and regard.

Dr. Harrison's lamentations, while justified, were not for complete demolition. In the minutes of the trustees, the fact is stated that the roof and cupola burned and fell in, destroying much of the interior woodwork, but not all. The walls and part of the galleries remained intact, Dr. Muir's tablet was uninjured, many windows were not broken, and the organ, at first thought destroyed, was very little injured; it remains in use to this day, and likewise the old clock. However the damage was terrific and there was only a nominal insurance to cover the loss.

Part of the congregation wished a new building site and it was given some thought, but the "siller" [silver] was found to be inadequate for the purpose. The amount in the treasury did cover the cost of restoration, and on April 5, 1836, it was "Resolved, That the congregation of the Church be called to meet at the Lecture room on Friday evening next at $\frac{1}{2}$ past 7 o'clock, to decide permanently on the location of the Church."[5] In November the committee minutes recorded that "The location of the Church was permanently fixed on the old site,"[6] and on February 7, 1837, "Mr. Smith, from the committee appointed to consult on the propriety of lowering the gallery, reported that it was thought to be inexpedient to do so."[7] The final notation on the new church read: "It was, on Motion Resolved that our New house of worship, be solemnly Dedicated to the Worship of Almighty God on the last Sabbath of July next—it being on that day two years before, that our former house of worship was consumed by fire . . ."[8]

It is distressing to think of the eighteenth century interior destroyed on that hot afternoon of July 1835, but we must be grateful for what the rebuilders of 1837 preserved as an outstanding example of Georgian architecture. In 1843 the tower was added: it was in the approximate location that the pulpit had stood for many years. In 1853 the front vestibule was constructed.

Dr. Harrison was a delicate man and for a long time his health was far from good. In 1848 he was so wretched that it was recommended he go south for his health. The firm of Lambert & McKenzie offered Dr. Harrison a free passage to and from the Barbados on the barque *Archibald Gracie*. The minutes of the committee record the motion of appreciation to the owners.

Mr. Robert Bell of the old printing firm of that name made a gift of letter paper to Dr. Harrison every Christmas for many years. In his latter years the Doctor in thanking Mr. Bell always said that he never expected to see another Christmas. He saw at least three after the first of these communications, for that many letters exist containing the same mournful allusion.

In 1862 the Civil War disrupted the Church. Dr. Elias Harrison died in 1863 after forty-three years of ministering to his congregation and with his death the Church ceased to function and its congregation scattered. During the Battle of Bull Run, it was used as a hospital for wounded soldiers, and from time to time it was used by other faiths, including a Negro Baptist congregation. Neglected, uncared for, the prey of thieves and vandals, the doors were finally closed.

The cemetery lies between the Church and the manse. Here John Carlyle sleeps. Cofounder and trustee of Alexandria in 1748; son-in-law to Colonel William Fairfax; brother-in-law to Lawrence Washington; commissary of the Virginia forces under Braddock in 1755; collector of customs on the South Potomac, and major in the Revolution; a Scottish gentleman, heir to a title, he cast his fate with the colonies. Nearby lies the tomb of William Hunter, founder of St. Andrew's Society, and that beloved friend and physician of General Washington, Dr. James Craik. Ramsay, McKenzie, Muir, Vowell, Harper, Hepburn and Balfour are among the names found inscribed upon the old stones. Their dust makes of this soil a part of Old Scotland.

Chapter 12
Presenting The Sun Fire Company

In the eighteenth century calamities visited Alexandria, and of these nothing was more feared than fire. To prevent and control such catastrophes the gentlemen of the town formed themselves into several companies of fire fighters. How and with what means the raging holocausts were controlled is revealed in an old, mutilated, leather-bound minute book of the Sun Fire Company.[1] The first entry in this treasure is part of the damaged record for the March meeting in 1775. The next page is numbered 9 and contains the minutes for the April meeting. This is evidence that the Company was formed in 1774 between August and December.

At this March 1775 meeting it was agreed to limit the number of the Company to forty-five persons. The clerk for this meeting was John Dalton; members served as clerks in rotation. Absent members were fined one shilling three pence. Members were to be provided with two buckets, a brown linen or oznaburg bag containing at least four yards of material, and a wicker basket as soon as possible after admittance. These were to be hung up in good order and always in place. There was a forfeiture of money for any neglect. The Company took some several months to acquire proper ladders and hooks. In April the "propriety of purchasing an Engine" was discussed and at the June meeting it was agreed to postpone the matter. Three ladders were then finished but most of the buckets were at the painters being marked with owners' names and numbers. By August the ladders had been completed by Thomas Flemming, and John Dalton was ordered to procure locks with proper staples for securing the ladders under the "piazza of the Court House."

As the Revolutionary War got under way many of the members were excused, "being frequently abroad on the Servis of Their Country." Among these were Captain Valentine Peirs, Captain John Allison, Colonel John Fitzgerald and J. Windsor Brown.

Unfortunately the clerks took for granted that everybody knew when there had been a fire and rarely are these important events mentioned in the minutes. In January 1777, "William Wilson lost a bucket at the late fire" and he was authorized to purchase another at the Company's expense; Robert Adam, who was clerk, forgot to "warn the Company and was fined Ten Shillings"; several members neglected to put up lights when the late fire happened at Zael Cooper's and the fine was two shillings. The next clerk was "desired to Enquire of the several members if they had candles at their windows and to collect Fines from such of them as had not."

The light begins to break—at the first hint of fire the Company member must, at the fastest possible speed, put lighted candles in the front windows of his dwelling. This was Alexandria's first alarm system! The member then dashed for four yards of material in an oznaburg bag, two leather fire buckets (they each weighed as much as a saddle) and a wicker basket and, without stopping, he raced to the fire, where he either pumped water, formed spectators in ranks for passing buckets, removed goods from burning houses in his bag or basket, climbed ladders or pulled down adjoining houses when necessary; and last but not least watched to "prevent evil minded persons from plundering sufferers." The only tranquil occupation was that of the "sentinels" who kept watch over goods removed from the conflagration wherever such goods were deposited.

What a spectacular sight a fire in Alexandria presented when one remembers the elegant dress of the day; short clothes, elaborate jackets or vests, ruffled linen, full skirted coats, perukes, queues braided and beribboned, powdered heads in three-cornered hats, silken and white hose, buckled shoes; and that fires generally occurred in winter upon the coldest days and in the worst weather, often at night, and that these firemen were the élite of the town, the serious, responsible merchants, doctors, masters, ship captains and owners.

There was some reward now and then for their efforts. At the April meeting in 1777, the "Succeeding Clerk is desired to warn the Company to meet next month at the *Ball Room* and to Desire the Treasurer to purchase Ten Gallons of Spirits, and one Loaf of Sugar Candles etc. The

Clerk to have the Ball Room cleaned and put in order." Alas, the members were either not warned or invited for only six showed up. The next month was worse, again no warning and only four came. The clerk was ordered to warn again and provide what spirit, sugar and candles may be necessary for the next meeting and "that the same be held in the Town House." The clerk was reimbursed "one pound Two Shillings for white washing and cleaning the Ball Room."

On February 22, 1779, a resolution was passed to fine the clerk refusing or neglecting his duty forty-two shillings, and absent members three shillings. There was a fine called the "Moreover Fine," which was increased from five shillings to nine shillings, and the Company voted to dispose of any sum not exceeding £5 "when less than 2/3 of the members are met." Besides funds in cash, the Company had 1,000 pounds of tobacco on hand. The following July the Company ordered the tobacco sold.

On Monday, October 27, 1783, nine years after the founding of the Company, the succeeding clerk is ordered to give notice that at the next meeting a proposal will be made to dispose of the money in stock in the purchase of an engine. Two months later, undaunted by the recent unpleasantness, the treasurer was requested to "Import from London on account of this Company a fire engine value from seventy to eighty pounds sterling." It took two years for the engine to arrive. Preparatory to its reception, officers were appointed for its direction. Nine stalwart members were chosen, and they were ordered to serve nine months. Six shillings each was collected from the members to help make up the deficiency, and a committee was appointed to wait upon the county court with a petition requesting ground sufficient for building an enginehouse upon the courthouse lot. This was granted and the enginehouse was built on Fairfax Street "adjoining the school House." The members were called on for a dollar each for this purpose and it was later necessary to borrow another dollar. Two keys were ordered labeled "Sun Fire Company."

The April minutes in 1786 contain the invoice for the engine:

To a Fire Engine Imported from London with 2 dozen buckets Amt
    p. invoice   £ 72.14
Commission on shipping D°—5%   3.12. 8
Insurance on £76 @ 2½pc   1.18
Freight from London   6. 6
                                                         £ 84.10. 8
Exchange 40 pc¹   33.16. 2
                                                        118. 6.10
Freight from Baltimore   1. 4
                                                        £119.10.10.

It was incorporated into the articles that the engine was to be worked for two hours every Monday of the meeting, and anyone neglecting to attend and work the engine was penalized nine pence. Moreover William Herbert, Dennis Ramsay and Isaac Roberdeau were charged with getting the engine to fires.

About this time (1788) the Virginia Assembly passed an act authorizing the different towns in the state to elect fire companies.

In May 1789, Dr. William Brown was elected treasurer to succeed William Hartshorne.

The first mention by the Sun of other fire companies in Alexandria is in the minutes of February 28, 1791. In July specific reference is made to the Friendship Fire Company and the Relief Fire Company.

In May 1793, the Sun Company was dissatisfied with the English engine, and they began correspondence with a Mr. Mason of Philadelphia with the intention of selling the old engine and acquiring a new one. Mason manufactured three engines. They contained 190, 170 and 160 gallons of water, respectively, which they discharged in one minute and a half and they were worked by twenty-four, twenty-two and eighteen or twenty men, respectively, and varied in price accordingly. The Sun Fire Company purchased the smallest engine for £125. It seems to have arrived in April 1794. Later the old engine "with the suction pipe" was thoroughly repaired by Mason and returned to the Sun Fire Company.

By 1796 such confusion reigned at fires that the three companies associated themselves together to make and sustain certain plans and rules for the management of fires. It was decided to have three directors or commanders, one chosen from each company, only one of whom was to act at a time, who were to have control of the engines, fire hooks, ladders and to be the judges of the expediency of pulling down adjacent buildings. In order that these gentlemen be more conspicuous (distinguished was the word) it was decided to "elevate their voices above the ordinary clamour on such occasions," each of them in action was ordered to carry in his hand a *"speaking trumpet, painted white, and not less than three feet long."* Each company was to keep such an affair in the enginehouse.

There were then chosen three subordinate directors who had immediate charge of the engine under the commander, then four persons from each Company, to be called regulators, who were to *"be diligent in searching for the most convenient source of water,* in forming lanes for the supply of the engines, and *preventing the use of dirty puddle water."* Upon these gentlemen fell the unpleasant task of "noticing remisness in the members and others and being obliged to give information to their respective companies whenever such shameful instances occured to their observation." Trustees were responsible for the removal of property, and the entire company was obliged to wear "at times of fire" by way of distinction, black caps with white fronts with letters thereon designating their company. Moreover these companies pledged themselves to "respect" the other companies when their property was in danger from fire, "in preference to persons who are members of neither."

Doctor Dick stated that he lost his fire bucket at the fire at William Herbert's house, then occupied by Edmund Edmunds, and the treasurer reimbursed the good Doctor eighteen shillings on October 24, 1796.

In July 1797, Dennis Ramsay was ordered to lower and enlarge the engine house to receive the old engine; the floor had given way in 1793. He presented his bills the following February for a total of £43 9s. 9d.

In 1799 it was decided to hold meetings at the courthouse, from May to October at half after seven o'clock, and from November to April at six o'clock.

One of the last mentions of the engines was in 1800. The engines were both worked at the January meeting, found to be in good order, except that the old one leaked a little.

Governed by a set of "articles" framed by themselves, to which they faithfully adhered, these firemen fined themselves and paid their fines, cheerfully or otherwise (they were mostly Scotsmen) when neglectful of their duty. A roster was kept each year, month by month, marking the members present or absent. The A's predominate. It was from these fines, plus others for neglect of duty that the Company's funds were formed. Many of these rosters have been destroyed, but enough remain to give an idea of the citizens who were members of the Sun Fire Company and lived near each other within a certain radius of the water front.

*   *   *

List of members of the Sun Fire Company of Alexandria for January 1777—being the first intact roster in the minutes:

William Ramsay
John Dalton
Robert H. Harrison
James Hendricks
Thomas Fleming
Richard Conway
William Hartshorne

James Kirk
Patrick Murray
Mathew Campbell
James Buchannan
William Hunter
David Jackson (Doctor)
John Mills

John Carlyle
John Harper (Capt.)
George Gilpin
Robert Mease McCrea
William Rumney
Richard Harrison
William Wilson
Thomas Kirkpatrick
Andrew Steward
James Stewart
Josiah Watson

William Herbert
Robert Mease
John Finley
William Brown (Dr.)
William Hepburn
Cyrus Capper
Robert Allison
James Muir
Robert Adam
George Hunter
Edward Owens

Added 1778

Dennis Ramsay (Col.)
John Fitzgerald (Col.)

David Arrell
Valentine Piers (Maj.)

Added 1780

James Adam
William Hunter, Jr.
Colin MacIver

David Steward (Doctor)
Peter Dow
Daniel Roberdeau (Gen.)

Added 1783 [Pages from 48 to 72 missing]

William Bird
R. Hooe (Col. Robert T. Hooe)
William Lyles
   (Col. Committee of Safety)
Dr. Elisha Cullen Dick

Samuel Montgomery Brown
Joseph White Harrison
Jesse Taylor
Charles Simms

Added 1784

John Sutton
Henry Lyles
John Hendricks (Col.)
George Richards
Daniel McPherson

John Oliphant
Michael Ryan (Col.)
John Allison
John Hawkins

Added 1785

Thomas Williams
Jonathan Swift
Randle Mitchel
William Baker (Doctor)
Jonah Thompson

William Lowry
Michael Madden
William Ramsay (Doctor)
Edward Harper

Added 1786

James Woodward (Capt.)

W. H. Vowel

Philip Marsteller
Joseph Greenway
William H. Powell

Cleon Moore
John Rumney
John Potts
Robert Donaldson

Added 1787

Baldwin Dade
Francis Peyton

John Long
John Love
George Deneale

Added 1789

Joseph M. Perrin
Richard Harrison

John Gill
John Forster

Added 1790

Jonathan Mandeville
John Carson Seton
Bernard Ghequiere

James Lawrason
Gustavus Brown Campbell (Doc.)
Joseph Riddle

Added 1793-4-6

James Douglas
John D. Orr (Doc.)
Stephen Cook (Doc.)
Robert Young
Henry Rose (Doc.)
Leven Powell, Jr.

James McRea
Augustine J. Smith (Doc.)
Jesse Wherry
Robert Hamilton
John Dunlap
Charles R. Scott
Abraham Faw

Added 1798

William S. Thompson
Joseph Saul
James Russell
William Hodgson
Nicholas Voss
Amos Allison, Jr.
Charles I. Stur
John T. Ricketts
Cuthbert Powell
John Ramsay
William Byrd Page

Joseph Mandeville
Guy Atkinson
Jacob Hoofman
Antony Vanhavre
Peter Wise, Jr. (Doctor)
Thomas Magruder
James Bacon
John Watts
Alexander Kerr
Walter Jones
Thomas Swann

Added 1799

William Groverman

John Dunlap

Added 1800

Michael Flannery

(Note: *Not all members at the same time.*)

By the turn of the century, the city of Alexandria boasted three fire companies whose membership rosters included the most responsible citizens. The year 1774, marking the formation of the Sun Fire Company, also saw the organization of the better-known Friendship Fire Company, claiming Washington as honorary member. The Star Fire Company was founded in 1799.

Alexandria property owners were quick to realize the advantages of membership in the Mutual Assurance Society, established in December 1794 and offering protection "Against FIRE on BUILDINGS in the State of Virginia." At the Alexandria office, leading citizens enthusiastically subscribed to a plan so soundly conceived and efficiently administered that the company which pioneered it is in operation to this day. The archives of the Mutual Assurance Society of Virginia constitute a mine of valuable information for the researcher. From General Washington's own files derives a broadside listing early subscribers throughout the state.[2] The Alexandria section includes a number of citizens whom we know to have been conscious of the ever-present danger of fire:

Name	Number Buildings Insured	Value	Name	Number Buildings Insured	Value
Wm. Hartshorne	3	7000	Wm. Brown	3	5500
John Potts	4	10000	Henry Stroman	1	300
Isaac McPherson	8	17700	Diedrich Schekle	2	3400
Rob. Hamilton	4	6000	E. Deneale	1	2000
J. B. Nickols	6	2000	Korn & Wisemiller	3	6000
Ch. Simms	4	3000	Rob. Lyle	4	7300
Lemuel Bent	1	400	Wm. Ramsay	2	2000
Thomas Rogerson	2	1000	Henry McCue	3	4000
R. T. Hooe	7	23500	Philip Wanton	1	800
John Dunlap	1	2000	Ephriam Evans	2	1600
Wm. Hodgson	3	10000	Dennis Foley	2	2000
Rob't Young & Co.	2	8000	Wm. Hartshorne	1	4000
Tho's Patten & Co.	12	14600	Philip G. Martsteller	2	3300
John R. Wheaton	2	3000	Joseph Thornton	1	2000
John Mandeville	10	15000	Stump, Ricketts & Co.	3	10000
Charles Lee	2	6000	Samual Davis	1	2000
Wm. Herbert	6	16000	Thomas Richards	5	15000
John Longden	3	3000	Adam Lynn	2	2000
Richard Weightman	4	4000	Mathew Robinson & Co.	2	3000
R. Weightman for the heirs of Ray's Estate	3	1000	Wm. Hoye	1	1600
Wm. Summers	5	8000	John Harper	4	8000
			Benjamin Shreve	3	9000

Name	Number Buildings Insured	Value	Name	Number Buildings Insured	Value
John Dundas	2	7000	John Fitzgerald	3	6000
Henry Walker	1	800	Thomas Forrell	1	800
John & Tho's Vowell	2	3000	Wm. Wright	3	2700
Ricketts & Newton	2	5000	James Kennedy	2	6000
George M. Munn	2	5000	Joseph Riddle & Co.	2	3500
Jonah Thompson	5	14000	Guy Atkinson	1	3000
Adam S. Swoope	1	2000	James Patton	2	6000
Mordecai Miller	1	3000	James Lawrason	1	1500
Wm. Bushby	2	4500	Shreve & Lawrason	7	12000
Philip Richard Fendall	7	10000	Geo. Hunter	5	2700
Wm. Hepburn	9	13500	Jacob Cox	4	3000
Tho's White	2	1600	Geo. Gilpin	3	6000
Richard Conway	8	15000	Isaac McPherson for N.		
Wm. M. McKnight	1	3000	Elliot	4	12000
Charles McKnight	1	2000	George Slacum	3	3000
P. Marsteller	1	2000	Geo. Slacum for Gabriel		
Adam Faw	1	2000	Slacum	1	2000
Wm. Halley	1	3000	Samuel Harper	1	1200
Jacob Schuch	3	1000	Jamieson	1	400
Peter Wise	3	9000	Chapin	2	2600

Chapter 13
Captain John Harper and His Houses

The streets of the old port of Alexandria bear royal names. Prince is one of those streets, shown in the first map of the town as surveyed in 1749. The 100 block is still paved with cobblestones "big as beer kegs" purportedly laid by Hessian prisoners during the Revolution.

The brick houses which sprang up in early days set the standard for the town. Many of these houses were erected prior to the Revolution and immediately after the signing of the peace in 1783. All original lots had been built upon by 1765 but there remained between these first houses empty spaces. There was a constant effort to have all vacant spaces of the lots built upon, so as to present an unbroken front. By 1790 the 100 and 200 blocks of Prince Street stood, very much as they stand today, the visible expression of the Scottish and English towns that our ancestors had left behind them.

These houses were nearly all built by Captain John Harper, and when not built by him, built on his land at a stipulated ground rent. The north side of the 100 block was part of lot No. 56 and until after 1771 no houses stood there. The ground rose here in a high bank above the Potomac, and the original lot contained less ground than a quarter of an acre. Bought by the Honorable William Fairfax at the first auction in

1749, in 1766 he was released from building thereon, as it was stated the improvement on his lot No. 57 was adequate for the two lots and "such was the true intent and meaning of the Trustees."[1]

The Honorable William Fairfax deeded this property to his son, Colonel George William Fairfax, who sold it on November 25, 1771, to Robert Adam. Adam in turn sold to John Hough of Loudoun County on December 11 and 12, 1771; and Hough, after disposing of several parts of the Fairfax lots, sold in June 1772, the remaining parts of lots Nos. 56, 57 and 58, fronting on Prince Street, to Captain John Harper of Philadelphia.

This is our first introduction to John Harper in the records of Alexandria. Apparently he must have made this purchase through someone else, for nearly a year later Washington received the following letter:

Philadelphia, May 5th 1773

Esteemed Friend
    Colonel Washington
    From the little acquaintance I had with thee formerly, I take the liberty of recommending the bearer Cap[t] John Harper who is in partnership with William Hartshorne—John Harper comes down in order to see the country, if he likes, they propose to come down and settle with you; they are Men that have a verry pretty Interest—W[m] Hartshorne lived with me some Time—They are Industrious, careful, Sober men; if Cap[t] Harper should want to draw on this place for Five hundred Pounds, I will engage his Bills shall be paid—Any Civilitys shewn him will be returned by
                    Thy Friend
                                    REESE MEREDITH[2]

Harper did nothing with these newly purchased lots until after the Revolution, when he began to sell and to build at astonishing speed. The number of deeds in the clerk's office in Fairfax and in Alexandria of property transferred to or from him fill page after page in the records. A book on John Harper's activities would be a good history of early town housing. Twice married, he had twenty-nine children—and to every one he left a house and lot.

John Harper's property housed many of Alexandria's important citizens. Two of Washington's physicians occupied adjoining houses built by him on Prince Street, though not at the same time. Dr. Craik lived at least three years and probably five at 209 Prince Street—from 1790 to 1793, and doubtless until 1796, when he moved to the house he purchased on Duke Street. Dr. Dick lived at 211 Prince Street from 1798 certainly until 1804, and then again at the same house in 1815. Surely it is safe

211 Prince Street was John Harper's gift to his daughter, Peggy Harper Vowell, April 10, 1793. Here Dr. Dick lived from 1796 to 1804. As he was here in 1815 it is safe to assume that he occupied this house for nineteen years. He paid John Harper £70 a year rent.

The Harper-Vowell Houses or the Sea Captains' Row

here to domicile the restless Doctor, for these ten undocumented years between 1805 and 1815. The Doctor paid for this house £70 per annum.

The early Harper houses which fill lower Prince Street are known in Alexandria today as "the Sea Captains' Houses" or "Captains' Row" and in truth they were either owned or occupied by captains or masters of vessels. After weathering the storms of a hundred and fifty years or better, their sea legs, or foundations, are well established in the soil of Alexandria, and they present one of the attractive sights of the town. The street slopes at a steep angle from the top of the hill, at Lee Street to the river, and the quaint old houses go stair-step down toward the Potomac in an unbroken line; sometimes a roof or a chimney sags with age, or a front façade waves a bit. The first house in the block on the northwest corner of Prince and Union was our stout Captain's warehouse and his wharf jutted out into the Potomac across the street from his place of business. A few years ago a great oil tank buried in the ground forced its way to the surface, bringing with it the enormous beams of John Harper's wharf and part of an old ship rotting in the earth. Real estate was only a side issue with the Captain. His main interest was the sea, his ships, and their cargoes.

On February 23, 1795 Harper sold to John Crips Vowell and Thomas Vowell, Jr., for £150, that part of lot No. 56 fronting on Prince Street, 24 feet 6 inches, 88 feet 3½ inches in depth, which begins on the "North side of Prince, fifty feet to the Eastward of Water Street, upon ye Eastern Line of a ten-foot alley, and all houses, buildings, streets, lanes, alleys, etc. . . ." The Vowells agreed to lay off and keep open forever an alley upon the northern back line of the premises, nine feet wide "Extending from the aforesaid ten-foot alley to the line of . . . William Wright."[3] This described property was one of those houses built by Harper. The two Vowells were his sons-in-law and both gentlemen in the shipping trade.

By this circuitous route we arrive at 123 Prince Street,* the house with a pure *Directoire* tent room, practically a duplicate of that at Malmaison, and another room with a magnificent painted Renaissance ceiling. How such work became a part of the sturdy two-story "Sea Captains' Houses" is one of Alexandria's mysteries. It is true that both rooms were in a deplorable state of repair, and it was necessary to trace the work on paper, repair the plaster and then continue the interrupted design. Naturally, the colors were freshened. It was exciting to watch this discovery unveiled, when sheets of shabby paper were pulled from the walls, and the artist repaired and restored the work of some itinerant master whose name has vanished with his dust these hundred years or better.

John Harper, a Quaker, was born in Philadelphia in 1728, and he was living in Alexandria in 1773, if not before. By his first wife, Sarah Wells of Pennsylvania, he had twenty children. He married at her death Mrs. Mary Cunningham, a widow, the daughter of John Reynolds of Winchester. By this lady he had nine children. In 1795 he was living at his residence on Prince Street, for William Hodgson's property was described in his insurance record as being next door to John Harper on the west. Captain Harper's house is now known as 209 Prince Street and today bears, erroneously, a plaque to the memory of Dr. Dick. This is the house in which Dr. Craik was living in 1790-93. Incidentally, no record viewed in a search of hundreds mentions Dr. Dick as occupying 209 Prince Street. On the contrary, Dr. Dick in 1796 was paying insurance on his dwelling on Duke Street.

In his old age Captain John Harper built two brick houses on the east side of Washington Street, south of Prince. In one of these he died in 1804, aged seventy-six years. Dr. Dick attended John Harper in his last illness and was paid sixty-five dollars by the executors for this service.

*Owner: Miss Margaret Frazer.

Wine for the funeral was eleven dollars, the coffin and case cost twenty-six dollars, and the bellman received one dollar for crying property to be sold. Captain John Harper lies buried in the cemetery of the old Presbyterian meetinghouse near two of his daughters, Mrs. John C. Vowell and Mrs. Thomas Vowell.

Captain Harper was an ancestor of Mrs. Mary G. Powell, author of *The History of Old Alexandria*. She tells of his patriotic action in procuring ammunition from Philadelphia for the independent companies of Prince William and Fairfax Counties: "Eight casks of powder, drums and colors for three companies."[4] His religion prohibited his taking part in combat, but his sympathy was manifested in a very practical fashion. John Harper was a member of the first city council in 1780 and of the congregation of the old Presbyterian meetinghouse. He was one of General Washington's Alexandria agents for Mount Vernon produce, doing an extensive business with the General in the matter of "Herring." At Washington's death he took part in the Masonic ceremonies at the funeral, and his son, Captain William Harper, commanded the artillery company on that eventful day. This son took an active part in the Revolution at the battles of Princeton, Monmouth, Brandywine, and Valley Forge, and crossed the Delaware with Washington. He succeeded to the business at Prince and Union. John Harper's third son, Robert, was a lawyer and married a daughter of John W. Washington, of Westmoreland County. John Harper, Jr., married Margaret West of West Grove, daughter of John West, and while acting as foreign agent for the Harper firm in the West Indies, was drowned in 1805.

Alexandria's Malmaison, or the Harper-Vowell house, listed as 123 Prince Street, was the residence of the eminent architect, Ward Brown, until his death in 1946.

Chapter 14

Dr. Elisha C. Dick and The Fawcett House*

The dashing Dr. Dick first appeared in Alexandria fresh from the tutelage of Drs. Benjamin Rush and William Shippen of Philadelphia. He was just twenty-one and of a figure to set feminine hearts aflutter; five feet ten inches, of commanding presence, very handsome, "playing with much skill upon several musical instruments" and singing in a sweet voice of great power; skilled and learned in his profession, "a strong and cultivated intellect," a genial spirit, witty and charming.[1]

The son of Major Archibald Dick (Deputy Quartermaster General in the Revolutionary Army in 1779) and his wife, Mary Barnard, Elisha Cullen Dick was born on March 15, 1762, at his father's estate near Marcus Hook, in Chester County, Pennsylvania.

His primary education was gained at the Philadelphia Academy, in the home of the Rev. Robert Smith, D.D., at Pegnea, and in his father's home, tutored by the Rev. Samuel Armor. In 1780 he began the study of medicine, graduating on March 21, 1782. Two days later he lost his father and came into his inheritance of half the estate. A year later he disposed of his Pennsylvania interest to Isaac Dutton and started for Charleston, South Carolina, with the expectation of settling there.

*507 Prince Street. Owners: The Fawcett Family.

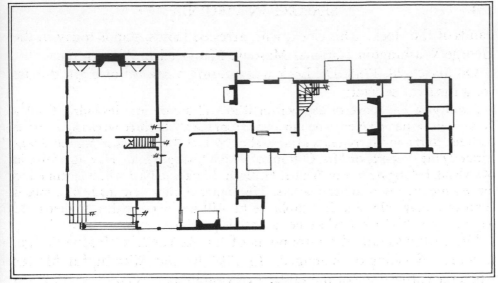

Floor plan of house

Armed with letters of introduction to General Washington, Colonel Fitzgerald, and Colonel Lyles, he stopped en route in Alexandria "to call upon a female relative" and to present his letters. He got no farther. "Influential persons" caused him to abandon his plans and remain in Alexandria, where the recent death of old Dr. Rumney left an opening which Dr. Dick filled for better than forty years. Alas, for the belles of Alexandria! In October 1783, Dr. Dick married Miss Hannah Harmon, the daughter of Jacob and Sarah Harmon of Darby in Chester County, Pennsylvania.

Two years after beginning his professional life in Alexandria, he pulled a tooth for one of the Mount Vernon house servants, and the following entry taken from Washington's diary for February 6, 1785, tells the results which do not seem to have been entirely satisfactory:

Sunday, 6th, Doctr. Brown was sent for to Frank (Waiter in the house), who had been seized in the night with a bleeding of the mouth from an orifice made by a Doctr. Dick, who some days before attempted in vain to extract a broken tooth, and coming about 11 o'clock stayed to Dinner and returned afterwards.[2]

So far as Washington's diaries show, Dr. Dick never crossed the threshold of Mount Vernon again until fourteen years later on a raw, cold day in December when the snow lay thick on the ground, he was sent for by Dr. Craik to attend Washington in his last illness. It was Dr. Dick who advised against additional bleeding and it was he, who, when Washington's last breath escaped, walked to the mantel and stopped the hands of the clock. This clock, with arrested hands, stands today in the George Washington National Masonic Memorial in Alexandria.

On March 28, 1788, Dr. Dick was offering a reward of eight dollars for a runaway servant:

I will give the above to any person who will secure in Alexandria Gaol a Negro fellow named Ned, who ran away from me about three weeks ago. He is between thirty and forty years of age, about 5 feet 7 or 8 inches high and was formerly the property of Mrs. Clifford of whom I bought him. Having a wife in Maryland, belonging to Mr. Samuel H. Bean, I imagine Ned will be inclined to make a nightly resort to her quarters. His winter clothes were made of a mixed cloth of a gray color and it is probable he will be found with a soldier's old napsack upon his back in which he carries his provisions.

Dr. Dick was one of the founders of the Alexandria Masonic lodge, to which Washington belonged. In 1791 he was Worshipful Master when the cornerstone of the District of Columbia was laid. Arm in arm with the President of the United States, who acted as Master, Dr. Dick led the procession with George Washington in 1793 at the laying of the cornerstone of the Capitol. This same year, as Master of the lodge, he solicited the President to "set" for the portrait by William Williams, which still graces the lodge room. In 1794 he commanded a company of cavalry raised in Alexandria and under "Light Horse Harry" Lee marched into Pennsylvania to help quell the famous Whiskey Rebellion. In 1795 he was superintendent of quarantine, an office he held for many years. In 1798 he was appointed coroner; in 1802, justice of the peace.

Dr. Dick amassed a great deal of property and was constantly buying and selling land, houses, ships, and so on. In April 1797 he disposed of the brig *Julia* to Robert Mease for ten thousand dollars, "with all her rigging and materials, together with the cargo of flour and corn now on board as she lies at Ramsay's Wharf in the Port of Alexandria."[3]

Two letters to the governor, written during his service as quarantine officer reveal the fact that he was alert to his responsibilities and give some idea of how grave they were:

Alexandria 4th Sept, 1795

Hon Robert Brooke
Sir:

Having received from various persons pretty certain information that a malignant fever is now prevalent in the town of Norfolk, I take the liberty of soliciting your instructions with regard to the propriety of interrupting the intercourse by water between that place and this. The inhabitants of Alexa. discover considerable signs of apprehension, and the corporation have entered into some temporary arrangements until more permanent ones can be obtained.

I have not yet received a compensation for the last year on account of my services as Superintendent of quarantine. Such sum as you may think me entitled to for last year as well as the percent you will oblige me by placing in the hands of Mr. Thomas Majore [?] subject to the order of Mr. Charles Turner of this place.

I am with great regard
Your Excellys
Obed Servt

ELISHA C. DICK

*   *   *   *

Alexander, 24th July 1800

Hon James Monroe
Sir:

The Ship Two Brothers on her voyage from New Orleans to this point having put into Charleston S. C. there contracted the yellow fever or some other infectious disease, by which two of her crew have died. Exercising a discretionary power given by the quarantine laws to the Superintendant, I have caused this ship to commence her quarantine near this place between Rozins Bluff and Jones Point. As the removal of vessels from this port to the mouth of Elizabeth River has been found to be attended with considerable inconvenience, the Executors have hitherto authorized me to use the situation above mentioned as the anchorage ground for all vessels bound here. I shall thank you sir for such instruction as you may deem it advisable to communicate on this subject, as well with regard to my present and future government.

I have the honor to be with the highest regard
Your obed. servt.

ELISHA C. DICK
Superintend. of quar.
Port of Alexa.

In 1801 Dr. Dick was declared bankrupt, but in 1811 he was setting free his Negro slave, Nancy, aged about forty. During these years he tended the sick (a bill for sixty-five dollars was tendered to John Harper's widow in 1804), fought the plague and fever, epidemics, and prescribed for his friends with time out for a song or a sketch. His copy of James Sharples' George Washington, now in the Mount Vernon collection, is a competent, artistic portrait. He was fond of good food, good talk, people and music. His genial spirit and charming wit graced many a festive board, and that he was hospitable as well needs no further proof than the following invitation:

If you can eat a good fat duck, come up with us and take pot luck. Of white backs we have got a pair, so plump, so sound, so fat, so fair, a London Alderman would fight, through pies and tarts to get one bite. Moreover we have beef or pork, that you may use your knife and fork. Come up precisely at two o'clock, the door shall open to your knock. The day 'tho wet, the streets 'tho muddy, to keep out the cold we'll have some toddy. And if perchance, you should get sick, you'll have at hand, Yours,

E. C. DICK[4]

Surely this friendly medical advice is well worth including in any sketch of Dr. Dick. A mature physician, he wrote to James H. Hooe:

Alexandria 20 of 2nd Month 1815

Respected friend:

I am in great hopes that the instructions I shall be able to give thee with regard to the general treatment of the prevailing disease, will be found on trial to be so far successful as to quiet in a good measure thy present apprehensions. Having received applications by letter from several physicians at a distance requesting information as to the character of the disease and the plan of treatment possessed by myself, I have thrown together a few practical remarks, which I shall here transcribe, and then add such other observations as may seem more especially necessary for thee in the present emergency.

The disease usually commences with a chill, succeeded by fever and accompanied either in the beginning or at a subsequent stage with pain in the head back breast or sides, and sometimes with an affection of the throat.

Though it is a disease attended sometimes if not generally with signs of local inflammation, yet owing to some peculiar affection or tendency of the nervous system, blood letting is in my opinion inadmissible. Of those who have been bled it has appeared that they either die or have tedious recoveries.

The disease is frequently though not always of a bilious character—that is an abundance of bile is found floating in the stomach or intestines. There seems to be neither torpor nor enlargement of the liver which have characterized the diseases of this country for 21 years past; hence culomel especially in the beginning has been avoided.

Emetics, if employed at all, (and in some cases they may be necessary) should not be given till the intestines have been well evacuated. The leading curative indication is purging, for which purpose Glaubers Salt has been preferred as acting upon the bowels with most ease and certainty. The purging process to be diligently persisted in, day and night or day after day according to the force and duration of the disease.

Warm, stimulating drinks such as toddy, made of whiskey, is frequently, though not in every case, indispensible. This stimulus, is to be resorted to whenever there are signs of prostration of body or mind, both in the beginning and after stages of the disease.

Excessive pain in the trunk may be generally mitigated in every stage of the disease by anodyne injections; for an adult two or three teaspoonsful of laudunum with a half pint of warm water. A beneficial persperation often follows this exhibition. Spontaneous sweats are commonly useful, but I have not found them critical.

The Fawcett House where Dr. Dick lived

Blisters may be employed for the mitigation of pain, and perhaps ought not to be omitted when . . . is either fever [?] is obstinate, but I have not found them in this disease to evidence their usually efficacy.

If the disease be attended with sore throat, swelling of the tonsils or palate, stricture of the trachea, with or without external swelling, a gargle of warm strong toddy, in the water of which has been boiled a pod of red pepper, will it is believed from past experience, be found uniformly and promptly effectual even in cases when suffacation seems immediately threatened. When this affection has existed to any considerable extent, I have generally with the use of the gargle also applied a blister around the throat.

In order that thou may not easily be discouraged in the prosecution of the purging plan, it is necessary to inform thee that I often find it expedient to give 3 to 6 ounces of salts in 24 hours. I usually divide 2 ounces into three portions giving one every two hours dissolved in a teacupful thin gruel. When the bowels are brought readily and freely into operation I have little difficulty in the management of the case—but I never discontinue the process till all fever and pain have subsided. Sometimes when the salts appear to be in operation I interpose with 60 or 70 grains of the cathartic powder repeated at intervals of two or three hours. When there is a despression of the pulse and something of coldness of the extremities, especially of the feet, I use with advantage mustard plaster to the feet, to which in such cases may be added with advantage hot bricks or bottles of hot water to various parts of the body.

There is one thing which particularly deserves thy notice and that is that this disease is in a majority of instances I believe preceeded by certain premonitory signs; such as flying pains about the chest or some other part, head ache, etc. A reasonable resort under such circumstances to one or two cathartics will pretty certainly avert a more serious attack.

I have directed Archy to forward thee a supply of salts and cathartic powder and I feel a persuasion that by the aid of the foregoing observations thou wilt be able to manage this disease to thy satisfaction. It indeed may be not expected that none should die of so formidible an epidemic, but I think I can with truth state to thee, that under this treatment 19/20s of those who fall under my care recover.

With regard to thy wife's present situation, I think it would be advisable for her to take occasionally a gentle laxative, and for that purpose I send a package or two of my saline purgative powders. Let her take one in a cup of gruel and repeat it as may be necessary.

Hoping that thou may be at least as successful as I have been in thy future management of this complaint, and that thy family may furnish no more victims is the sincere wish of

Thy friend

ELISHA C. DICK

Tobacco	1
Magnesia	1.50
Newspaper	7
Ginger Cake	12
Tavern	1.50
Turnpike	18
	4.37

Tablespoon vingar with 10 gns of salts of Tartar in teacup swallowed in effervescent state—slight sweat.

Dr. and Mrs. Dick were the parents of two children, Julia and Archibald. Julia married Gideon Pearce of Maryland and their son, James Alfred Pearce, became a United States senator from Maryland.

Dr. Dick, who began life as an Episcopalian, became a Quaker and

Mrs. Dick became an Episcopalian. His dueling pistols are among the curios in the Masonic museum, but if he ever used them, it is not known in Alexandria.

Writing to her son, Smith Lee, April 10, 1827, Mrs. R. E. Lee commented: "Poor Alexandria has suffered much by fire this winter. Mr. Dulaney will give you the particulars, it has lost some of its old inhabitants too. Capt. Dangerfield, Mr. Irvin, dear Dr. Dick, and Sam Thompson. . . ."[5]

Dr. Elisha Cullen Dick rests in the Friends burial ground in an unmarked grave, but his spirit hallows several houses in Alexandria. With such a wealth of dwellings to choose, it has been difficult to settle Dr. Dick for long; nor really does he want to be settled. He was full of surprises during life, and it will be another to most Alexandrians when we place him in the old clapboard house known for better than a century as "the Fawcett house."

On December 20, 1774, John Alexander sold to Patrick Murry a certain lot or half acre of land situated and adjoining the west side of a lot or half acre of land lying in the town of Alexandria and represented by lot No. 112. This lot, lying on the north side of Prince Street, between Pitt and St. Asaph Streets, was described as: "Beginning on the Southwest corner of the said lott No. 112 and running thence with it to the Northwest corner thereof 176 feet 7 inches, thence Westerly with a line at right angles with the last 123 feet 5 inches thence Southerly with a line parallel to the first one and of the same extent thence Easterly with a straight line to the beginning."[6]

There was a ground rent upon this property every year forever of £13 5s., and the provisions that Patrick Murry or his heirs should build within the space of two years from the date of purchase a brick, stone or wooden house, twenty feet square, to cover four hundred square feet, with a brick or stone chimney or chimneys. At the same time John Alexander bound himself to lay out and keep free forever a street sixty-six feet wide binding on the west side of the granted lot or half acre of land, by the name of St. Asaph Street: "Beginning at a straight line produced and extended from the termination of Cameron Street in the said town of Alexandria until it extends sixty-six feet to a direct line to the Westward beyond the breadth of the other lott or half acre of land, thence Southerly and parallel to Pitt Street in the said town, until it intersects a street of the same width called Wilkes Street . . ."[7]

Patrick Murry built and resided in this completely charming clapboard

Patrick Murray's parlor. The picture over the mantel is needleworked, a polite accomplishment taught to females and the product of the gentle hands of a Fawcett ancestor

house until the year 1786, when the wheels of fortune forced him to dispose of all houses, yards, gardens, ways, advantages, and so on, to Ann English and William McKenzey, executors of Samuel English to secure the payments of the sum of £348, Virginia currency, with interest from August 22, 1775. Alas, for compound interest! Ann English and her husband, James Currie, did convey and sell the lot with all improvements unto Elisha Cullen Dick on April 15, 1794. Two years later Dr. Dick and his wife, Hannah, disposed of the house and grounds to John Thomas Ricketts and William Newton for and in consideration of £1000 current money.

On July 2, 1806, William Newton and wife conveyed the property "including all that framed dwelling house lately occupied by the said William Newton" for the sum of four thousand dollars to William Smith;[8] thence again in 1816 the Smiths, William and Margaret, disposed of the frame dwelling house for three thousand dollars to John D. Brown.

The descendants of John Douglas Brown have occupied the home for the past one hundred and thirty-three years. His great-grandchildren, the Fawcett family, are the present owners of the house. The Fawcett house has been little changed, and is kept in excellent repair. The woodwork in the drawing room is true to the period; that throughout the house is quaint and interesting. In the great room the fire breast is outlined with a dog-eared mold. The mantelshelf, attached without brackets, has a punch-work motif. The heavy raised panels on each side of the chimney, and the paneled closets enclose the entire west wall.

There are many levels, and the house goes back in a surprising brick ell that is not seen from the street. The exterior presents the appearance of a story-and-a-half cottage. Two windows, with their uncommon blinds, break the wood-shingled roof. The blinds' slats are wide and heavy, and the shutters are held in place when opened by the traditional molded iron holdbacks. The east gable end of the house is shiplap. From this side projects the entrance porch, added about 1816, and protected by "jalousies."

Portraits, old silver, glass, and china, prints and mahogany, with great grandmama's best brocade dresses, are the fruits of more than a century of the family's inheritance. The picture over the mantel is done in embroidery—the product of one of the Fawcett ancestors, worked in 1814, while a pupil at one of Alexandria's schools where young ladies were taught the fine arts, and the curriculum included every form of needlework.

Dear Dr. Dick. By Saint Mèmin.
(Courtesy Corcoran Gallery of Art)

Benjamin Dulany's Town House

Chapter 15

The Benjamin Dulany House*

On February 15, 1773, George Washington wrote to a friend, "Our celebrated Fortune Miss French, whom half the world was in pursuit of, bestowed her hand on Wednesday last, being her birthday (you perceive I think myself under the necessity of accounting for the choice) upon Mr. Ben Dulany, who is to take her to Maryland in a month from this time."[1]

Miss French, the heiress, was a ward of Washington and lived at Rose Hill, not far from Mount Vernon. Benjamin Dulany Sr., a wealthy and cultured gentleman of Maryland, born of distinguished Irish parentage, was of the third generation in America. He and the celebrated Miss French moved to Alexandria before the Revolution and settled at Shuter's Hill overlooking the town, where they reared a large family. Ben Dulany is often mentioned by General Washington in his diaries. He was a frequent visitor at Mount Vernon, a companion in the chase

*601 Duke Street. Owners: Mr. and Mrs. John Howard Joynt.

Benjamin Dulany of Shooter's Hill and Alexandria

and the race, at dinner and overnight, sometimes with his lady, but more often without.

In 1785 Washington concluded a bargain for the exchange of some land with the Dulanys and made several references to the transaction in his diary. Under the entry for Monday, February 21, 1785, he wrote:

Went to Alexandria with Mrs. Washington. Dined at Mr. Dulaney's and exchanged deeds for conveyances of land with him and Mrs. Dulaney, giving mine, which I bought of Messrs. Robert Adam, Dow and McIver, for the reversion of what Mrs. Dulaney is entitled to at the death of her Mother within bounds of Spencer and Washington's patent.[2]

Entrance hall, Dulany House. Fine woodwork in arch and cornice

Tradition says Dulany served with Washington as steward of the Jockey Club. An amusing anecdote has come down to us of a race in which both gentlemen had entered horses. The race was close—Washington's horse won. For some reason the governors awarded the prize to Dulany. The General left in high dudgeon and wrote a letter resigning from the club, saying that he was under the impression that he belonged to a club the members of which were gentlemen. Whereupon the governors reversed their decision and awarded the General the prize! This extraordinary action is reported to have placated him, for he appears to have continued a member of the Jockey Club.

Mr. Dulany's house, now 601 Duke Street, is one of those famous houses where it is claimed General Washington slept. An agent of the General, Peyton Gallagher, occupied this house at one time, and—so the story goes—when Washington had sat too long at accounts and the evening was bad, his man of business put him up for the night.

The tradition is firmly entrenched that the Marquis de la Fayette addressed the citizens of Alexandria from the front steps of this house in 1824. The General was occupying the house across the street, which was given to the Marquis and his party by the owner, Mrs. Lawrason, for the duration of his visit. Alexandria was more excited by this visit than any other occurrence in her history, and gave La Fayette a resounding welcome. When citizens came surging in great crowds around the Lawrason mansion to do him honor, the old gentleman, finding the steps too low for speechmaking, walked across the street, climbed the steps of 601 Duke Street, where he could be seen, and there made his expressions of good will and appreciation in broken English to "the assembled multitude."

Tradition also reports that Benjamin Dulany was a handsome, arrogant gentleman, a fine horseman, superbly mounted. In those days the streets of Alexandria were not as smooth nor as dry as today. Irate pedestrians often found themselves bespattered and befouled by some passing horseman or vehicle and in danger of their very lives. "Bad Ben" Dulany thundered up and down the streets, riding a spirited horse, sparing no wayfarer, causing men to rush for safety to the nearest doorway. At Shuter's Hill, his estate just outside Alexandria, he maintained well appointed stables and owned fine-blooded horses. A "stranger" traveling in America records a rather interesting horse story in connection with one of Mr. Dulany's sons:

Throughout his campaign he [Washington] was attended by a black man, one of his slaves, who proved very faithful to his trust. This man, amongst

The beautiful drawing room

others belonging to him, he liberated, and by his will, left him a handsome maintenance for the remainder of his life. The horse which bore the General so often in battle is still alive. The noble animal, together with the whole of his property, was sold on his death under a clause in his will, and the charger was purchased by Daniel Dulaney, Esquire, of Shuter's hill, near Alexandria, in whom it has found an indulgent master. I have often seen Mr. Dulaney riding the steed of Washington in a gentle pace, for it is now grown old. It is of a cream color, well proportioned, and was carefully trained to military manoeuvres.[3]

* * * *

The Dulanys were hospitable folk, and many were the guests entertained both at their country estate and at their Alexandria home. A

revengeful guest, or a malicious wit, startled the town one morning by
the following poem entitled

THE BALL AT SHOOTER'S HILL
By A. X.—Georgetown

Ben Dulany of Shooter's Hill,
Once said to his wife, "Our rooms we'll fill
With all the beauty, and all the style
And all of the rank and some of the file
That flourish in Alexandria
Alias 'Botany Bay',"
(Which was ever his subsequent say
When speaking of Alexandria).
Mrs. Dulany said with a sigh
"If such is your fancy, so will I".

Ben Dulany of Shooter's Hill
Said to his wife, "We will fulfill
Our social trust and invite them all,
The great and the wealthy to come to our ball,
The handsome and ugly, the pretty and plain,
The learned and the silly, the wise and the vain."
He was a man of great learning and wealth
And the name that he bore was a power itself,
For his Tory father was great among men
And smote hard on the rebels with voice and pen,
But Mrs. Dulany said with a sigh,
"This fancy of his, I cannot tell why".

Ben Dulany of Shooter's Hill
Said to his wife, "I wish you to fill
The pantry and larder, the shelves and the table
With all the most excellent things you are able,
And spare neither trouble or money, for when
(Tobacco remember was currency then),
I offer a banquet my guests must behold
Something more on my table than china and gold".
And Mrs. Dulany said with a deep sigh,
"This fancy of his, I cannot tell why".

Ben Dulany of Shooter's Hill,
Said to his wife, "Of course we will
Have music, the best that can be found
And we, dear wife, will dance one round.
Many years have passed since you agreed

The original dining room at Mr. Dulany's, now the library

To slide down from your window and marry with speed,
And we'll show our children how to dance
After the fashion I learned in France".
Mrs. Dulany sighed and said
"What could have put this whim in his head".

The guests arrived at Shooter's Hill,
Names of renown the chambers filled,
Masons and Carters, Stevens and Balls,
Rosiers and Fendals, Marshalls and Halls,
Daingerfields, Herberts, Craiks, Tuckers a few,
Platers, Custis, and Randolph and Washingtons, too,
Blackburns, Hunters and Forrests and Taylors a lot,
Lees, Seldons, Fitzhughs, Wests, Dandridge and Scott,
Pope, Ramsey and Graham, French, Lewis and Key,
Lloyd, Taylor and Wellford, Ridout, Beverly,
Simms, Peters and Lightfoot, Lyles, Murray and Beall,
Fauntleroy and Grey and Carroll they tell,
Berkley, Fairfax and Bladen, Powell, Chase, Montague,
Bassett, Harrison, Tasker, Gant, Stoddert and Chew,
Spotswood, Lomax and Taliaferro, Grymes, Rutherford,
Snowden, Fontaine and Pendleton, Moncure and Bushrod,
But if all were put down, the unlearned might insist,
The names had been taken from off the tax list.

Ben Dulany of Shooter's Hill,
Received them with grace and courtly skill,
When all of a sudden he started to dance,
And teach them the lessons he learned in France,
He drew them up in a regular line
And marched them around while he kept time,
Shouldered a blunderbuss, stuck on a hat,
Called it a helmet, and drilled them in that.
Thundered and threatened and ordered them all
To know he was giving a marching ball.
Round through the parlors, out on the grass
Down through the garden and back did they pass,
Not for a moment he left them to rest,
Forward and backward, and wearied he pressed.
Mrs. Dulany appealed to his pride,
But unceremonious he thrust her aside.
Many the terrors, the words and the fright,
But he marched them and marched them till far in the night.
Mrs. Dulany again essayed
To urge him to cease his desperate raid,

Then bending before her his handsome form,
He declared no lovelier woman was born
Than she, his own, his beautiful wife
Then he vowed to love and cherish through life;
And to prove to all how he loved her then,
He'd embrace her before all those women and men,
Which he certainly did, for he clasped her waist,
And raising her high, strode off in haste.
In vain she screamed, in vain besought,
All her entreaties he set at nought,
Into the pantry he quickly passed
And stuck her up on the vinegar cask
Then locking her in, he lovingly said,
"Dear wife you are tired, 'tis time for bed".

And away he stalked to pick up his gun
For a panic and flight had already begun,
He ordered a halt, but they faster ran,
Urging each other, woman and man.
Wholly regardless of dresses and shoes,
Thorns or stones, or damps or dews.
Halt! he cried again more loud
Then fired his blunderbuss into the crowd,
Which only helped to increase their speed.

They thought he was crased, and he was indeed!
Into the town at dead of night
Forlorn and weary, half dead with fright,
Into the town the company came,
Draggled and straggling, half dead with shame,
That they should have marched and tramped about
At a lunatic's whim, now in, now out,
The livelong night, through garden and hall,
Would they ever forget Ben Dulany's ball!

Mrs. Dulany in grief had passed
The rest of the night on the vinegar cask.
Trembling the servants unlocked the door,
And the wrathful lady stood before
Her . . . lord, but never a word
Between them passed, or afterward was heard.
He ordered his horse and from that day,
As I have heard the old people say,
He rode unceasing, nor ever still,
Was Ben Dulany of Shooter's Hill.[4]

The front bedroom, Dulany House

On August 5, 1779, the executor of John Alexander, William Thornton Alexander, granted by deed to David Arrell the tract of land located at the northwest corner of Duke and St. Asaph Streets, which held an annual ground rent of £14 10s. On September 6, 1783, David Arrell of Alexandria and Fairfax County in the Dominion of Virginia, sold this same lot on Duke and St. Asaph Streets for £50 to Benjamin Dulany of the same place, charged with an annual ground rent of £14 10s., payable on the fifth of August forever. Very shortly thereafter the house now known as 601 Duke Street was completed for a town residence. During some recent repairs letters and bills for purchases made by Mrs. Dulany were found under a partition, bearing dates from 1785 to 1796. Two of these are quoted:[5]

Mrs. Delasia   Balto. 24 Feby 1793
   For Mrs. Dulaney Bo[t] of George Wily
1 pair of sattin shoes 16/8   £   16.   8
1 p[c] Roses   22d   1. 1. 18
     Rec[d] payment   £   1. 18. 6
Benjamin Dulany Esq.   *   *   *   GEORGE WILY
   Bo[t] of Bennett & Watts
1 pr Slippers 9/—3½ yds Lute string @ 10/   £   2.   4.
Alex[a] May 25th 1796

Probably the best example of Georgian architecture in Alexandria, the plan of the house is common to this town. Two-storied, dormer-windowed, detached brick, the house faces south with a large garden to the left taking up half a square.

A hall runs the length of the house. Two large parlors, one behind the other, on the right, open into the hall. The dining room, in an ell at the rear, is entered from the hall by a small flight of steps leading to a lower level. The long, narrow, low-pitched room has an off-center fireplace and is papered at both ends in old wallpaper of Chinese design. When seen from the front doorway, the room presents an unexpected and charming view. This wing was added after 1800, probably 1810. A very nice tradition exists about the building of this wing. Robert I. Taylor bought the house from the Dulanys in 1810. He was a vestryman of St. Paul's Church and very much interested in its construction. Benjamin H. Latrobe was the architect for the church and it is believed that he designed the wing connecting the kitchen with the big house. The story is more than plausible since the high, narrow arches and pilasters are characteristic of his work.

The woodwork in the two parlors is massive. The heavy cornice is similar to that in the blue room at the Carlyle house. A thick dentil cornice is surmounted by modillions, and they in turn are surmounted by a heavy molding. The drawing room mantels, capped by the traditional broken arch, dominate these rooms. All openings are dog-eared, as well as the panels of the chimney breasts. The hall arches, wainscoting, hand-rails, and stairways are noble examples of early craftsmanship. Upstairs the woodwork is equally good, though more delicate, while the paneled mantels lack the broken arch.

It is a satisfaction to see these old rooms, graced by fine furniture, draperies, portraits, and silver of local origin, restored again to the dignity and graciousness of days long past.

Chapter 16
Dr. James Craik and His Dwelling*

Of the many quaint, historical figures whose memories haunt the old streets and houses of Alexandria, none is more interesting than Dr. Craik.

He is remembered as a "stout, hale, cheery old man, perfectly erect, fond of company and children, and amusing himself with gardening work." But this was when the sands were running out. The good Doctor had passed fourscore years, and his share of history-making was over. Let us turn back some two hundred years and begin.

There is a little village near Dumfries in Scotland called Arbigland or Obigland. In the year 1730 on a cold December day a baby boy began an eventful life. He was destined to bring to the New World the skill to heal and succor the wounded, to ease the dying, to administer the primitive hospitals of the American Revolution, and to move for a span of forty-five years as the close and intimate friend of George Washington.

The names of his parents have been lost in the Scottish fogs. A story

*210 Duke Street. Owner: Mr. Merle Colby.

that his father employed a gardener by the name of John Paul, sire of another young Scotsman who distinguished himself in our naval history under the patronymic of John Paul Jones, is all we can glean of our Craik's paternal parent.[1]

The Scottish baby, christened James Craik, grew to young manhood in his native country, going in proper time to the University of Edinburgh and there was educated in medicine for service in the British Army. After leaving the university he set sail for the West Indies; from there he came to Virginia in 1750 and settled in or near Winchester.

We pick up his trail four years later on an April morning in the town of Alexandria. The occasion is both historic and dramatic. The market square was filled with "two companies of foot," a hundred and twenty soldiers; a drummer wielding his sticks fiercely; two wagons, loaded with provisions, and well guarded by officers and soldiers; a captain, a lieutenant, five subalterns and a "Swedish Gentleman" going along as a volunteer, and one *surgeon*. This military assembly under the command of Lieutenant Colonel George Washington was marching out of Alexandria for points west "to the Ohio" to fight the Indians and the French, to build forts, and to defend the possessions of His Majesty. The commander of the purposeful outfit was twenty-two years old, and the surgeon, Dr. James Craik, twenty-four.

Did the two meet in the City Tavern, in the market square, or upon that first day's march of six miles when the troops bivouacked for the night? Wherever the acquaintance was made, the beginning of a friendship that was to last the lives of both men was cemented on this expedition. From the battles of Great Meadows and Fort Necessity, our warriors returned to accompany Braddock to the Monongahela and Fort DuQuesne where Dr. Craik nursed Washington through an illness and was with Braddock from the time he was wounded until his death.

In August 1755 Dr. Craik was back from two unsuccessful expeditions. He was one of a group of officers addressing the august assembly sitting at Williamsburg, by letter, who informed the Burgesses that they had lost horses, furniture, tents, marquees, clothes, linens—in short, all their field equipage—and asking that body to compensate in some measure for their misfortunes, reminding the House that it was customary among British troops by way of a contingent bill, and suggesting that the colonial troops were equally deserving. The letter was ordered tabled, but later £30 was voted as compensation.

After this second disastrous campaign, Dr. Craik was lured into domesticity by Miss Marianne Ewell, whom he married in 1760. This young lady drew the ties closer to Mount Vernon. Her mother, first cousin to George Washington, was Sarah Ball Conway, who married Charles Ewell. After his marriage, Dr. Craik moved across the Potomac to Port Tobacco, Maryland, where he built a house and proceeded to raise a family of six sons and three daughters.

In 1754 Governor Dinwiddie offered as bait to officers who would enlist for service in the French and Indian Wars, two hundred thousand acres of land in the Ohio country. Sixteen years later this land had not been distributed. Washington was selected as agent to represent the officers of the First Virginia Regiment, and at their request, he left early in October 1770 to inspect and locate lands to be patented in their names. He was accompanied by Dr. Craik. The two set off on horseback with three Negro servants, two of the General's and one of Dr. Craik's, and a pack horse, spending two months in surveying and plotting these wild lands. Despite bad weather, cold, and early snow, it was a journey enjoyed by both men.

The route was charged with memories of Fry and Braddock's campaign. Washington wished to retrace these rivers and streams. The possibility of connecting the Potomac with the west by canals, opening up the country for settlement and trade had come to the engineer even while the soldier was fighting. As they rode he dreamed of tilled fields and settled communities in the path of his horse and used his instruments to measure distances and to plumb the depth of streams. That he revealed his plans to this congenial friend of his travels seems certain. Fourteen years later, in 1784, he took Dr. Craik over the same terrain when these dreams appeared to attain realization in the contemplated canal to connect the Potomac with the Ohio.

During his entire life, Dr. Craik was a steady visitor at Mount Vernon, on social occasions or on professional calls. He could be counted on for a visit at least once a month; sometimes he remained four or five days at a time, but more frequently he only passed the night. It is rather strange that the good Doctor is never mentioned as a companion of Washington's favorite sport. That he was an able horseman, covering the roughest terrain in arduous campaigns, a seasoned sportsman, a hardened athlete but no fox-hunter, seems borne out by the fact that he is never mentioned as sharing in the chase, although the gentleman to whom it meant so much noted almost every hunt and rider in his daily journals.

Politically the two friends were united. When Virginians were becoming dissatisfied and impatient with England, Dr. Craik and Washington thought alike, attending county meetings and councils, acting together. When the colony was disrupted by revolt and Washington appointed commander in chief of the Continental forces, he at once had Dr. Craik appointed Surgeon-General in the Continental Army. In 1777 he was made Assistant Director General of the Hospital of the Middle Department of the Army. Throughout the war he was part of Washington's military family.

At Cornwallis' surrender, Dr. Craik was in command of the hospital corps at Yorktown and present on that occasion. It was his painful duty to attend the fatally injured Hugh Mercer at Princeton, to dress the wounds of La Fayette at Brandywine, to nurse during his last hours young Jacky Custis, only surviving child of Martha Washington. It was Dr. Craik who learned of the Conway Cabal in 1777 and warned Washington of the conspiracy to remove him from command. To him we also owe the Indian legend of Washington's immortality. When Braddock was defeated and killed at Monongahela, Washington, with four bullets through his coat and two horses shot from under him, the chosen target of the Indian chief and his braves, was unharmed, and the Indians believed him immune to poisoned arrow or blunderbuss.

It is said that Washington persuaded Dr. Craik to move to Alexandria after the Revolution. We find him renting a house on Fairfax Street from one Robert Lyles in 1788 for £45. In 1789 he rented a house on Prince Street from John Harper for £25, and in 1790 one on the same street for £35. He rented and occupied a house belonging to John Harper from 1793 to, or through, 1795, for £60, a residence which has been so closely associated with Dr. Dick that it bears a memorial tablet in his memory.

In October 1795, Dr. Craik bought the property on Duke and Water (now Lee) Street, which he occupied for several years, and owned until 1810. Tradition, in this case false, says the house was built by George Coryell, and the story of how he came to Alexandria as a builder is a very interesting anecdote. On one of Washington's trips to Philadelphia after the Revolution, the story goes, he admired a well designed and constructed gate at the house of Benjamin Franklin, and inquired the name of the artisan. It was the work of one George Coryell of Coryell's Ferry. The young man's father, Cornelius Coryell, had acted as guide during the New Jersey campaign and the family had rowed Washington across the Delaware in that surprise attack upon the Hessians on Christmas

Night, 1776. The General, interested in building, and something of an architect himself, with an eye to securing competent workmen near home, is said to have persuaded George Coryell to move to Alexandria. Here Coryell bought a lot on Duke Street in 1794 where he lived for many years. That Coryell set up in the building and lumber business and was very active is better documented, for this advertisement appeared in the *Gazette* for October 23, 1793:

George Coryell
Has for Sale
At His Board Yard on Mr. Mease's Wharf and
at his Dwelling House on Duke Street
Two-inch, Inch, and Half-Inch and
etc. Plank. House frames of dif-
ferent sizes, Cypress shingles
Locust and Red Cedar Post
Scantling

Many houses in the town are perhaps his handiwork, but the statement that he built Dr. Craik's house or the frame cottage next door, which tradition says was his Alexandria home, is open to grave doubt. Recorded deeds at Fairfax Court House testify that the house and lot east of Dr. Craik were owned by Joseph Robinson, a sailmaker, in 1783, and used descriptively in a deed dated 1795. Coryell's lot was two doors below Dr. Craik's house (the lot now in possession of General Carl Spaatz) which Coryell purchased from William and Sarah Lyles of Prince Georges County, Maryland.

Coryell served for a time as clerk of the market and sealer of weights and measures. He did some repair jobs on Washington's town house. At the General's funeral, when Lieutenant Moss was unable to carry the heavy weight of the casket, George Coryell took his place as one of the pallbearers. He remained in Alexandria some fifty-odd years, returning to Coryell's Ferry a few years previous to his death in 1850, at the advanced age of ninety-one.

At the first auction of lots in Alexandria town in 1749, the lots numbered 80 and 81 were sold to Anne West. The trustees upset this sale in 1754, reselling lot No. 80 to George Mercer for £9 13s. 10d. and lot No. 81 going to Daniel Wilson for £10 10s. By devious transactions these parcels of land were divided and sold. The property of Dr. Craik was in the ownership of John Short, a watchmaker, in 1783. Due to inability to repay John Harper money advanced, Short, then of the borough of Norfolk, sold his house and lot at auction on November 30, 1789 to

Rear of house and courtyard built by John B. Murray and bought by Dr. James Craik. The leanto at right replaces the frame building of Joseph Robinson, sailmaker

John Murry for £234. This same property was sold by John B. Murry and Patty, his wife, of the city and state of New York on October 26, 1795, along with another lot belonging to Murry, to Dr. James Craik for £1,500. Allowing for the additional lot, for which Murry had paid £71 10s. 1d. in 1787, and on which Dr. Craik's stable stood, for inflation and increase in value of property in Alexandria following the Revolution, this price of approximately $7,500 indicates beyond question that John Murry made very substantial improvements upon this property. It was subject to a ground rent of £11 forever, and it is only within the last few years that the present owners have satisfied this rent.

The house is a typical Alexandria town mansion. With three stories, dormer widows, of salmon brick, laid in Flemish bond, it faces the street as sturdily as when first built.

All the chimneys in Dr. Craik's house are handsomely paneled, as well as the window frames. Cornices, chair rails, stairway, six-panel doors, old pine floors, H&L hinges are part of its attractions. It is believed that Dr. Craik used the front rooms on the first floor of his house as his office. Washington was a visitor in this house. He frequently mentions in his journal dining or supping with his friend. The last time seems to have been in July 1798, when he "went up to Alexa. with Mrs. W. and Miss Cus[tis] dined at Doct^r Craik's, ret^d in ye aft^n."

One of the Craik boys was named after George Washington. In September 1785, Washington makes this entry in his diary: "Wed. 31st . . . This day I told Dr. Craik that I would contribute one hundred dollars pr. ann. as long as it was necessary towards the education of his son, George Washington, either in this country or in Scotland."

George Washington Craik studied medicine, and was, for a time during Washington's second administration, his private secretary. He was one of the young people of the town who was a constant visitor at Mount Vernon up to Washington's death. In 1807 and 1808 he was postmaster at Alexandria. He married Maria D. Tucker, daughter of Captain John Tucker, and their son, James Craik, was an Episcopal clergyman. Another son, William, married the daughter of William Fitzhugh and became the brother-in-law to George Washington Parke Custis. William Craik was a member of Congress, judge of the District Court of the United States, and chief justice of the Fifth Maryland Judicial Circuit Court. Craik lost two sons, James and Adam. James Craik Jr. set up in the drug business in Alexandria, dissolving his current business of James Craik & Company in 1787, but continued "the drug business at his store next door to Col. Ramsays'." At the time of this announcement he advertised for a young man well recommended as an apprentice for the druggist profession. He died, poor young man, without attaining any great success. The Doctor was appointed administrator and failed to give any accounting of the estate. As a result Dr. Craik was haled before the court to show the cause of his failure to comply with the order. He was somewhat riled as appears from the following:

James Craik this day appeared at the Register office and being duly sworn, gave the following statement: That when the said James Craik, Jr., departed this

"To my compatriot in arms, and old intimate friend, Dr. Craik I give my Bureau, (or as the cabinet makers call it, Tambour Secretary) and the circular chair —an appendage of my study." *(Mount Vernon Ladies' Association)*

life all the personal estate he had consisted of a Medical Shop furniture, and medicine, to what amount or value he cannot ascertain, nor did he ever think it necessary he should render any appraisement of them, as he was security for the payment of the money they were purchased for, and since the deceased death has paid the same, and every debt he owed; in speaking of the said shop furniture and medicine being all the personal estate of the deceased his cloathes are excepted of which the said administrator saith he considered it unnecessary to render any account for the reasons above mentioned. Sworn to before me at the Register office on Tuesday, the 26th day of April, 1803.

CLEM MOORE

James Craik Adms.[2]

Of the three daughters, one married a Mr. Harrison, one Daniel of St. Thomas Jenifer, and the third married Colonel Roger West of West Grove. The daughter of this union married John Douglas Simms, son of Colonel Charles Simms of Revolutionary fame. Mrs. James Craik Jr., was Sarah Harrison, daughter of Robert Hanson Harrison, one of Washington's military secretaries.

On November 27, a little over two weeks before Washington's death, Dr. Craik delivered Nellie Custis, wife of Washington's nephew and private secretary, Lawrence Lewis, of a daughter, her first child.

December 12, 1799, was a bad day. General Washington, making the usual rounds of his farms, was not deterred by snow, sleet, nor the cold rain that followed. Coming in late to dinner, which was awaiting him, his clothes soaked, snow clinging to his hair, he did not take time to change his wet things. The next day he had a sore throat and was very hoarse. During the night he felt ill and awoke his wife. As soon as it was daylight, Mrs. Washington sent a messenger posthaste for Dr. Craik. Before he arrived, Washington insisted upon being bled, and his secretary, Tobias Lear, sent across the river to Port Tobacco for Dr. Gustavus Brown. When Dr. Craik arrived he was alarmed at the condition of his friend, bled him twice, and asked to have Dr. Dick called for consultation. The three doctors battled with their primitive knowledge as best they knew how. Dr. Craik rarely left the room, sitting by the fire, his hand cupped over his eyes. Mrs. Washington sat at the foot of the bed, while Tobias Lear noted every passing moment for posterity and gave what aid he could to make the patient comfortable. About five o'clock Washington said to Craik, "Doctor, I die hard but I am not afraid to go. I believed from my first attack that I should not survive it. My breath cannot last long." Life dragged five hours more, and when the end came Dr. Craik closed the eyes of him who was his best friend.[3] The watch

Mantel in the house at 209 Prince Street which John Harper rented to Dr. Craik from 1790 to 1795 at £60 per annum and which bears a plate erroneously marking the domicile of Dr. Dick, who lived next door

which ticked off these awful moments is preserved in the Museum at Mount Vernon. When the General's will was opened one of the clauses read:

To my compatriot in arms, and old & intimate friend, Doct[r] Craik, I give my Bureau (or as the Cabinet makers call it, Tambour Secretary) and the circular chair—an appendage of my Study.[4]

This desk and chair migrated with a later generation of Craiks to Kentucky and afterward the heirloom chair was presented as a token of esteem to General Andrew Jackson. Happy to relate, both pieces are again united in the library at Mount Vernon.

There remained for Dr. Craik one more duty to perform at Mount Vernon. In May 1802, two and a half years after the death of her husband, Martha Washington fell ill. This old friend of her married life of forty years watched over her for the seventeen days that remained and was with her, too, when she breathed her last.

Doctor Craik lived for fifteen years after the death of his friend and patron, hale and hearty to the end. In 1810 he put up his Alexandria house as security for a loan and it was sold at public auction March 23, 1810, to Rebecca Taylor.

Doctor Craik died on February 6, 1814, in his eighty-fourth year at his country estate, Vauclause, near Alexandria. He lies in the graveyard of the old Presbyterian meetinghouse.

His house in Alexandria, at 210 Duke Street, was fittingly enough in 1943 made habitable once again by another physician, Dr. Laurence A. Thompson, and Mrs. Thompson.

Dr. James Craik and Dr. Elisha Dick

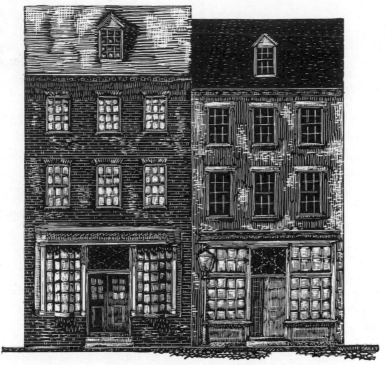

Chapter 17
Alexandria's Old Apothecary Shop*

Among the Quakers who settled in Alexandria there was a young man by the name of Edward Stabler, who came from Petersburg, Virginia. By 1792 he had established himself in the drug business on Fairfax Street between King and Prince. The major portion of his first stock of drugs came from London and cost about £106. Today his shop is famous as the second oldest apothecary shop in the United States in continuous operation and has been conducted by five generations of Stabler's descendants, the name of the proprietor changing to Leadbeater in 1852.

Always the proprietors maintained the most unique relations, business and social, with their patrons. Extant today are orders for one quart of castor oil from Martha Washington, an order for paint from George Washington Parke Custis, and many other curious and historical records, including the comments on a bad debt. In 1801 Mr. Stabler ordered from his dealer in London:

---

*With the settlement of the Leadbeater estate in 1933, these two adjoining buildings were acquired by the Landmarks Society of Alexandria and the contents purchased by the American Pharmaceutical Association. Under the direction of Mrs. Robert M. Reese the buildings have been restored and opened to the public as a museum with displays generously lent by the American Pharmaceutical Association. Entrance at 107 South Fairfax Street.

Alexandria's Old Apothecary Shop, where Georgian and Victorian meet

One medicine chest, complete with weights, scales, bolus knives, etc. I want this to be mahogany, of good quality as it is for the granddaughter of the widow of General Washington, the cost to be about 12 guineas.

There is a story in Alexandria that it was in this shop that the messenger, Lieutenant J. E. B. Stuart, from the War Department, found General R. E. Lee chatting with the proprietor, his old friend, the senior Leadbeater, and delivered to the then Colonel Lee sealed orders from General Winfield Scott ordering him to Harpers Ferry to take command during John Brown's raid. It may be safely said that this shop was commonly used as a place of meeting by the gentlemen of the town who gathered there to exchange views and hear the latest news.

There remain in the old pharmacy early hand-blown bottles, counters and showcases, weights and scales, mortars and pestles, prescriptions, old ledgers, and much unidentified impedimenta of these early apothecaries. The decoration of the interior is indicative of the five generations who have lived and worked here. Georgian and Victorian blend in a harmonious whole. The exterior has been admirably restored to eighteenth century correctness—semicircular windows and all. The shop proper is the ground floor of a three-story business structure. Adjoining is an associated gift shop, also on the ground floor of a three-story building, and the two structures must appear very much as they did when built.

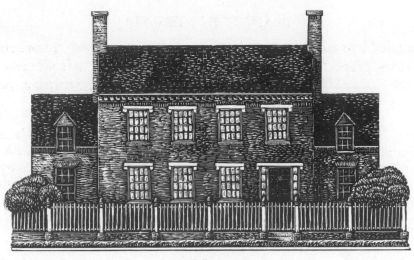

Chapter 18
Spring Gardens*

The stranger arriving in Alexandria by ship, coach, or horse could be sure of a welcome. The old port was noted for her taverns. They were numerous and good. At the taverns the gentlemen of the town were wont to gather for an oyster supper, a turtle feast, or a cockfight. The Masonic brothers sought these places for their banquets, and often for their meetings. Here stagecoaches drew up with bustle and excitement to put out the mail, change the horses, set down and take up the passengers, and let the traveler call for a draught of ale. Here the mail was collected and distributed. Here sailors could find a berth, the stranger a roaring fire, a glass of grog, food, bed and forage for his weary horse.

In 1753 at a court held at Fairfax, the rate for a night's lodging with clean sheets was fixed at 6d., "otherwise 3 pence." For a quart of punch with loaf sugar, 1s. 3d.; for a quart of punch with brown sugar, 10d. For a hot dish with small beer or cider, 1s.; for a cold dish, 4d. Stablage and fodder for a horse for twenty-four hours, 6d.; pasturage for twenty-four hours, 4d. It was ordered that "the several and respective ordinary keepers in this county do sell according to the above rates in money or tobacco at the rate of twelve shillings and six pence per cubic weight, and that they do not presume to demand more of any person what so ever."[1]

Among the Alexandria taverns of note that flourished in the late eighteenth century was Spring Gardens or Yates' Tavern, as the place was known in comparatively recent years. The little brick buildings were

---

*414 Franklin Street. Owners: Mr. and Mrs. Harry W. Harris.

surrounded by spacious grounds, the walks edged in box, arbors covered with vines, grapes, fruit and shade trees all but hiding it from view.

In the *Columbia Mirror and Alexandria Gazette* of Saturday, January 12, 1793, the following advertisement appeared:

Oyster House—Spring Gardens. The subscriber informs his Friends and the Gentlemen of Alexandria that he intends providing oyster suppers at his house this winter on the most moderate terms and at the shortest notice. Those who may incline to favor him with their custom, may rest assured that there shall be nothing wanting on his part to give general satisfaction.

ABEL WILLIS

Again Spring Gardens figured in the news of October 5, 1795, when this advertisement appeared in the *Virginia Gazette and Alexandria Advertiser* of that date:

To be sold by Private Contract. The unexpired term of the lease or covenant of that desirable lot called Spring Gardens with all its extensive improvements. The lease or covenant has many and great advantages annexed to it. Apply to the proprietor on the premises.

H. WILBUR.

Some time previously, in 1793, H. Wilbur in the same publication announced that the "Late Master of the Steine House Academy Brighthelmstone, Begs leave Respectfully to inform the Public in General that his Academy will open on Monday next, the 27th, inst. for the reception of ten young Ladies at Two Dollars per month, pens and ink included."

Was Spring Gardens a young ladies academy as well as oysterhouse, tavern and jockey club?

The tradition that Spring Gardens was the second Jockey Club seems to be borne out in the announcement of the spring races which appeared on Saturday, May 20, 1797:

Red House Spring Races

To be run for on Thurs. 25th inst. over Jockey Club course. A subscription purse of 100 dollars, three mile heats, free for any horse, mare or gelding. Aged horses to carry 126 lbs; six year old 118; 5 years old 110; 4 years 98 and three years old feather.

On Friday, a Purse of $50.00, 2 mile heats, Saturday a Purse of $50.00, mile heats. The Purses shall be at the Post.

The horses to be entered the day preceding each race with me or pay double on entrance; the winning horse on each preceding day only excepted. I have expended a great deal of money in altering and improving the course it is now

Rear of Spring Gardens or Yate's Tavern

approved by the best judges of racing. No exertion shall be wanting to give satisfaction by the publics devoted servent.

JAMES GARDINER

Last day a feather.

N.B. The Jockey Club Races will commense on Wed. 20th, Sept. next.

The Races were intended for the 18th, 19th, and 20th, but the commencement of the District Court being altered from the 12th to the 18th inst. was only known this day by the public's obedient servant

JAMES GARDINER

N.B. On the 15th June following a colts purse or sweepstake will certainly be run for; each subscriber putting five guineas in the purse the day before starting. Several are already entered. The Colts that are admissable may be known by an application to J.G.

General Washington was a visitor many times and on July 4, 1798, he recorded in his diary: "Went up to the Celebration of the Anniversary of Independance and dined in the Spring Gardens near Alexa. with a large Compa. of the Civil and Military of Fairfax County."[2] His cash accounts for the day set his expenses in Alexandria "at the Anniversary of Independance" as £1 4s.[3] A Philadelphia newspaper gave a full account of the festivities:

Alexandria, July 7—The 23rd [*sic*] Anniversary of American Independence was celebrated by the inhabitants of this town, on Wednesday last, with the greatest harmony and conviviality.—Every thing conspired to render the business of the day a varied scene of patriotism and social joy; and the dignified presence of the beloved WASHINGTON, our illustrious neighbor, gave such a high colouring to the tout ensemble, that nothing was wanting to complete the picture. The auspicious morning was ushered in by a discharge of sixteen guns. At 10 o'clock the uniform companies paraded; and, it must be acknowledged, their appearance was such as entitled them to the greatest credit, while it reflects honor on their officers and the town—it was perfectly military: . . . . . The different corps were reviewed in King street by General Washington, and Col. Little, who expressed the highest satisfaction at their appearance and manoeuvring; after which they proceeded to the Episcopal Church, where a suitable discourse was delivered by the Rev. Dr. Davis. Of this discourse I may say, with the expressive Collins, it was
"Warm, energetic, chaste, sublime."
A dinner was prepared at Spring Gardens by Mr. John Stavely; which, considering the number of citizens and military that partook of it (between 4 and 500) was conducted with the greatest propriety and decorum.—Ludwell Lee, esq. presided at the head of the table—the foot was honored by Col. Charles Little. . . . GEN. WASHINGTON was escorted into town by a detachment from the troop of Dragoons. He was dressed in full uniform, and appeared in good health and spirits. The troops went through a number of military evolutions during the day, with all of which the General was particularly pleased, and bestowed many encomiums on their martial appearance.—*Claypoole's American Daily Advertiser,* July 19.[4]

In the last years of his life, the General again "Went up to Alexa. and dined with a number of the Citizens there in celebration of the Anniversary of the declaration of American Independence."[5] And again the Philadelphia newspaper reported:

Alexandria, July 6.—The 23rd anniversary of the American Independence was celebrated in this town with the greatest harmony and decorum. The military commands agreeably to orders previously given, mustered in the court house square, and the line was formed in Fairfax street. After going through the manual, which was performed with the strictest exactitude, Col. John Fitzgerald, accompanied by John Potts, Esq., passed the line in review, and expressed his satisfaction at their military and elegant appearance. The battalion then marched, by sections, up King street, and formed the line there to receive their beloved chief General GEORGE WASHINGTON. On his passing the line the usual military honors were paid; and it is with pleasure I remark, that the Cincinnatus of America appeared in excellent health and good spirits.

Lieutenant General Washington dined at Col. Kemp's tavern, with a select party of friends.—*Claypoole's American Daily Advertiser,* July 11.[6]

Whether Colonel Kemp at this time kept the Spring Gardens Tavern, the deponent sayeth not!

Thrilling tales of long departed patrons who haunt the old red house are told by the Misses Lewis and Evans, who lived in this house for several years. When the family of three sat down for their evening meal, they were disturbed by the consciousness of the presence of unseen persons. Often they raised their wine glasses in a silent toast to the invisible guests and empty chairs. On several occasions a brave spirit clad in buff and blue was clearly seen, only to vanish into the heavy six-panel door—to the utter astonishment of three pairs of eyes. Once on a clear moonlight night, a great brick barn appeared in the place of a modest wooden structure which stands today. The lady who first saw it called her companion and asked her what she saw. The immediate reply was "An enormous brick barn." For a while they thought it an optical illusion produced by moonlight and clouds and waited at the window to see the bricks disintegrate into the factual wooden structure. But the ladies retired leaving the great brick apparition still standing. Colonel W. H. Peake, the recent owner, when told this story, confirmed it to the extent of admitting that there was a large brick foundation under the present frame building.

Colonel and Mrs. Peake added a half story to the two wings and increased the length of the ell. The old tavern faces the street bravely, and the sturdy, paneled front door swings on H&L hinges as in days long past. In the brick-walled garden behind, arbors are fragrant with grape and wisteria. Hollyhocks flourish in the borders. A modern garage replaces the stables where the gentry of Alexandria and the neighborhood put up their horses when they frequented the "Oyster House." In this mellowed atmosphere of Spring Gardens, it is pleasant to turn one's thoughts backward and reflect on the gay evening when it cost the General £1 4s. to celebrate "Independance."

Chapter 19
William Fitzhugh and Robert E. Lee

Another fine example of late eighteenth century federal architecture in Alexandria is the residence at 607 Oronoco Street,* commonly spoken of as the boyhood home of Robert E. Lee. This house abounds with memories of Alexandria. Her history, romance, and past are interwoven here in a perfect pattern. Washington, perhaps, frequented this house more than any other save Dr. Craik's after the Fitzhughs moved to Alexandria from Chatham near Fredericksburg.

Built by John Potts in 1795 on land purchased from Charles Alexander, the date is attested by the stone fixed high in the wall under the carved cornice. Potts and his wife, Elizabeth deeded the property to William Fitzhugh in 1799 for the sum of twelve thousand dollars.

The house and garden occupy half a city block. A central hall runs through the house and every room opens by window or door into the garden. The woodwork in the house, while simple, is in the best tradition and, save for two missing mantels, is undisturbed. The stairway rises on the left of the hall in a series of easy steps to a landing that crosses one end of the hall and then mounts on the right side to the second floor. The decoration of the risers and landing, in a diamond motif paneled in a

*Owners: Mr. and Mrs. Robert C. Goodale.

delicate mold, is reminiscent of the designer, Adam. Two superb rooms open off the hall on each side, and the dining room and offices are in an ell on a lower level. There are Adam mantels of great beauty in the two master bedrooms on the second floor. The doors, chair rails, cornices, floors, and locks are in a fine state of preservation throughout the house.

In the kitchen is the brick oven with patent doors made in England and inserted in the chimney about the time the house was built. A few years ago, the former owners, Dr. and Mrs. R. R. Sayers, went to the address of the manufactory at Stratton, 173 Cheapside, London. It was still in operation and there they were able to purchase needed parts for the faithful old oven.

Virginia is more like the mother country in the relations that exist between her aristocratic classes, than any other part of the Union save, perhaps, South Carolina. These people moved in one large circle, marrying and intermarrying, related and associated as one enormous family. Welcome in one another's homes, they kept alive family ties by visits and letters, both of considerable length. It was quite possible to go away from home for several years for a series of visits, moving from one estate to another and remaining for the season—all the while renewing associations within the chosen orbit.

Of this hierarchy was William Fitzhugh. A man of charm and culture, reared in the days and traditions of the great planters, he kept open house at Chatham, near Fredericksburg, the year around. Travelers en route to and from Williamsburg and Richmond were entertained in a lavish fashion. With the formation of the new government, the stream of visitors increased to such an extent that the Fitzhughs were being eaten out of house and home, and found it necessary to escape from their friends. They selected Alexandria as a place of domicile. Chatham was placed on the market in 1796.

A lifelong friend and associate of George Washington, there was great intimacy between the two families. Fitzhugh contributed two fine does to the Mount Vernon deer park in 1786, and the same year forwarded a supply of orchard grass seed for the General's use. A year before Washington's death his good offices as neighbor and friend were directed toward the acquisition of a horse that would best serve Washington's purpose. Entries in George Washington's diaries attest the many times that the Fitzhughs were at Mount Vernon, and the Washingtons at Chatham or Alexandria. On January 3, 1798: "Mrs. Washington, myself, etc., went to Alexandria and dined with Mr. Fitzhugh,"[1] and on April 3, 1799,

The Alexandria home bought by William Fitzhugh of Chatham to escape from his friends

"went to Alexandria and lodged myself with Mr. Fitzhugh";[2] the next day he "returned to Alexandria and again lodged at Mr. Fitzhugh's."[3] The last mention in Washington's diary of his old friends is in the last month of his life, dated November 17, 1799, "went to Church in Alexandria and dined with Mr. Fitzhugh."[4]

To Fitzhugh's house came Washington Custis wooing, and successfully, too, Mary Lee Fitzhugh. George Washington did not live to see the marriage between the daughter of this old friend and his adopted son, George Washington Parke Custis; nor the splendid Arlington mansion, following that new fashion of likeness to a Greek temple, that was to house the Custis and Lee families for three generations. He knew those rolling acres of the Arlington plantation, but never dreamed they were destined to become the emerald pall for America's warrior dead.

In the *Alexandria Daily Gazette, Commercial and Political* of Friday, January 12, 1810, appeared the following advertisement:

On Wednesday, the 17th instant will be sold between the hours of ten and eleven at the house of William Fitzhugh, esquire, deceased, a quantity of
Household Furniture
consisting of carpets, chairs, tables, bedsteads, etc., as also a carriage and one or

The Alexandria home of "Light Horse" Harry Lee's widow. The house that
General Lee loved

two horses. Of all sums of twenty dollars or under, immediate payment will be
expected, on all over a credit of six months will be given, and bond with
approved security required:

Robert Randolph
Executor of Wm. Fitzhugh

William Fitzhugh's will was probated on December 23, 1809. To each
of his two daughters who had "made themselves as dear as children can
be to an affectionate Father," he left the sum of two thousand pounds,
certain slaves (about sixteen) and lands containing eight hundred acres,

General Lee's bedroom, showing the railing of the little stair leading to his mother's room

for since they were "equal in his affections" he wished them to have an equal quantity. After other bequests, the residue of his estate passed to his only son, William Henry Fitzhugh, with the admonition and hope that he would make proper use of it. He appointed his two sons-in-law, William Craik and George Washington Parke Custis, also Edmund I. Lee and Robert Randolph, as guardians of his son's estate until he came of age, and as executors of his will. The inventory of the contents of his house is that of a rich man, who lived in the comfort and elegance of his time. Appropriately enough, a pair of his knife boxes have found their way to Mount Vernon.

William Henry Fitzhugh married Anna Maria Goldsborough of Maryland and built the house on the Ravensworth estate so intimately associated with the Fitzhughs and Lees. In September 1820, he sold the house in Alexandria to William Brent of Stafford for ten thousand dollars. William Brent Jr., lost the house by indebtedness to the Mechanics Bank of Alexandria in 1824. The bank was the highest bidder at $3,500.

Young Fitzhugh met an early death shortly after his marriage when thrown by his horse. He was an only son and he died childless so that

The mantel in Mrs. Harry Lee's bedroom

branch of the clan ended with the death of Mrs. George Washington Parke Custis. Fitzhugh's widow lived for forty years at Ravensworth.

Later William Hodgson and his family owned the Oronoco Street house for a couple of generations and in turn sold the house to William C. Yeaton, who owned it for some twenty-odd years. This family planted many tropical trees, the unique magnolia and the lemon trees among them. In 1883 the house was sold at public auction for one thousand dollars to Mary E. Fleming, widow of Dr. Robert F. Fleming, "she being the highest bidder."

It is a strange coincidence that to this Alexandria home of the Fitzhughs came, about 1818, the widow of a gentleman active in the affairs of the nation. He had commanded, during the Revolution, a Legion bearing his own name; he had served as governor of his state from 1792 to 1795; as a member of Congress from 1799 to 1801, and he it was who prepared the memorial resolutions which were presented when word reached Philadelphia of Washington's decease, declaring him in immortal words: "First in war, first in peace, and first in the hearts of his fellow citizens." In fact, he liked the phrase himself and used it with a slight modification in the halls of Congress when making his celebrated eulogy of Washington.

This widow then resident in the former home of William Fitzhugh was Mrs. Henry Lee, born Anne Carter of Shirley. Exiled from Stratford when her eldest stepson came into his patrimony, she and her husband, General Lee, known to all Virginians as "Light Horse Harry," moved to Alexandria. The Lees occupied several houses from time to time, but on October 14, 1824, Mrs. Lee was at home in the house on the northwest corner of St. Asaph and Oronoco Streets and she received a visitor of such importance that it made history. The guest, who was no less a personage than General the Marquis de la Fayette, came to pay his respects to the wife of his friend. This visit was witnessed by the young Quaker, Benjamin Hallowell, who had moved into the house next door with his bride of a day, and stood in the doorway to watch the Marquis go by. Moreover, the Marquis saw the young couple and "made a graceful bow."

Mrs. Henry Lee, with her family of boys, occupied this house for seven years. Robert Edward's room adjoined hers, on a lower level, being connected by a small stairway.

Shortly after Mr. Hallowell opened his school, Robert E. Lee went to him in February 1825, for instruction in mathematics, preparatory to going to West Point to prepare himself for the Army.

Naturally the friendliest intimacy existed between the family at Arlington and the house on Oronoco Street. And so, two years after leaving West Point, Lieutenant Robert E. Lee, Corps of Engineers, married, on June 30, 1831, Mary Custis, granddaughter of William Fitzhugh, and great-granddaughter of Martha Washington.

General Lee always loved this house and after defeat he came back to Alexandria, which for some time had been in command of the Union forces, to take farewell of his family and friends and went again to look once more upon the scenes of his childhood. The story is told that people next door were startled to see a man peeping over the wall. Upon investigation, it proved to be General Lee, who had climbed upon the wall to look into the garden. He apologized, saying, "I just wanted to see if the snowballs were in bloom."

To this day the garden, as the house, retains its integrity. All the growing things associated with old gardens are there—the lilacs, boxwood, magnolias, lemon trees, iris, syringa, lilies, jonquils, jasmine, honeysuckle —and General Lee's remembered snowballs.

George Washington Parke Custis; grandson of Martha; adopted son of George Washington; husband of Mary Fitzhugh; father-in-law of Robert E. Lee. By Saint Mèmin. (Courtesy Corcoran Gallery of Art)

Chapter 20
George Washington's Tenements*

On the corner of Pitt and Prince Streets stand two little frame houses that possess the distinction of being the only buildings in Alexandria built on George Washington's lots and dating back to his time. Their history is fairly complete and may be compiled by anyone taking the trouble to search the records housed in the Alexandria clerk's office and balancing those data against the well kept accounts and writings of General Washington.

Alexandria had outgrown her swaddling clothes by 1761 when the trustees petitioned the assembly for permission to extend the limits of the town. This was promptly granted. New acreage was added, divided into lots and sold at auction as formerly. General Washington bought, at the sale held on May 9, 1763, two half-acres of ground, numbered on the plat as 112 and 118, which he took up later for approximately £48. For the former, the subject of this sketch, on the northwest corner of Pitt and Prince, he paid £38. On the latter lot at Pitt and Cameron Streets he built his town house six years later. As early as 1760 Washington spoke of "my House in Town," but this earliest reference[1] is believed to have related to Lawrence Washington's estate, for which he was one of the executors. Its subsequent story has not been unwound, but all facts point to the house at South Lee Street as having been built by Lawrence.

General Washington acquired the deed to lot No. 112 in 1765 and mention was made of it in his will and in the accompanying inventory of his property. At the time of his death the lot had been subdivided for building and let on ground rent, for purposes of revenue. The two small frame houses standing today at 123 Pitt and 501 Prince Streets unquestionably date from this period.

Time did not deal gently with these little houses and a few years ago they were condemned by the city council as unfit for habitation and ordered to be destroyed as they created a fire menace. Former owners succeeded in allaying the ultimatum of the council, reclaiming them from oblivion. Unaware that the story of Washington's ownership was true, the wing of one was demolished, the other is a new addition and replaces a smaller one too dilapidated to restore. The floors, mantels, much of the trim, some hardware and two chimneys are original. The uprights were found to be mortised together and numbered in Roman numerals. Handmade nails and split wood laths formed part of the original construction. Preservation of the structure was the urgent concern.

In her *History of Old Alexandria* Mrs. Powell tells an interesting anecdote relating to the construction of these houses. The mention of "Mr. La Fayette" identifiable as the son of the Marquis, fixes the period at 1797. It seems that the coach had been sent to Alexandria from Mount Vernon for repairs and stood in the courtyard of the coachmaker's waiting to be called for. Two little children, Hannah Taylor and Joe Peters, were playing hide-and-seek in the courtyard. The little girl opened the door and hid in the coach. Joe failed to find her, and she fell asleep. The carriage was called for, the horses hitched and driven to Mount Vernon, without awakening the child. Only when the coach came to a standstill in the stable yard did she awake, much frightened and in tears. She was carried at once to the house, soothed and petted. The General dispatched a servant on horseback to tell Mr. and Mrs. Taylor that the little girl was safe and would be returned in the morning. She dined with the family, sat next to Miss Nelly, and was laughed at by a young man called "Mr. La Fayette" whom she did not like. She was put to bed by the Negro maid, Caroline Brannum, in a little room at the head of the stairway, wearing one of Miss Nelly's gowns, much too large, but with beautiful lace on neck and sleeves, her sheets warmed by the first copper warming pan she had ever seen. Caroline left the candle burning until Hannah fell asleep, to keep the little girl from being frightened. She had a splendid breakfast and was returned home in the coach wrapped in a large shawl and with a piece of cake as booty.

After that she frequently saw General Washington on the streets of Alexandria. "He often walked past her father's shop to the corner of Pitt

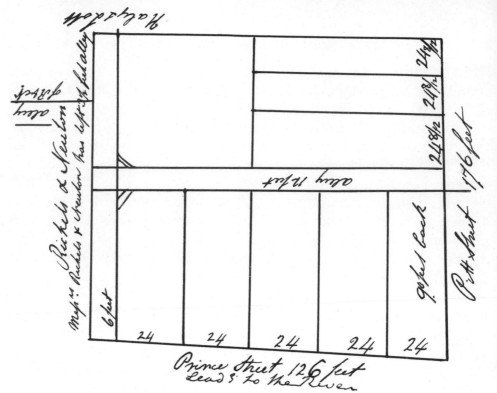

Washington identified this sketch: "Col° Fitzgerald respect[g] my Vacant Lot-in-Alexandria" and the notation under Prince Street is also in his handwriting. This rough draft seems to have been done by Fitzgerald pursuant to the General's letter to him, dated June 12, 1797. (Courtesy *Library of Congress*)

and Prince, where two small frame houses were being built, and he seemed to be giving some directions to the carpenters, but he did not recognize Hannah who stood in too much awe of the great man to make herself known."[2] Hannah was all of seven years old at the time of the visit. Her trip to Mount Vernon furnished her with conversational matter for the rest of her life.

The little houses, known in Alexandria for many years as the Washington Tenements fell to the lot of his nephew, Lawrence Washington, in the division of the estate.

Now to explore the title for those whose time does not permit or whose inclination does not incite to delving into old and dusty records.

In February 1767 Washington, in an irate letter to Carlyle & Adam, who had neglected to pay for some wheat, soundly berates them, complaining that in September 1764, he passed his bond for the wheat for "some lotts in Alexandria as payment," only to have the money demanded again with interest and "was at some pains to convince Mr. John Alexander of the unreasonableness of paying twice for the same thing."[3]

The Washington Tenements

Writing to his friend, the Secretary of War, Henry Knox, in January 1785, he says, ". . . Rents have got to such an amazing height in Alexandria, that (having an unimproved lot or two there) I have thoughts, if my finances will support me in the measure, of building a House, or Houses thereon for the purpose of letting."[4] Later in that same year he confides to Knox that his finances were not equal to undertaking the projected building in Alexandria.

Ten years later the lot was still unimproved, when Halley, who owned abutting property, was desirous of acquiring ten feet of Washington's land for an alley. The deal did not go through and a year later William Summers offered the owner three thousand dollars for the lot in question, which was declined. President Washington wrote Tobias Lear, his secretary, under date of March 21:

I have no wish to part with the lot unless I can do it upon advantageous terms, and can dispose of the Money in a more productive manner. I had thoughts of building on it, but this would be attended with trouble, and perhaps a good deal of impositions; as it could not be properly attended to in the execution of the work. And besides workmens wages and materials are very high at this time.[5]

Shades of a later postwar era!
By June 1797, Washington had determined upon the subdivision as a

solution. This was time-honored practice locally. To John Fitzgerald, on June 12 he wrote, "If you have had leizure to examine my unimproved lot in Alexa, more attentively, and have digested any plan in your own mind for an advantageous division of it, I would thank you for the result, as I wish to fix on a Plan." A plot plan, docketed by Washington "my vacant lot in Alex" has been found among his papers preserved in the Library of Congress,[6] and is worthy of reproduction. That this plan was carried out almost to the letter is revealed by the text of an advertisement prepared in July to be set up in the gazettes:

The Subscriber having resolved to lay off the half acre lot which he holds in the town of Alexandria (bounded by Prince and Pitt Streets) into convenient building squares, gives this public notice thereof; and of his intention to lease them forever, on ground Rent. Five and a half feet extending from Prince Street, will be added to the alley already left by Mr. Rickets, across to Mr. Halleys lot; and another Alley of ten feet will be laid out about midway the lot from Pitt Street until it intersect the former Alley. All the lots on Prince Street will extend back to this Alley, and be about 83 or 4 feet in depth. And the lots North thereof will extend from Pitt Street to the first mentioned Alley, and be four in number of equal front (about 21 feet each). The other lot will have a breadth of 26 feet on Prince Street and about 83 or 4 on Pitt Street, or may be divided into [illegible] remaining front on the former street will be divided into [illegible] lotts, equal in size and abt. 24 or 5' feet front each. If any persons should be inclined to make offers for the lots here described, or any of them, Mr. Jas. Anderson (my manager) will receive the same [illegible] shortly, the lotts will be exposed at public sale, of which notice will be given.[7]

The following September, writing to James Harrison, he said, "The Ground Rent of the lot I have offered to Lease, in Alexandria, is three dollars a foot, for what it measures on *each* Street. This I must obtain as an annual Rent or the lot will not be disposed of in that way."[8]

Washington died on December 14, 1799, and his will, written July 9, 1799, was probated January 20, 1800. In an annexed schedule of property which he directed be sold (some conditionally disposed of) with explanatory notes relative thereto appears this entry:

Alexandria
Corner of Pitt & Prince Stts. half an Acre—laid out into build-⎱ 4,000 (t)[9]
[in]gs 3 or 4 of wch. are let on grd. Rent at \$3 pr. foot.   ⎰

Under the note "t" the property is further described: "For this lot though unimproved, I have refused \$3500.—It has since been laid off into proper sized lots for building on—three or 4 of which are let on ground Rent—forever—at three dollars a foot on the street.—and this price is asked for both fronts on Pitt & Princes Street."[10]

These lots were included in the estate left to his wife for her lifetime. Martha Washington died on May 22, 1802. On June 7, 1803, the executors of Washington's estate sold this half-acre lot divided into nine lots, Nos. 1 to 4 on Pitt and Nos. 5 to 9 on Prince. An alley ten feet wide separated the Prince Street lots from those on Pitt. Only one lot was unimproved. The executors submitted this sale along with others made the same day to be recorded at Fairfax July 15, 1811.

The lot at the intersection of Pitt and Prince, bearing the number 5 in the division, was sold to L. A. Washington for $1,613.33, bringing more by nearly four hundred dollars than any of the other eight.

Lawrence Augustine Washington's deed for this property was dated August 7, 1804, and calls for "twenty-five feet four inches on Prince Street, beginning at the intersection, running in depth parallel to Pitt eighty-three feet to a ten-foot alley, and all Houses, Buildings, Improvements, Streets and Allics."[11]

On the death of Lawrence A. Washington the little houses and the lot on the corner of Prince and Pitt Streets became the property of his son, Robert W. Washington. He in turn sold the property to Alexious Johnson, at whose death it was sold at public auction by Samuel Bartle, commissioner, to William Gregory for $605.00 on July 11, 1844. Three years later, September 13, 1847, Will and Mary Gregory sold the same property to Benjamin Huges. Benjamin and Susan Huges divided the property, selling 30 feet 10 inches on Pitt Street to Joseph Francis Cook on July 15, 1874, and on July 26, 1887, the Huges sold the house and lot on the corner of Prince and Pitt, running 25 feet west on Prince and 52 feet north on Pitt to J. Frank Taylor. On July 17, 1874, Joseph Francis Cook and his wife, Georgeanna, conveyed to Taylor the part they had previously bought from the Huges.

On April 20, 1897, J. Frank Taylor conveyed this same property to Walter G. Rogers, and on April 20, 1900, Walter G. Rogers and his wife, Matilda A. Rogers, sold to George T. Klipstein. In 1935 the property was purchased by Charles B. and Gay Montague Moore, and in 1945 the property was again divided, and the house on Pitt Street was sold to Mr. Charles Francis Alexander, and the Prince Street House to Colonel Hubbard.

In England a Georgian Cottage, but in Alexandria a great house

Chapter 21
The Georgian Cottage*

Alexandria was never a large town. The thrifty merchants of this Scottish trading center built well, and their dwellings abound in architectural interest, but really great houses are rare. On the 700 block of Prince Street, behind a picket fence, guarded by a tall magnolia and several gnarled box trees stands what is called in England a "Georgian cottage," which in Alexandria is an important house.

On November 2, 1797, William Thornton Alexander and Lucy, his wife, sold to James Patton, of Fairfax County, half an acre of land situated in Fairfax County in the state of Virginia, adjacent to the town of Alexandria and bounded as follows:

Vizt: On the South by Prince Street, on the West by Columbus Street. Beginning at the corner formed by the intersection of the East side of Columbus Street and with the North side of Prince Street and running Eastwardly with Prince Street 123 feet 5 inches, thence Northerly and parallel with Columbus Street one hundred and seventy six feet seven inches, thence Westerly and parallel with Prince Street 123 feet 5 inches thence Southerly with Columbus Street to the point of beginning.[1]

This was subject forever to a ground rent of £30 in good and lawful money of Virginia. On this lot James Patton erected a type of house well known locally as a "flounder," because of its narrow width. Such a build-

---

*711 Prince Street. Owner: Mrs. Andrew Pickens.

ing was usually set back from the street, anticipating fuller architectural development when the flounder became the ell of the larger house. Patton's home, though diminutive, was comfortable and it had convenient gardens and pleasant surroundings. Here he lived until overtaken by that ogre of all Alexandria shipping merchants—compound interest.

He became indebted to the firm of Marsteller & Young to the amount of ten thousand dollars and sundry notes discounted for his use at the Bank of Alexandria to the amount of nine thousand dollars. To afford full indemnity, he sold in November 1809, to Robert I. Taylor, twenty-five shares of Potomac Bank stock, six shares of Little River Turnpike stock, ten shares of Great Hunting Creek bridge stock, a house and lot on Fairfax Street, and two squares of ground under the charter of Alexandria, adjoining Spring Gardens, bought of Jesse Sims, and the brig *John* of Alexandria. Also relinquished to Taylor in the settlement of his debts was the half-acre on Prince and Columbus Streets "with the buildings and improvements thereupon erected."[2]

A year later William Fowle with "the consent and concurrance of all parties," purchased the said lot of ground and improvements from James Patton at the price of $6,550.

William Fowle had come to Alexandria in 1800 from Boston to enter, as a partner, the important shipping firm which became Lawrason & Fowle. He married Miss Esther Taylor, daughter of George Taylor of Broomalaw and they are purported to have had eighteen children, eight of whom they reared to maturity. Fowle's father-in-law is remembered as the last gentleman in Alexandria to hold to the fashion of knee breeches and silk stockings. As he lived well into the nineteenth century, his figure clad in "short clothes" and leaning upon a high cane (similar to those associated with the Court of Louis XVI) was a familiar sight upon the streets of Alexandria long after such a costume had become a curiosity. Taylor entertained no idea of giving up the habits of his ancestors, nor of complying with any such folderol as high choker collars and pantaloons so tightly strapped under a gentleman's gaiters that someone had to invent a machine for jumping into them.

The Fowles were agreeable hosts and the Georgian cottage was the scene of many gay gatherings and fine dinners. The family took part in all the festivities of the town—balls at Gadsby's, the theatre; trips to Boston, doubtless in their own ships, were frequent. William Fowle was senior warden at Christ Church for many years.

Thirty-six years after Fowle moved to Alexandria the following notice

Elegance and grace, harmony and beauty in brick and wood and iron.
Regency at its best in Alexandria

The stair sweeps up, circular wall, window and door in hall

appeared in one of the papers. It is interesting to observe that the firm was now "William Fowle & Co."

The splendid ship Alexandria, about 500 tons burthen, built under the superintendence of Captain William Morrell, for William Fowle & Co., and others, and to be commanded by Capt. Charles W. Turner was launched in beautiful style on Thursday.

William Fowle was a man of taste as well as means. He improved his garden by acquiring adjoining property and extending his grounds as far east as Washington Street and as far north as King, adding several new outbuildings. Nor did he stop with horticulture. He took up architecture and deftly transformed his home to the ample size and satisfactory design all admire. The earlier flounder house became one of the fine houses of Alexandria—and one of the loveliest. By the addition of a wing to the left of the present doorway, a beautiful Palladian window, and new entrance porch set in a gabled bay, Fowle changed the front façade into the latest mode. The house has an individuality and appeal unlike anything else in town.

The outstanding architectural interest is in this entrance. Inside as well as out the design and wood carving are chaste and elegant. Four slender columns support a shallow balcony whose grace and lightness is produced in a great measure by the fragile spindles carrying the weight of the projection. The delicate inclosure of wrought iron is Regency at its best in this medium. It is said he imported the plans for this arresting doorway from New England. The interior focal point is again the doorway, for here the beauty in design and wood carving equal the elegance of the exterior. An added interest is the circular wall, window and door in the entrance hall.

The drawing room mantel is of gray marble, early Empire in design, a style which dominates the lower floor. The walls support the original old whale-oil lamps, complete with engraved shades and prisms. Interesting family portraits and fine furniture have occupied the same places for over a century and a quarter. The Sheraton sideboard is exceptional.

In the garden court, box bushes cluster close to the doorway, perfuming the air after a summer's shower. Enormous pink poppies, phlox, and roses grow in riotous abandon, while old-fashioned periwinkle covers the roots of ancient trees.

It is a satisfactory thought that Fowle's descendants still inhabit his house, using many of his possessions, for this is one of the few old residences in Alexandria still in the family. Five generations have called it home. Two wings, or dependencies, of this house have been demolished and the garden reduced by time and the inroads of "progress." What is still a large city garden, no longer touches Washington and King Streets.

Chapter 22
The Vowell-Snowden House*

Presently the residence of Mr. Justice and Mrs. Hugo L. Black, this house has been known in Alexandria for about a hundred years as the Snowden home; and so it was from 1842 to 1912 when it passed from the hands of that family.

The Snowdens have long been prominent in the old town. Samuel Snowden became sole owner and editor of the *Alexandria Gazette* in 1800, a paper that traces its ancestry back to 1784, and boasts of being the oldest daily newspaper printed continuously, still in circulation in the United States. Edgar Snowden succeeded his father as editor, at the age of twenty-one years. Active in civic affairs, interested in politics, he was the first representative of Alexandria to the Virginia Assembly after the retrocession of Alexandria to Virginia in 1846. He ran for Congress on the Whig ticket when Henry Clay was defeated for the Presidency and went down with his party.

He was mayor of Alexandria in 1841, and Mrs. Powell states in her *History of Old Alexandria* that in a collection of silhouettes in London is one of "Edgar Snowden, Mayor of Alexandria."

Snowden married Louisa Grymes of the prominent family of Grymesby, Brandon, and Marmion on the Rappahannock. From this union there were three sons, Edgar, Jr., Harold and Herbert, "each of whom in turn upheld the traditions and honor of the old paper."[1]

---

*619 South Lee Street.

The Vowell-Snowden House. The widow's walk is missing

Edgar Snowden purchased the Lee and Franklin Streets property from Lawrence B. Taylor, who had the house from Thomas Vowell Jr. In a deed granted August 29, 1798, William Thornton Alexander and Lucy, his wife, let this property with all houses, buildings, streets, lanes, alleys, and so on, to Thomas Vowell Jr., for the yearly ground rent of $61.66. The fact is cited that William Thornton Alexander had the property from his father, John Alexander. In 1802 Thomas Vowell was released from this obligation upon payment of £200.

In 1826, in a deed of trust, the house is referred to specifically as a two-story brick dwelling, with other buildings and improvements. There is doubt as to whether the present house was built by Alexander or by Vowell. William Thornton Alexander mentions in the deed of 1798, "all houses, buildings, streets, lanes, alleys, Etc." The front of the house is a typical federal house, hardly earlier than 1790 to 1798, and similar to the New City Hotel, built in 1792. The doorway is almost a replica of the doorway taken from the tavern to the Metropolitan Museum of Art and since restored. The transom above the entrance door, in a deeply recessed arch, is interesting in design. The unusual cornice excites attention.

Thomas Vowell, in partnership with his brother, John, operated for a long while a successful mercantile business. The firm of John & Thomas Vowell owned a large wharf on the east side of Union between Prince and King Streets and sent out its own ships to the far corners of the earth, advertising its wares upon their return. George Washington ran an account with the Vowells and receipts preserved at Mount Vernon tell of purchases made by James Anderson, his manager. One of Anderson's dockets, dating from 1798, reaffirms in the inscription the age-old system of barter, "For Lint seed Sold them & Salt in Exchange." Lean and hard times were Thomas Vowell's lot. He overreached himself in speculation—buying and selling property until "by reasons of losses and misfortunates in trade" we find him mortgaging his warehouse and wharf, even his house; finally he was forced to part with his home.

Thomas Vowell's first wife, Mary Harper, died in 1805, aged twenty-three years, and was buried in the old Presbyterian meetinghouse grave-yard. She was the daughter of Captain John Harper; her sister, Margaret, married Thomas Vowell's brother, John. The graves of the two sisters lie near the north wall of the church, while their father's remains rest within.

The Vowell-Snowden house, in splendid condition, stands flush with the street, surrounded by a half-acre of garden, defying the elements as well as the hand of time. Much of the fine woodwork has been removed or destroyed, but the perfect proportion of the rooms is indestructible. The hall arch and stairway remain untouched and convey some idea of the former beauty of the woodwork and elegance of the house.

There are people still living in Alexandria who as children played on the "Widow's" or "Captain's Walk" that formerly topped the old mansion. A magnificent view up and down the Potomac River could be had from that vantage spot, long since disappeared.

Chapter 23

The Edmund Jennings Lee House*

Many of the citizens of this community bore the greatest names in the Commonwealth. Henry Cabot Lodge's description of Virginia society in the eighteenth century might aptly be applied to Alexandria: "We must go back to Athens to find another instance of a Society so small in numbers and yet capable of such an outburst of ability and force."

Among the great Virginia names closely associated with Alexandria is that of Lee. Virginia's (and America's) patriot, Arthur Lee, was born at Stratford, in Westmoreland County, on December 20, 1740, and died at his residence, Lansdown, in the old town of Urbanna, Middlesex County, on December 12, 1792. These fifty-two years he filled with deeds and action. His primary education was gotten at Eton. From there he went on to the great University of Edinburgh to study medicine. For a while he practiced this profession in Williamsburg, but in 1766 we find him reading law at the Temple in London. By 1770 he had begun his role as a barrister in London and there he practiced until 1776. For five years of this time he acted as London agent for Virginia and Massachusetts. Thus began his diplomatic career. With Benjamin Franklin and Silas

*428 North Washington Street. Owners: Mr. and Mrs. Franklin F. Korell.

Deane he was one of the commissioners to France in 1776, and from this he went on to other negotiations between America and Europe.

Arthur Lee returned to America in 1780, and from 1782 to 1785 he served as a member of Congress. During these years he entered somewhat into the real-estate business in Alexandria. When his will was probated, he left to his niece, Hannah Washington, wife of Corbin, a half-acre lot on Washington and Oronoco Streets.

Hannah and Corbin Washington sold a half-acre lot to Charles Lee on March 19, 1796. It is described as beginning at the intersection of Washington and Oronoco on the southwest side, running west on Oronoco 123 feet 5 inches and south on Washington 176 feet 7 inches.

Charles Lee and Anne, his wife, sold this property to their brother, Edmund I. Lee, for five thousand dollars in January 1801. Part of the lot was rented at that time to Henry Zimmerman, subject to a ground rent, and part to Howard Beale, and there were houses, ways, advantages, and so on.

Edmund Jennings (always called Edmund I, following the eighteenth century usage of I for J) Lee was born just prior to the Revolution in 1772, when great events were stirring. He grew to young manhood in the post-Revolutionary days, and developed into an able lawyer, one of those stalwart citizens, giving his time and energy to his family, his church, and his city. He has been overshadowed by his more famous brothers, "Light Horse Harry" and Charles Lee, Attorney General in Washington's cabinet, and his immortal nephew, Robert Edward Lee.

At twenty-four, Edmund Jennings Lee married Sarah Lee, daughter of Richard Henry Lee of Stratford, his near cousin, and that same year, 1796, settled in Alexandria. Nearly everyone of local prominence dined at Mount Vernon on some occasion or another—and so did Edmund Lee and his wife. Washington's diaries record three dates when the former was present and one when the latter accompanied Attorney General Charles Lee and his wife. Mrs. Edmund Lee as "Miss Lee" had visited General and Mrs. Washington innumerable times with her father. As a matter of statistical interest, the General's diaries enumerate more than one hundred visits of various Virginia Lees to Mount Vernon.

Edmund I. Lee is remembered in his native city for saving the Glebe lands for Christ Church. Glebe lands were property belonging to the Church of England, and used for the support of the rector and the needs of the parish. After the Revolutionary War the Virginia Assembly confiscated these lands for the use of the poor. On behalf of the Alexandria church, now called Christ Church, Edmund I. Lee took this case to the United States Courts in 1814, protesting the unconstitutionality of the act. His eloquence, legal knowledge and labors resulted in the return of the Glebe lands to Christ Church. The case was won on a technicality, *i.e.,* the Virginia Assembly had no jurisdiction over the District of Columbia, and Alexandria lay in the District.

In 1810 Lee was president of the common council of the city, a thankless task which he performed faithfully and cheerfully. The year 1832 saw "his house and half an acre lot at Washington and Oronoco Streets in which he now resides for sale or rent." It was not sold, for in his will, Lee left this dwelling and lot to his two daughters, Sally Lee and Hannah Stewart, jointly. To his son he left the family Bible and a cane-bottom settee, formerly owned by William Lee of Green Spring, and a house and lot at the "bottom of his garden" on Washington Street, and the "arm-chair" from his drawing room. His son, Cassius Lee, fell heir to his father's home and there brought up a large family of handsome children.

Family tradition names Edmund I. Lee as the builder of his home, which would fix the date of the house at 1801 or later. Everything about the house is typical of a late eighteenth century federal building. It is certain that Charles Lee built the mansion around 1796 and that Edmund I. Lee lived there from the time of his marriage. The price of five thousand dollars at the time of purchase is also indicative of a substantial and elegant residence.

This house is a fine federal example and is handsomely fitted out. The Lee family seems to have had a leaning toward brass hardware, and like the hinges in the great hall at Stratford, unusual brass latches and locks are here plentiful. Unquestionably the handsomest brass locks in Alexandria are in this house. A rare latch in addition to the great locks is attached to the Washington Street door. This double doorway, deeply recessed, in a hand-carved Georgian frame, arched and paneled, challenges the attention of every passer-by. The colonnaded rear gallery is hung with festoons of wisteria and is the most picturesque and lovely spot when the great lavender bunches of bloom are scattered and draped around the vine and against the white columns and railings. The woodwork throughout the house is in keeping with the dignified exterior. The rooms are large and inviting; the mantels' trim and stairway are better than pleasing.

Robert E. Lee was first cousin to Cassius Lee. They grew up together,

Edmund I. Lee's doorway, an inviting entrance

were of the same age and generation, devoted and sympathetic friends throughout their lives. For advice and counsel they sought each other.

On April 21, 1861, the Sunday following General Lee's resignation from the United States Army, he attended Christ Church in Alexandria, and left his carriage and horses at Cassius Lee's house. Sometime during the morning, commissioners sent by the Virginia convention arrived at Arlington House and found General Lee gone to church in Alexandria. They followed him to the home of Cassius Lee, and there awaited his return from church. When the two Lee gentlemen, who had walked home from church together, entered the house, they found the waiting delegation. Realizing at once that only grave considerations had brought these gentlemen to his home, Cassius Lee left the room, and dispatched his family of children to the house of his sister, Mrs. Lloyd. General Lee had written to General Scott only the day before—on April 20:

Since my interview with you on the 18th inst. I have felt that I ought no longer to retain my commission in the Army. I therefore tender my resignation, which I request you will recommend for acceptance. It would have been presented at once but for the struggle it has cost me to separate myself from a service to which I have devoted the best years of my life, and all the ability I possessed. . . . Save in the defense of my native State, I never desire again to draw my Sword.[1]

For this purpose the commissioners from the governor and convention had come, to ask Robert E. Lee to draw his sword—to accept the office of commander in chief of the Virginia forces.

General Lee arrived in Richmond on April 22, and the next day accepted from the Secession Convention the command just offered him:

Trusting to Almighty God, an approving conscience and the aid of my fellow citizens, I will devote myself to the defense and service of my native State, in whose behalf alone would I ever have drawn my sword.[2]

EPILOGUE

WASHINGTON IN GLORY—AMERICA IN TEARS

The effect of the sudden news of his death upon the inhabitants of Alexandria can better be conceived than expressed. At first a general disorder, wildness, and consternation pervaded the town. The tale appeared as an illusory dream, as the raving of a sickly imagination. But these impressions soon gave place to sensations of the most poignant sorrow and extreme regret. On Monday and Wednesday the stores were all closed and all business suspended, as if each family had lost its father. From the time of his death to the time of his interment the bells continued to toll, the shipping in the harbor wore their colors half mast high, and every public expression of grief was observed. On Wednesday, the inhabitants of the town, of the county, and the adjacent parts of Maryland proceeded to Mount Vernon to perform the last offices to the body of their illustrious neighbor. All the military within a considerable distance and three Masonic lodges were present. The concourse of people was immense. Till the time of interment the corpse was placed on the portico fronting the river, that every citizen might have an opportunity of taking a last farewell of the departed benefactor.
—*The Alexandria Times and District of Columbia Advertiser,* December 20, 1799.

PART THREE

Five Sketches of the Nineteenth Century

Chapter 24

The Yeaton-Fairfax House*

William Yeaton was born in Portsmouth, New Hampshire, in 1766, and migrated to Alexandria to enter the shipping business when a young man. In the early nineteenth century he launched into the building trade —an "undertaker" he would have been called in the eighteenth century— an architect and contractor today.

On July 15, 1805, he purchased from Cuthburt Powell a part of a lot, granted unto Levin Powell by James Irvine in a deed dated September 10, 1795, and described as situated at the intersection of Cameron and St. Asaph Streets, running west on Cameron for the distance of one hundred feet and north on St. Asaph for ninety-eight feet. The consideration involved one thousand one hundred dollars.

The elegant three-storied square brick house which William Yeaton

*607 Cameron Street. Owners: The Misses Crilly.

Recessed and panelled doorway to my Lord Fairfax's town house

erected upon his land is a monument to his talent as a designer. His residence is an individualized interpretation of the best Georgian traditions. The façade of the house is broken in the middle by a long recessed shallow arch, beginning flush with the first belt line, and continuing nearly to the modillioned cornice. In this recess the middle, second and third story windows, are centered, giving the effect of a very high Palladian window. Large arched windows flank each side of the entrance, while windows of the second and third stories are quite ordinary, save in

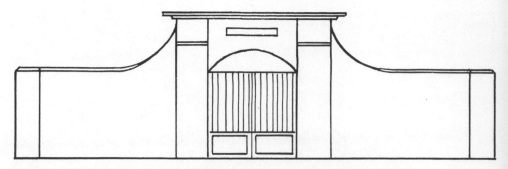

Washington's Tomb at Mount Vernon. From a sketch appearing in a letter of William Yeaton to Lawrence Lewis under date of April 4, 1835. (Courtesy Mount Vernon Ladies' Association)

proportion. Every window has outside shutters and molded iron hold-backs.

The entrance, a flat arch flush with the house, opens into a deeply recessed and paneled vestibule. Side lunettes, leaded transom, double doors supported by reeded half columns, and an elaborate fret decorate the arch and door trim, making the doorway a very important element of the design. Stone front steps and double flights of outcurving steps, banded by iron railings, contribute emphasis. The watersheds and belt lines are white, as is the recessed arch, adding a dramatic touch to the dull red masonry.

To the right, upon entering, runs a long room the entire length of the house; to the left a small chamber faces the street. A large arch frames a graceful stair, which winds up to the third floor in a circular movement. Newel post and stair ends are carved. While woodwork throughout the house is elaborate, the difference between the first and second floors is marked. That of the first floor is massive, rather more dull than interesting, but the second floor, especially the large room, is startling in that mantel, door trim, chair rail, and baseboard are carved with the delicate lightness of Adam. The feature of this room is, of course, the mantel which is centered between two large shell-like shallow recessed arches, reaching from the floor to the ceiling. The room might have been done by McIntire at his best.

In 1814 the Yeatons sold their home to a man who immediately disposed of his interest in the property to the Bank of the Potomac for ten thousand dollars. Sixteen years later, on December 9, 1830, the house was purchased as a town residence by Thomas, Ninth Lord Fairfax, for five thousand dollars, and remained in the Fairfax family for thirty-four years. Thomas, Ninth Lord Fairfax, in 1800 married Margaret Herbert,

William Yeaton produced this fine Federal Mansion. A sample of the interior woodwork

eldest daughter of William and Sarah Carlyle Herbert and granddaughter of John Carlyle. They had ten children. Mrs. Robert E. Lee (*née* Custis) was an intimate of the girls of this family and a frequent visitor in the house.

Doctor Orlando Fairfax succeeded his father as owner from 1848 to 1864. He bore the title of the "Beloved Physician." The following advertisements, taken from the files of the *Alexandria Gazette,* give a brief glimpse of his activities in the 1830s:

Dr. Fairfax has returned to Alexandria, and is ready to resume the practice of his profession in the town and its neighborhood. His office is at the N.W. corner of Pitt and Cameron Streets.

Dr. Fairfax in his late absence of five months, has been constantly engaged at Philadelphia in increasing his medical acquirements. [1831]

Dr. Fairfax has returned to Alexandria and is ready to resume the practice of his profession. He has, during his late absence from Alexandria, witnessed many cases óf the epidemic cholera. [1832]

In 1829 Dr. Fairfax had married Mary Randolph Cary, daughter of Wilson Jefferson Cary. They had nine children.

Arch and staircase in the Yeaton-Fairfax House

In a deed of April 14, 1864, the fact is revealed that this property was condemned according to an act of Congress in 1862 "to suppress insurrection, to punish treason and rebellion to seize and confiscate property of Rebels and for other purposes."[1] It further records that on the preceding day, April 13, 1864, Gouverneur Morris, attorney for Patsy J. Morris, of Westchester County, New York, purchased for four thousand dollars, he being the highest bidder therefor, all the right, title, interest and estate of Dr. Orlando Fairfax.

Gouverneur Morris was a brother-in-law of Dr. Orlando Fairfax, and while living in France sent the Fairfaxes from the palace at Versailles a very large and elegant mirror which hung in the drawing room, filling one of the alcoves from floor to ceiling. This mirror is still in existence and in the possession of Dr. Fairfax's granddaughter, Mrs. Donald MacCrea.

Mrs. Burton Harrison in her *Recollections, Grave and Gay,* relates the wartime experiences of her uncle and his family who were forced to seek refuge in Richmond, of their sufferings and privations, and of the death of the young son of the family, Randolph, barely twenty, killed in action in mid-December 1862.

During the years of Fairfax occupancy, this mansion was one of the social and cultural centers of the town; the Fairfaxes were the important noble family of the "upper reaches of the Potomac." They intermarried with the Carlyles, Washingtons, Herberts, and Carys. Their contribution to Alexandria cannot be overrated, for in their personal lives and public service, they set an example of chivalry and courage. They have been distinguished by handsome men and beautiful women, by gentleness and courtly bearing. They have had great wealth and used it generously; have lost great wealth and borne it nobly. The family is represented in England today by Thomas Brian, Thirteenth Lord Fairfax, great-great-grandson of Thomas, Ninth Lord Fairfax.

Let us return to William Yeaton, builder of the mansion on Cameron Street. It is of vital interest that he was the designer and contractor for the inclosure of the Tomb of the *Pater Patriae.*[2] The archives at Mount Vernon contribute a number of papers dealing with this construction. Here is the proposal which Yeaton addressed to Major Lawrence Lewis, of Woodlawn, General Washington's nephew and the executor who supervised the work:

Alex April 4th 1835.

Dear Sir

I have sent you a sketch of the wall & have anticipated a *Gate* way on one of the sides which I expect will be necessary.

If you wish the Gate, one something like the sketch will be appropriate, you may have the gate made solid—or open as you prefer, to releive the dead wall, between the arch and copen there may be placed a slab of stone 4 Feet long & one foot wide, or a pannell may be formed in the wall.

I will engage to have the wall erected and find all materials, say Forty Five Feet square, ten Feet high, from the bottom of the foundation, which is to be two Bricks thick 2 feet high, the peirs to continue the same thickness to the copen, the pannells between the piers to be one brick & one half thick, the copen to be formed with best Brick three courses above the square—the Gateway & Gate similar to the sketch the work to be well done, & materials of the best quality —For Six hundred dollars,—

Very respectfully
Your Obed Servt

W. YEATON

This addition was completed by the end of the year at a cost just slightly in excess of the original six-hundred-dollar estimate. Designed primarily as a protective wall to inclose the burial vault built in 1831, it contributed an appropriate architectural character to the tomb lot. The Gothic arch of the completed entrance was in sympathy with a funereal scene enhanced by willowlike foliage observable in certain views of the period.

Alterations were made in 1837 which created a vestibule between the vault and the outer wall and gateway constructed by William Yeaton. It is not known whether Yeaton again participated in the construction. It was in 1837 that the bodies of General and Mrs. Washington were removed from this closed vault behind and permanently entombed in marble sarcophagi, which the visitor views today in the outer chamber at Mount Vernon.

William Yeaton, builder and "undertaker" (architect) of Alexandria. By Saint Mèmin. (*Courtesy Corcoran Gallery of Art*)

Chapter 25
The La Fayette-Lawrason-Cazenove House*

The presence of La Fayette was nothing new to Alexandria, yet his official visit in 1824, as the nation's guest, created a turmoil in the town. As soon as the news was received of his arrival in New York (it took two days to reach Alexandria) Captain A. William's company of artillery arose before dawn to fire a national salute at sunrise, and at noon the same company fired seventy-six rounds. During the day the harbor presented the spectacle of all ships displaying their flags at masthead. When the Marquis reached Baltimore, on October 8, representatives from the Alexandria city council were on hand to extend an invitation (in the form of an address) to visit the town, which the distinguished visitor was pleased to accept.

He was met on the south side of the Potomac River on the 16th by that same Captain Williams and his company, firing a salvo in salute, and was addressed in a "neat and handsome" manner by General Jones and

*301 South St. Asaph Street. Owners: Mr. and Mrs. Nathan Wallack.

Left: Thomas Lawrason, builder, and the first owner of the La Fayette House.
Right: Mrs. Thomas Lawrason *née* Elizabeth Carson

suite. He "then entered a splendid barouche, drawn by four fine grays, with postilions dressed in white with blue sashes," and thus was escorted by a company of cavalry under the command of Captain Andrews and a civilian escort led by Captain James Carson, dressed in blue "with sashes of the same color." To this splendor add marines, fire companies, the Alexandria Battalion (1,500 men) all saluting, firing salvos, presenting arms—two bands playing, reception committees, constant alighting from and entering the barouche, and you have some idea of the excitement as the procession passed under the triumphal arch spanning Washington Street.

This arch was a masterpiece. It has been described by Benjamin Hallo-well in his *Autobiography* and by the *Alexandria Gazette* at the time, and memories of it linger in old tales told in many homes. Built in three sections, a large arch spanned the street, with smaller ones the sidewalks. The columns were decorated with portraits of Washington and La Fayette. Noble and patriotic sentiments were inscribed: "Welcome La Fayette —A Nation's Gratitude Thy Due"—"For a Nation to be Free, it is Sufficient that she wills it." A fully rigged ship hung beneath the central span, and the whole was decorated with cedar, laurel and oak, set off by a Liberty cap and "a real mountain eagle which had been politely furnished by Mr. Timothy Mountford of the Museum." When the column passed under the arch, the eagle "politely furnished" opened wide his wings and

The doorway to the elegant house built by Thomas Lawrason and loaned by
his widow to La Fayette

gave a mighty screech, produced, 'tis said, by a small boy and a pin placed in close proximity for this very purpose. From the windows of the houses ladies waved handkerchiefs and threw nosegays in fiesta fashion.

When the parade reached Royal Street and Gadsby's Tavern, we are told that a ceremony took place there which, "in sublimity and moral effect surpassed all." "One hundred young girls and one hundred boys from seven to twelve years of age were arrayed in lines extending to the Reception Room." They were neatly dressed, the "females" in white with blue sashes and badges and leghorn bonnets, the boys in blue with pink sashes and badges. As the General approached, a little girl, Rosalie Taylor, stepped out and "spoke with becoming grace and manner" a poem several verses long that began:

> Fayette, friend of Washington.
> *Freedom's* children greet thee here;
> Fame for *Thee* our hearts has won
> Flows for thee the grateful tear.
> Chorus
> Happiness today is ours;
> Strew, ye fair! his way with flowers!

After being wined and dined at Claggett's Hotel, formerly Gadsby's, the barouche was again brought forward and General La Fayette, escorted by the procession, "moved on to the house which had been procured for his accomodation."[1]

And so we arrive at the home of Mrs. Thomas Lawrason, the most elegant house of its day and time in Alexandria, lent by this charming Irish lady to the great Frenchman, thereby endowing it with imperishable fame as the La Fayette house.

On August 5, 1779, the executors of John Alexander sold to Thomas Wilkinson "a half acre lott lying and being upon the South side of Duke Street and the West Side of St. Asaph Street and described by the number 175," the ground rent of which was £14 10s. In September 1795, William Thornton Alexander, one of the heirs of John Alexander, released Benjamin Shreve and James Lawrason from this ground rent upon the payment of the sum of £300, and in this indenture of September 14, the fact is cited that this was the property sold by Thomas Wilkinson and that Shreve and Lawrason divided the property.

On September 27, 1819, in an indenture between James Lawrason and Alice, his wife, and Elizabeth Lawrason, widow of Thomas Lawrason,

The hall

son of the said James, lately deceased, and their five children, the fact is cited that Thomas Lawrason bought for five hundred dollars the lot at the intersection of St. Asaph and Duke Streets, described as running "West on Duke 120 feet to an alley 6 feet wide 10 inches to be held in common with the heirs of Benjamin Shreve, thence on said alley South 55 feet, thence East, parallel to Duke 120 feet to St. Asaph and thence on St. Asaph North to the beginning." This same document further described that "the said Thomas entered on said lott and erected thereon a three story brick tenement and other buildings and improvements and afterwards departed this life intestate without having received a deed for the same," which deed James was at this time executing, conveying this property to his son's widow and orphans.

The three-story brick tenement, built by Thomas Lawrason for his young wife, is one of the important federal houses in this ancient seaport. High upon the roof a white railing incloses the "Captain's Walk" from which point of vantage the Fowle & Lawrason ships could be sighted far down the Potomac. The doorway is the outstanding feature of the house. The fanlight over the door is a true fan in shape and design, and the lunettes on each side of the double doors are unique. The interior of the mansion is commodious and comfortable with well proportioned rooms of agreeable size and beautiful woodwork.

James Lawrason of Sussex County, New Jersey, married Alice Levering. Their son, Thomas Lawrason, builder of the house, was born in Norfolk, Virginia, in 1780. The Lawrasons lived for a while in Canada, where life for those with Tory sympathies was more agreeable, but after the Revolution, and prior to 1795, the family returned to Virginia and settled in Alexandria, where the senior Lawrason was associated for a time with Benjamin Shreve.

Thomas Lawrason, a member of the important shipping firm of Lawrason & Fowle, married Elizabeth Carson, the sixteen-year-old daughter of Dr. Samuel Carson of Armagh, Ireland, in October 1808. To them were born five children: Samuel Carson, October 18, 1809; James Thomas, July 28, 1811; William Wilson, 1814; George Carson, 1816; and Anne Carson, 1818.

Thomas Lawrason died on June 7, 1819, before he could enjoy his fine, new home, leaving Elizabeth to struggle with a house and family. She never remarried, remaining in Alexandria until her children were reared and settled in life. Then she followed her youngest son, George Carson Lawrason, to New Orleans. An entry in the family Bible reads: "Elizabeth Lawrason, consort of Thomas Lawrason died at the residence of her son George C. Lawrason in New Orleans on the 11th of April, 1851, aged 59 years." A curious and sad sequel to her death is that some years later her grave was washed away and swallowed by the Mississippi. When General Lee's body lay in state at Washington College (now Washington and Lee University) her grandson, Samuel McCutcheon Lawrason, then a student at Virginia Military Institute, was one of the bodyguards at the bier.

The rear parlor. These rooms are spacious and well proportioned, the woodwork in style of McIntire after Adam is worthy of the master builders

The original portraits of Elizabeth and Thomas hang in the Lawrasons'
Louisiana plantation home at St. Francisville. Some of the family silver,
made in Alexandria by I. Adam, belongs to her granddaughter, Mrs.
Kirkpatrick.

The La Fayette-Lawrason association rightfully includes the name
Cazenove to commemorate the role played by Alexandria's noble French-
speaking citizen on the happy occasion of La Fayette's visit. Really his
name was De Cazenove for his family was both Huguenot and noble.
They had fled France in 1688 and settled in Geneva, Switzerland, where
they were prominent bankers for over one hundred years. When the
French Revolution broke out, the radical Swiss threw the French aristo-
crats into jail; then, becoming frightened at their tyranny, they released
the patricians. Among those incarcerated were the De Cazenove family.
After their release Antoine Charles de Cazenove and his elder brother
were sent by their parents to America to avoid the Revolution. They
landed in Philadelphia and were the guests of some cousins there by
the same name. The two brothers married sisters, the Misses Hogan of
Philadelphia.

Later, the elder brother returned to Geneva. Antoine Charles Cazenove (for by this time our young Frenchman had become imbued with the spirit of republicanism and dropped the De as un-American), moved to Alexandria about 1794 and founded the banking house of Cazenove & Company. Head of a large shipping business, he maintained his own wharf and warehouses; was French consul; one of the founders of the Alexandria Water Company and of the cotton factory; and an active member of the old Presbyterian Church. He owned three or four black slaves who spoke only French. During the yellow fever epidemic in 1803, when forty to fifty people were dying in a day, Cazenove refused to leave Alexandria. He contracted yellow fever and was one of the few persons to have the disease and survive.

After Mrs. Lawrason put her Alexandria home at the disposal of General La Fayette, Antoine Charles Cazenove was invited to act as host. When the Alexandrians crowded outside the Lawrason house demanding a sight of and a speech from La Fayette, Cazenove introduced him. La Fayette was *"chez lui"*; the whole visit passed off with great *éclat*.

The great General on departure referred to his entertainment in Alexandria as "the most pleasing hours of his life." A gratified city council presented Mrs. Lawrason with a silver cup in recognition of her generous and hospitable act. This, duly inscribed, is cherished to this day by her great-granddaughter, Mrs. Donald M. Hamilton of Georgetown, in Washington, D. C.

Chapter 26
Enter the Quaker Pedagogue: Benjamin Hallowell

Benjamin Hallowell came to Alexandria in 1824 to open a school for boys. He was then twenty-five, with no fortune, a large debt, a dependent mother, a new and young bride.

For his first school he rented the building on the northeast corner of Oronoco and Washington Streets, next to the house where the widow of General Harry Lee resided!

Alexandria was in a turmoil of hospitality, welcoming the Marquis de la Fayette. Hallowell and his wife of a few hours stood in their front door the morning after their marriage and saw the famous Frenchman paying his *devoirs* to Mrs. Lee. Hallowell's autobiography pictures the occasion: "When he got opposite," he wrote, "he looked at us, took off his hat, and made a graceful bow, not knowing it was to a lady who had been married the day before." Nor that his liking for a fresh smiling face inspired the schoolmaster to immediately express his emotions in the following verse:

Each lover of Liberty surely must get
Something in honor of LaFayette
There's a LaFayette watch-chain, a LaFayette hat,
A LaFayette this, and a LaFayette that.
But I wanted something as lasting as life
As I took to myself a LaFayette wife.[1]

The school of Benjamin Hallowell filled slowly at first. The ninth boy to enroll was Mrs. Harry Lee's son, Robert Edward. Edmund Lee and Thomas Swann sent their boys, who were "ten dollar" scholars. The time was to come when Hallowell would turn away more than a hundred applicants, but that was after Robert Edward Lee had gone to West Point and distinguished himself.

At the end of his year in Alexandria, Hallowell's child was born. Both he and the mother were very ill, "seemingly with bilious fever." Then, for the first time, Hallowell heard that the "situation on Oronoco Street, on the edge of town as it was, had always been regarded as unhealthy."[2] He could not bear the idea of his wife and family continuing in a place that was so evil, or of inviting his scholars to share such an environment. Then it was that he got in contact with the widow Hooe, made arrangements to give up his first schoolhouse and immediately engaged the more healthy situation on Washington Street.

The house which was so "unhealthy" is a replica in almost every respect of Mrs. Harry Lee's house, but there is no record of Mrs. Lee complaining of the situation nor of the health of her boys.

The new schoolhouse, so commonly spoken of as the Lloyd House* by Alexandrians, was built by John Hooe in 1793. In 1826, Benjamin Hallowell rented it from the widow Hooe and in the spring vacation with his ill wife in his arms, moved into this building so admirably adapted to his purpose.

"My school room," he tells us, "was on the first floor, north end, all across the house. I having obtained permission of my Landlady, in our arrangements, to remove the partition on condition of replacing it by one with folding doors, when I should leave the property, which was done. My lecture room was the back room over the school room. . . . The very day the quarter's rent was due the widow Hooe's carriage was at the door, and this continued to be her custom as long as she lived. If I had not the money, which was generally the case, I would frankly tell her so, and add that the first money I could get, and could possibly spare, I would take to her, with which she was always satisfied. She never said a word like urging me, or being disappointed in not getting the rent due, and I did take her the very first I received, never permitting it to be in my possession over night."[3]

The frail Mrs. Hallowell opened a school for girls in the front room over the schoolroom, and Hallowell lectured to her scholars. Money

*220 North Washington Street.

Entrance to Benjamin Hallowell's first school. A fine type of Georgian doorway

being very scarce with them at this time, they could not afford two stoves, so Hallowell and the servant, Nancy, carried the stove from schoolroom to lecture room as needed.

"On the 17th of Ninth month, 1830," the autobiography continues, "commenced giving private lessons to Angela Lewis, daughter of Major Lawrence Lewis (who was a nephew of General Washington, and it was said a good deal resembled him in appearance). These lessons continued through the year, for which I charged fifty dollars, and the Major

The Lloyd House and Benjamin Hallowell's second school

promptly sent me his check for the amount. Eleanor Lewis, Angela's Mother, always attended at her daughter's recitations in English Grammar, Parsing, Natural Philosophy, etc., so that her influence, which she afterwards exerted in my favor, and her praise of my method of teaching, was of greater value to me than the amount I received in hand for teaching her daughter."[4]

In the meantime, he struggled along with debt, with illness, with sorrow. Scarlet fever wiped out three of the four little Hallowells in nearly the same number of weeks. He witnessed the cholera in Alexandria and had the unhappy experience of seeing a man drop dead of the plague before his eyes; he heard the market square echo to the feet of soldiers mustering and drilling in preparation for war in Mexico.

This man had the most singular relationships in his business dealings. When he bought the lot and buildings of his school from the bank, it was two years before any papers were signed, interest paid, or deed given, although he had made extensive improvements during that time. He never failed to meet an obligation although at the beginning it took him ten years to pay back the two hundred dollars plus five per cent interest,

When the blast of winter chilled the great rooms at Woodlawn the Lawrence Lewises came into warmer quarters in Alexandria and occupied this cottage. 'Twas here that Benjamin Hallowell came to improve the mind of Nelly Custis' daughter

that he had from his Uncle Comly in Philadelphia. Everyone trusted him, the merchants in Philadelphia from whom he had his school supplies and chemical apparatus; his grocer in Alexandria, John P. Cowman, not only never dunned him, but invited him to come to his store and get what was necessary, and never sent bills unless requested.

Hallowell was city surveyor, but accepted no fee because it afforded a fine opportunity to instruct his pupils in "Field Practice with the Odolite and Level." He was something of an architect, improving every place he occupied, and building two fine structures in the town.

In 1831 the widow Hooe died and in the spring of 1832 the house which he had acquired for a school in 1826, was put up at auction. Hallowell hoped to possess this property, having put both his time and money into the remodeling. He had already enlarged and improved a sugar house adjacent to the building. His school was growing in reputation and size, he becoming more prosperous. Gathering together all the cash he could put his hands on, he attended the auction where he had the misfortune to be outbid. The property was purchased by John Lloyd, and remained in the Lloyd family for nearly one hundred years.

Early nineteenth century mantel in the home of Mr. and Mrs. Ford Swetnam at 815 Franklin Street. The original use of reeded work to form a beautiful design, the shell-like ornamentation and diagonal bands make this an attractive piece of wood carving. (Nelly Custis Town House)

Ancient mahogany filled the rooms, portraits of ancestors lined the walls. General Lee was a frequent visitor in this house. The Lloyds intermarried with the Lees, and Mrs. Lloyd was General Lee's first cousin. His daughter, Miss Mary Custis Lee, always stayed here when visiting in Alexandria. The last Lloyds to live in this house were two very old ladies. What follows will serve to reveal why their neighbors considered them "quaint."

Following the death of Prince Albert, Queen Victoria's consort, a fashion grew up in Virginia affecting widows. At the death of the husband a real Victorian Virginia lady simply went to bed and awaited death. It did not always follow that a broken heart put her in her grave as readily as was anticipated, and many of these brokenhearted widows lived to a ripe old age. Such was the case with one of these piously saddened ladies. When she heard the doorbell, she at once put herself between the sheets of her high poster and covered herself to the chin. Under the cover went such things as high button shoes, a "reticule" and any other regalia that was in service at the moment. If the caller was familiar, or after the formalities had been observed, proper sympathy for the heart palpitating between the sheets, the head languishing upon the pillow noticed and condoned, the sufferer would arise, hop out of bed fully clothed and partake of cookies and wine passed by the black dwarf, Selena. This small creature, after fulfilling her part in the social amenities, seated herself upon a small stool, joined in the conversation, and when amused (which was often) broke into a high falsetto laugh. In the last years of these two ladies she gained a most unholy influence over her charges and took cruel advantage of their helplessness.

Another peculiarity of this household was the fashion of being admitted to the mansion. After repeated ringing of the bell, a second-story front window would open—those not in the know often left—and in a leisurely fashion a grape basket was lowered by a long string. Inside the basket, those who were familiar with the proceeding would find the front-door key, a large, heavy iron affair, somewhat like that to the Bastille, now on display at Mount Vernon, and with this they let themselves in.

The Lloyd house, a large rectangular brick building, divided by a central hall with rooms on each side, is two and a half stories high. Three dormer windows pierce the roof, front and back, and four great chimneys rise from the gable ends. Flush with the street, on a corner, with a handsome garden behind a pale and paneled fence adjoining to the left, the house is a model federal town mansion. Pedimented doorway, window caps, keystones, cornice and dormer trim follow the best mid-Georgian tradition. This house is one of Alexandria's finest homes. It was for many years the residence of Mr. and Mrs. W. A. Smoot.

Chapter 27
The Alexandria Lyceum*

Benjamin Hallowell, our Quaker pedagogue, was not content with improving the minds of the young. He soon realized the necessity of furbishing up the cranial contents of his associates.

An able propagandist, Hallowell set himself to interest his friends in founding a lyceum. This was accomplished in 1834, just ten years after his entrance as a schoolmaster. Naturally he was the first president and naturally the early lectures were held in his school. Here the erudite of the town were wont to gather to express themselves in lecture and debate. Hallowell does not give the date of the actual building of the lyceum, saying merely:

At length a lot was purchased on the Southwest corner of Washington and Prince Streets, on which was erected a fine building, a little back from the street, with a pediment front supported by four fluted Doric columns with a triglyph cornice, and surrounded by an iron railing, and a beautiful yard of flowers and ornamental shrubbery. In this building was placed the Alexandria Library, and there was besides, on the first floor a large reading room, and a room for a cabinet of minerals, and specimens in Natural History. On the second floor was a well arranged and handsome lecture room, with marble busts of Cicero and Seneca, one on each side of the President's desk and seat. In this room lectures were given by John Quincy Adams, Caleb Cushing, Dr. Sewell, Samuel Goodrich (Peter Parley), Daniel Bryan, Robert H. Miller, William H. Fowle and several others. I gave the introductory lecture (which was published) and several

---

*201 South Washington Street.

others afterwards. Attending the Lyceum was a very interesting and improving way of spending one evening in the week (Third-day evening), and the citizens would adapt their visiting and other arrangements so as not to have them come on Lyceum evenings.[1]

Thus came into being one of the finest examples of the Classical Revival in American architecture. When the portico was under construction, bricks salvaged from old St. Mary's Catholic Church were used for the columns (afterwards plastered). This is an interesting fact, but another Quaker-Catholic relationship merits recalling here. Old St. Mary's Church stood on South Washington Street on land donated by Robert Townsend Hooe, a Quaker. Built in 1793, it was abandoned in 1826 when the new church on Royal Street was opened, but the early graveyard which adjoined the old church continues in use. A small detail this of the bricks—yet it commemorates the friendly ties ever maintained in Alexandria between the two congregations.

It was appropriate that the new lyceum should provide facilities for the Alexandria Library Company, the city's first organization for the advancement of learning dating back to 1794. Insight into the early efforts to establish a library and the bid made for its public support is revealed through announcements of the type which follow. This one appeared in the local gazette for the year 1797:

ALEXANDRIA LIBRARY COMPANY

The President and Directors of the Alexandria Library Company desirous of promoting the influence which they conceive eminently calculated to diffuse useful knowledge, establish the morals of the rising generation, and afford rational entertainment for a vacent hour, earnestly recommend it to the attention and support of their fellow citizens. The utility of a public circulating library is too obvious to need arguments to demonstrate it. The friends of Literature, of Virtue, and refinement of manners, will, no doubt duly appreciate its value, and interest themselves in its advancement.

The addition of a number of valuable books has lately been made to the former selections; to which the American edition of the Encyclopoedia is directed to be super added as soon as it can be procured.

The President and Directors have ordered a catalogue of all the books in the library forthwith to be printed, with their respective prices annexed; to which will be prefixed the existing laws of the company, together with the names of all the actual subscribers to the institution. As they can determine between real and nominal members only by the fulfillment of their engagements, they solicit those who are in arrears to come forward and pay their respective balances to Samuel Craig, Treasurer, before the fifteenth of the next month, otherwise their names will be omitted in the list and their shares, agreeably to the condition, will be deemed forfeited to the company without respect of persons. Also all such as incline to become subscribers are desired to call on Mr. Craig on or before the above date, and pay their subscriptions, that their names may be inserted with the rest.

Signed by order

JAMES KENNEDY, Librarian.

That the Alexandria Library Company merited and met with cordial and generous support is shown by the fact of its perpetuation to this day within the structure of the Alexandria library system. The Library Company has been called one of the "time-honored heirlooms of the town."[2]

The Alexandria Library has had a nomadic existence from the time it was called into existence in 1794 until it was moved into its new home on Queen Street in 1937. At least five buildings other than the lyceum have doubled for home during this period; but the lyceum is the first location mentioned in the extant minutes of the company. The author nostalgically hopes the lyceum may know a renaissance and that it may again serve as the city's library and a historical museum.

Hallowell tells us that the books were housed on the first floor. His autobiography also contributes an interesting note on the busts of Cicero and Seneca which stood in the lecture room upstairs: "The marble busts spoken of above," he added, "were purchased in Italy in the time of Cromwell by one of the Fairfax family; they were brought to this country by Lord Fairfax, and had come into the possession of Daniel Herbert, whose mother was a Fairfax. I purchased them of him for the price he asked (one hundred and twenty-five dollars), but permitted them to remain in the Lyceum while it continued in operation." Benjamin Hallowell served as president of the lyceum until 1842.

After the War Between the States, the lyceum was abandoned, the society dissolved. The town was rife with rumors that a Negro organization was making plans to acquire the building. By order of the court in 1867, the stockholders of the Alexandria Lyceum Company were compelled to sell the property. Advertisements were set up in the *Gazette*. W. Arthur Taylor and Reuben Johnston were appointed commissioners, and having given thirty days' notice of the time and place of sale, the building was offered at public auction in front of the mayor's office on May 16, 1868 and "struck off" to John B. Daingerfield for the sum of $6,800.00, being the highest bid. The sale was confirmed by the court and the deed ordered executed, describing the lot of ground with buildings and improvements, southwest corner of Prince and Washington Streets,

The old Lyceum and Library

commonly called the Lyceum Hall, fronting on Washington Street 92 feet 7 inches and on Prince 101 feet 5 inches and bounded on the south by the property of H. W. Vandergrift and on the West by Mr. Henry Daingerfield's estate.[3] John Bathurst Daingerfield and his brother, Henry, owned almost the entire square bounded by Prince, Duke, Columbus and Washington streets, where now stands the Alexandria Hospital.

John B. Daingerfield turned the lyceum into a residence for his daughter, Mary, at the time of her marriage to Captain Philip Beverly Hooe, 17th Virginia Regiment, C.S.A. The house remained in the Hooe family until 1900, when John Daingerfield Hooe and his wife, Mary, the daughter of Colonel Arthur Herbert, sold the property to Sara J. McGuire. In 1913 Mrs. McGuire transferred the property to her husband, the late Dr. Hugh McGuire. The lyceum was used for many years as a private residence by Dr. and Mrs. McGuire, and the interior has been much changed. The exterior is quite untouched, triglyph cornice, Doric columns, all well past the century mark. It stands today one of the best examples of the Classical Revival in architecture, not only in Alexandria but in America.

The corner of Prince and Washington Streets is hallowed ground to Alexandria. From here the 17th Virginia Regiment, C.S.A., marched gallantly off to war, and when the fighting and turmoil died, the remnant of this regiment was wont to gather on Confederate Memorial Day and hold services for those left behind on Virginia's bloody battlefields. This custom continued long after the bronze monument of a Confederate soldier was placed in the center of the street. If, today, hurrying automobiles are forced to slow up to pass the circle enclosing the Confederate warrior, it is well. For this spot, while marking a lost cause, does not mark a forgotten one.

Chapter 28
The Sea Captain's Daughter and Her House*

This large, almost square house, rises three stories in a stately pile of soft red brick, flanked by two ancient tulip trees towering twenty-five feet above the pavilion roof, while a great box hedge partially hides the front façade and large garden. Five generations of the same family have called it home.

It is a romantic and interesting house. Built prior to 1853 by Reuben Roberts on a half-acre of unimproved ground, it lay "in the country" for some years. Roberts, a Quaker of the family of Cameron Farms, died in 1853; his widow moved to New Jersey, and the house stood new and tenantless until 1857, when it was purchased by Captain Samuel Bancroft Hussey of Portland, Maine, as a bridal gift for his only daughter, Melissa Ann. And thereby hangs a tale.

Gallant Captain Hussey is reported to have been a descendant of that

*617 South Washington Street. Owners: Mr. and Mrs. Malcolm Westcott Hill.

Presented by E.P.Johnson to S.B Hussey. Hong Kong. January 10th 1859.

The Stag Hound, one of the great clipper ships in the China trade

Christopher Hussey who arrived in Charlestown, Massachusetts, in 1630 and became one of the large proprietors. Intended for the Navy at an early age he ran away to sea and became a master of Clipper ships that raced the seas in the China trade. Captain in succession of the *Reindeer,* the *Strabo,* earlier and smaller vessels, he became Captain of the *Westward Ho* on which, in 1854, he made a record trip of eighty-five days from Canton to New York. In 1857 he speeded the same vessel from Boston around the Horn to San Francisco in a hundred days. Two years later he died on the *Stag Hound* of which he was master and part owner.

The *Westward Ho* was a great and beautiful ship of sixteen hundred tons, outfitted with every comfort and luxury of her day, including crystal, books, silver, and a melodeon on which to while away the hours at sea. Captain Hussey was frequently accompanied on his voyages by his wife, and for a time they lived in India, as well as many other far-off and curious ports.

Melissa Ann Hussey[1] after her graduation from the Charlestown Female Seminary, near Boston, made the grand tour with her father. This was not her first voyage, as he had entrusted her to Captain Creesy, master of the *Flying Cloud* on a long journey from China. But on the occasion of this grand tour graduation gift, he directed the *Westward Ho* up the Potomac and anchored in the then busy port of Alexandria. The city of Washington was not very sophisticated in those days, so the official and

To this house came the Portsmouth bride, Melissa Ann Hussey Wood, with parakeets and nonpareils

social set of the capital sought the theatres, taverns, and balls of Alexandria. Statesmen had apartments at the new and elegant Braddock House or Green's Mansions on Fairfax Street, and at this hotel the Captain engaged a suite for himself and daughter.

While in Alexandria, a romance developed which resulted, in 1857, in the marriage of Melissa Hussey and Robert Lewis Wood. Their wedding took place in New York, and the young couple returned to take up life in Alexandria. No colonial house was desired by this bride of nineteen. She must have something new and fresh and modern, and as though preordained, they came upon the large red brick house at Franklin and Washington Streets, much like those so well known to her in Portland, Longfellow's "beautiful town that is seated by the sea."

With Melissa came to her new home a collection of rare birds in such numbers that the room over the kitchen was devoted to the cages of cockatoos, parakeets, parrots and nonpareils. Here these feathered friends in spectrum-hued plumage lived among the potted plants and charmed the little bride with their beauty and sweet tricks. Other appendages included a chimpanzee, and a small Chinese slave boy, bought by her father from one of the innumerable sampans in the harbor of Canton. "Chinese Tom" was reared and educated by Melissa Wood and after the War Between the States she gave him his freedom. For years he was the only Chinaman in Alexandria. Mrs. Wood's granddaughter remembers the visits of this man to her grandmother. He would station himself at the entrance to her door and a long conversation would go on between the guttural-voiced Oriental and the gentle little "Missey" whom he adored.

Almost unchanged is Melissa Hussey Wood's house. Her exquisite wax flower arrangements, colored and molded by her hands, her mother's tête-à-têtes, made in England and purchased in India, paintings of her father's ships and his ivory chessmen, her silver wedding bouquet holder, her baby's shoulder clips, her brass and crystal girandoles, her pictures, books and chairs, have all been used by her two daughters, her granddaughter, and her great-granddaughters. Old pressed brass cornices decorate the windows above the lace curtains. Unusual, too, are the very large silver daguerreotypes, made in California for the new house, and the haircloth "pouf" rocking chairs. An Italian clock, bought by her father in Florence, which arrived in Bangor, Maine, on the day Melissa Ann was born in 1838, stands on its original music box base upon the dining-room mantel. Strangest contrast of all, above the doors of this high-ceilinged room are steel engravings in their contemporary oval frames of Generals Joe Johnston, Stonewall Jackson, and Robert E. Lee, placed there by the Yankee bride, who after three years in Alexandria became an ardent champion of the Confederacy and never took the oath of allegiance while Alexandria was under Union jurisdiction.

Acknowledgments

It would be impossible to write a book of this kind without a great deal of help from many sources. This help was given by very busy people with knowledge or documents, which inspired the historian to further impositions upon their useful persons.

An expression of appreciation, always banal, is nevertheless an attempt to express gratitude—and this is my only means of acknowledging my obligations to friend and stranger. Without such help this book, such as it is, would never have been written and so my lasting gratitude goes:

First, to my father, who said I would never finish it, and to my husband, who said I would.

To Mr. Walter Wilcox, American Photographical Society, and Royal Photographical Society, for his labors and beautiful photographs which illustrate this book.

To Mrs. George Kirk, for endless and patient typing and sustained enthusiasms.

To Miss Virgila Stephens, for intimating that I might be able to write anything that anybody would ever care to read, and to Mrs. Worth Bailey, who said I had.

To Mr. Worth Bailey, curator of Mount Vernon, for numerous historical contributions, rare and authentic, for the finished seal of Alexandria, the endpapers, the charming drawings, for editing; and lastly, for wise and useful advice. Mr. Bailey's historical knowledge and artistic training have been invaluable.

To Mrs. Louis Scott, for permission to see the scrapbook of her mother, Mrs. Mary G. Powell, and family papers; for the Harper family records, for her gracious assistance and advice, and for the use of her late mother's *The History of Old Alexandria, Virginia*.

To Mrs. Robert M. Reese, for long and helpful hours and the generous use of the Ramsay family records, and historical documents.

To the Lady Regents of Mount Vernon and to Mr. Wall, the superintendent, for the use of the Mount Vernon library, the photograph of Lawrence Washington, the choice bill of lading, and Dr. Dick's *George Washington*.

To Miss Frances Herbert, for information about the Carlyle, Herbert and Fairfax families, and for the photograph of John Carlyle's mother, Rachel Carlyle.

To the late Mrs. Charles R. Hooff, for loan of the Carlyle genealogy and for permission to photograph John Carlyle's snuffbox.

To Mrs. William Boothe, for Lee family notes and Christ Church anecdotes.

To Mrs. Charles Baird, and her sister, Mrs. Gerhard Dieke, for permission to quote from the books of their father, the late Fairfax Harrison, and from the books of their late grandmother, Mrs. Burton Harrison; for photographs of Sally Cary, George William Fairfax and Ben Dulany.

To Mr. Taylor Burke, for the anecdote of the purchase money for Mount Vernon.

To Judge Walter T. McCarthy, for permission to open court-sealed deed books.

To the late clerk and assistant clerk of the Fairfax Court House, Messrs. F. W. Richardson and Alton R. Holbrook, and to the present clerk, Mr. Thomas P.

Chapman Jr., for documents, photostats and unfailing patience and courtesy.

To the attendants of the manuscript division, the map room and the rare book room of the Library of Congress.

To the attendants of the Virginia state archives in Richmond, for assistance in uncovering Alexandria records.

To the ladies at the Alexandria library.

To Miss S. Frances Leary, for the Michael Swope family notes.

To the late Mr. Charles Callahan, and to Mrs. Callahan, for permission to quote from Mr. Callahan's works and for many inspirational talks with Mr. Callahan.

To Captain George H. Evans for old photographs.

To Mrs. Arthur Herbert, for photographs of Herbert furniture from the Carlyle house.

To Mr. Courtland Davis, for generous aid and valuable Alexandria records and the use of his personal manuscripts and to Mr. Davis and the Reverend Doctor William B. McIllwayne, for access to the old Presbyterian meetinghouse session books.

To Miss Cora Duffy, for the records of the Sun Fire Company.

To Mrs. Margaret Gill Davis, for use of an old customs house journal.

To the late Mr. Ward Brown, for loan of architectural documents.

To Messrs. I. D. Matthews and Milton Grigg, for floor plans.

To Mrs. Howard Tolley, for the photograph of Dr. Brown and his obituary.

To Mr. Gardner L. Boothe and the vestry of Christ Church, for permission to photograph the church.

To Mrs. Helen Lawrason Kirkpatrick, Miss Margaret Lawrason and Mrs. Edward Butler, for a wonderful day at the Lawrason plantation, Greenwood, in Louisiana, and the photographs of the Lawrason portraits.

To the Misses Carne, for the loan and use of valuable Alexandria documents.

To Miss Belle da Costa Green, of the Pierpont Morgan Library, for use of an important Martha Washington letter.

To Dr. St. George L. Sioussat, chief of the division of manuscripts of the Library of Congress.

To Mr. Allen L. Reese, for exciting finds among the Washington papers in that library.

To Mrs. Andrew Pickens, for notes on the Fowle family.

To Mr. Louis de Cazenove, for information on the Cazenove family.

To the late Mr. Cazenove Lee, for the story of General Robert E. Lee and the Edmund I. Lee house.

To Mr. W. B. McGroarty, for the letters and biographical information on Dr. Dick and permission to quote from his works.

To the Corcoran Gallery of Art for photographs of St. Mèmin's Alexandrians.

To Mr. John O. Brostrup, Mr. Thomas Neil Darling, Mr. Lewis P. Woltz, and others, for the use of photographs.

And last but not least, to Lena Harris, my old and faithful maid, who made it all possible.

Chapter References

PART ONE: PROLOGUE

An Account of the First Century of the Seaport of Alexandria.

[1]Caton, *Jottings from the Annals of Alexandria*, 3-4; and Powell, *The History of Old Alexandria, Virginia*, 25.

[2]Hening, *Statutes at Large*, IV, 268.

[3]*Journals of the House of Burgesses of Virginia*, Session 1727-34, 1736-40, 204.

[4]*Ibid.*

[5]*Ibid.*, Session 1742-47, 1748-49, 30.

[6]Fairfax County was formed from Prince William in 1742 (*Journals of the House of Burgesses, Virginia*, 1742-47, 70; and Hening, V, 207-8) after numerous petitions to this effect had been presented to the Burgesses, beginning as early as 1732 (*Ibid.*, 1727-34, 1738-40, 146), with a request to divide the county into two parishes.

[7]*Journals of the House of Burgesses of Virginia*, 1748-49, 1742-47, 265.

[8]*Ibid.*, 375.

[9]*Ibid.*, 404-5.

[10]Hening, *Statutes at Large*, VI, 214; and Caton's *Jottings*, 6-8.

[11]Caton's *Jottings*.

[12]*Ibid.*

[13]*Ibid.*

[14]*Ibid.*

[15]*Ibid.*

[16]In 1748 George Washington made a survey of the site of Belle Haven, and the following year, 1749, a plan of the town, doubtless for his brother, Lawrence, who purchased lots. Now with the Washington papers in the Library of Congress.

[17]*Minutes of the Trustees of Alexandria*, 1749-1767.

[18]*Ibid.*

[19]From data contributed by Robert C. Gooch, Chief of General Reference and Bibliography Division, Library of Congress, Letter dated April 11, 1947.

[20]*Minutes of the Trustees of Alexandria*, 1749-1767.

[21]*Ibid.*

[22]*Ibid.*

[23]*Journals of the House of Burgesses of Virginia*, 1752-1755, 1756-1758, 21, 24 and 31.

[24]*Ibid.*, 27.

[25]*Ibid.*, 34.

[26]Analoston Island, formerly My Lords Island, was part of the Alexander purchase.

[27]*Minutes of the Trustees, Recorded Deeds;* and Carne's *Tiny Town* notes.

[28]Fitzpatrick, *Diaries of George Washington*, I, 74.

[29]*Ibid.*

[30]Fitzpatrick, *Writings of George Washington*, I, 148-150, Washington's Report to Governor Dinwiddie, July 18, 1755.

[31]Burnaby, *Through the Middle Settlements in North America* (1759-60), 40.

[32]Fitzpatrick, *Diaries of George Washington*, I, 163.

[33]*Ibid.*, 294.

[34]*Ibid.*, 294.

[35]Fitzpatrick, *Writings of George Washington*, II, 338.

[36]*Minutes of the House of Burgesses*, November 5, 1762, 76, (Vol. 1761-1765); *Minutes of the Trustees of Alexandria*, 1749-1767.

[37]*Minutes of the Trustees of Alexandria*, 1749-1767.

[38]*House of Burgesses Journal*, 1761-1765, 246.

[39]*Minutes of the Trustees of Alexandria*, 1749-1767.

[40]*Order Book*, Fairfax Court House, 1768-1770, 338.

[41]*The Charter and Laws of Alexandria, Va.*, 78.

[42]Harrison, *Landmarks of Old Prince William*, II, 416, note 46.

[43]Letter to George Washington from Lund Washington, April 28, 1792. *Toner Transcripts*, Library of Congress. Copied from notes in Mount Vernon Ladies Association Library.

[44]Wilstack, *Mount Vernon*, 138.

[45]*Ibid.*

[46]Fitzpatrick, *Diaries of George Washington*, II, 209.

[47]Letter of Olney Winsor to his wife in Providence, Rhode Island. Original in archives, State Library, Richmond, Virginia.

[48]Harrison, *Landmarks of Old Prince William*, II, 409.

[49]Morse, *The American Geography*, 381.

[50]Harrison, *Landmarks of Old Prince William*, II, 408.

[51]*Ibid.*

[52]*Ibid.*

[53]*A Stranger in America* (Anonymous), 213.

[54]Snowden, *The Laws of the Corporation of the Town of Alexandria from 1779 to 1811*, 32.

[55]Fitzpatrick, *Writings of George Washington*, III, 18.

[56]Caton, *Jottings*, 115.

PART TWO: THE PRESENCE OF GEORGE WASHINGTON, 1749-1799.

Chapter 1. WILLIAM RAMSAY: *Romulus of Alexandria.*

[1]Harrison, *Landmarks of Old Prince William*, II, 371, quoting President Madison in 1827.

[2]Harrison, *Landmarks of Old Prince William*, II, 406.

[3]*Ibid.*, 663. Alexandria, 1749. Record Hening, I, 214, C.O. 5, 1895, No. 20. Description: "60 Acres . . . parcel of the land of Philip Alexander, John Alexander, and Hugh West, situate . . . on the south side of Potomack River about the mouth of Great Hunting Creek in the county of Fairfax." Trustees: Thomas, Lord Fairfax, William Fairfax, George William Fairfax, Richard Osborne, Lawrence Washington, William Ramsay, John Carlyle, John Pagan, Gerard Alexander, Hugh West, Philip Alexander.

[4]Hamilton, *Letters*, II, 164.

[5]Harrison, *Landmarks*, II, 414; Hayden, *Virginia Genealogies*, 88; *William and Mary College Quarterly Historical Magazine*, IV, 17; *Maryland Gazette (Copy in Ramsay Family records)*.

[6]*Maryland Gazette*, December 1761, Ramsay Family records.

[7]Lipscomb, *The Writings of Thomas Jefferson*, IV, 90, Memorial Edition.

[8]Letter of Martha Washington to Betty Ramsay, dated Cambridge, December 30, 1775. Courtesy Pierpont Morgan Library.

[9]*Ramsay Family records.*

[10]See reference No. 8, *supra*.

[11]*Deed Book P*, 365, December 20, 1784. Fairfax Court House.

[12]*Deed Book B*, 168, July 14, 1785. Alexandria Land Records.

[13]Fitzpatrick, *Diaries of George Washington*, II, 342.

[14]From a newspaper clipping in *Ramsay Family records.*

[15]Fitzpatrick, *Diaries*, II, 356.

[16]From a newspaper clipping in *Ramsay Family records.*
Alexandria Deed Book F, 331.
Alexandria Will Book 4, 92.
Fairfax Deed Books: D, No. 1, Part I, 436; *D*, 380; *M*, No. 1, 286.

Chapter 2. JOHN CARLYLE AND HIS HOUSE.

[1]*Will Book I-D*, 368. Fairfax Court House.
[2]*Minute Book*, 1753 Fairfax Court House.
[3]*Will Book, I-D*, 368. Fairfax Court House.
[4]*Will Book I-D*, 203-207. Fairfax Court House.
[5]Harrison, *Early American Turf Stock*, I, 152, 155-156.

Chapter 3. THE MARRIED HOUSES.

[1]Fitzpatrick, *Diaries*, I, 308.
[2]*Ibid.*, 366.
[3]*Deed Book E*, 63. Alexandria.
[4]From information furnished by Mr. Taylor Burke.
Alexandria Deed Books: 43, 445; *E*, 90, 316; *L-3*, 474; *P-3*, 650; *Q-3*, 19; *T-3*, 537;
V-3, 383; *W*, 398; *W-3*, 453.
Alexandria Will Book 4, 63.
Fairfax Will Book D, 17-20.

Chapter 4. THE FAIRFAXES OF BELVOIR AND ALEXANDRIA.

[1]Neill, *The Fairfaxes of England and America*, 49.
[2]Fitzpatrick, *Writings*, I, 166.
[3]*Ibid.*, 122-123.
[4]Cary, *Sally Cary*, 50.
[5]Neill, *The Fairfaxes of England and America*, 95-97.
[6]*Minute Book*, Court held August 15, 1758, 501-502.
[7]Fitzpatrick, *Diaries*, II, 118.
[8]Fitzpatrick, *Writings*, XXVII, 58.
[9]*Ibid.*, 57.
[10]*Ibid.*, XXXVI, 262-265.

Chapter 5. THE GEORGE WILLIAM FAIRFAX HOUSE.

[1]*Minutes of the Trustees of Alexandria, 1749-1767; Deed Book G-1*, 116. Fairfax
Court House.
[2]*Minutes of the Trustees of Alexandria, 1749-1767*.
[3]Fairfax Court House Records. Missing Liber K (now in the Library of Congress),
124-127.
[4]Fitzpatrick, *Diaries*, II, 42.
[5]Personal Property Tax, Fairfax County (1782-1793). Virginia State Library Archives,
No. 400.
[6]Lee, *Lee of Virginia*, 235-254.
[7]Shepperson, *John Paradise and Lucy Ludwell*, 98.
[8]Fitzpatrick, *Diaries*, IV, 270, 280.
Alexandria Deed Books: B, 364; *D*, No. 2, 177.
Alexandria Will Book 2, 278 (Orphans' Court).
Fairfax Deed Books: C-1, 382; *G-1*, 116.
Fairfax Deed Book K, 119-127; 302-307, 368, 370. Now in Library of Congress.

Chapter 6. JOHN GADSBY AND HIS FAMOUS TAVERN.

[1]*Tyler's Quarterly Historical and Genealogical Magazine*, XVI, No. 4, 233.
[2]So-called by Thomas T. Waterman, author of *The Mansions of Virginia*.
[3]*Columbia Mirror and Alexandria Gazette*, October 30, 1793.
[4]*Ibid.*, November 6, 1793.

[5]*Ibid.*

[6]A number of years ago the Metropolitan Museum acquired by purchase the woodwork of the great ballroom, where so many of Alexandria's social events had taken place. It is an outstanding exhibit in the American wing.

[7]Custis, *Recollections and Private Memoirs,* 451-452.

[8]*Liber R, No. 2,* 372. 1809. Alexandria.

[9]*Alexandria Gazette,* October 19, 1824.

[10]Fitzpatrick, *Diaries,* IV, 298.

[11]*Tyler's Quarterly Historical and Genealogical Magazine,* XVI, No. 4, 238.

[12]*Ibid.*

Alexandria Liber P, No. 2, 421. Indenture, July 8, 1802.

Chapter 7. THE MICHAEL SWOPE HOUSE.

[1]*Minutes of the Trustees of Alexandria, 1749-1767.*

[2]*Liber D* (1755-1761), 452. Fairfax Court House.

[3]*Ibid.*

[4]*Liber B,* 375. July 25, 1786. Alexandria.

Alexandria Deed Book X, 330.

Fairfax Liber I, No. 1, 321-322; *N,* No. 1, 226.

Chapter 8. DR. WILLIAM BROWN *Author of the First American Pharmacopoeia* AND HIS DWELLING.

[1]Fitzpatrick, *Diaries,* II, 64.

[2]Fitzpatrick, *Writings,* XXX, 133.

[3]Lund Washington's ledger, 148. Manuscript Collection of the Mount Vernon Ladies Association.

[4]Washington's Papers, Ledger B, 119. Library of Congress.

Alexandria Liber B, No. 3, 273; *H,* No. 1, 140.

Fairfax Deed Books: D, No. 1, Part 1, 436; *M,* No. 1, 25, 261; *O,* No. 1, 82.

Fairfax Liber M, 259; *S,* No. 1, 419.

Chapter 9. THE PERUKE SHOP.

[1]*Order Book,* 333-334. (April 18, 1759.) Fairfax Court House.

[2]*Liber J* (I), 236. Alexandria.

Alexandria Deed Books: F, 483; *S,* 420; *V,* 114.

Alexandria Liber O, No. 2, 453.

Fairfax Deed Books: C, 306; *G,* 119; *P,* No. 1, 385.

Fairfax Liber D, 169.

Chapter 10. HISTORIC CHRIST CHURCH.

[1]Truro Parish Vestry Book (Manuscript), *sub.* June 4, 1753.

[2]*Ibid.,* November 22, 1754.

[3]*Ibid.,* November 29, 1756.

[4]Slaughter, *Truro Parish,* 96-100.

[5]Papers of George Washington, Library of Congress, Vol. 258.

Chapter 11. THE PRESBYTERIAN MEETINGHOUSE.

[1]Dr. Muir's Report, in the files of the Presbyterian Historical Society, Philadelphia.

[2]*Minutes of the Session.*

[3]*Committee Book,* October 4, 1825, 132.

[4]*Alexandria Gazette,* 1831
[5]*Committee Minutes,* 208.
[6]*Ibid.,* 209.
[7]*Ibid.,* 212.
[8]*Session Book,* Session 210, 134 (April 29, 1837).
Fairfax Liber L, No. 1, 215.

Chapter 12. PRESENTING THE SUN FIRE COMPANY

[1]*Minutes of the Sun Fire Company.* Courtesy of Miss Cora Duffey.
[2]Papers of George Washington. Library of Congress. Vol. 275 (August 24-October 19, 1795), *sub.* October 7, 1795.

Chapter 13. CAPTAIN JOHN HARPER AND HIS HOUSES.

[1]*Minutes of the Trustees of Alexandria, 1749-1767; Deed Book G. No. 1,* 116. Fairfax Court House.
[2]Hamilton, *Letters to Washington,* IV, 196.
[3]*Liber G, No. 1,* 28, Fairfax Court House.
[4]Powell, *Old Alexandria,* 313-314.
Alexandria Deed Book E, 128.
Alexandria Land Book (1798-1800), Virginia State Library and Archives.
Alexandria Will Book B, 16-161.
Fairfax Liber K, No. 1, 270-275.

Chapter 14. DR. ELISHA C. DICK AND THE FAWCETT HOUSE.

[1]Letters of his great-grandson, J. A. Pearce, to Dr. A. M. Toner, August 30, 1885. From copies given the author by Mr. W. B. McGroarty.
[2]Fitzpatrick, *Diaries,* II, 340.
[3]*Deed Book I,* 41. Alexandria.
[4]Lindsey, *Historic Homes and Landmarks of Alexandria, Virginia,* 37.
[5]Freeman, *R. E. Lee.*
[6]*Liber M,* 121. Fairfax Court House.
[7]*Ibid.*
[8]*Liber N. No. 2,* 42. Fairfax Court House.
Alexandria Deed Books: A, 53; *B,* 23; *C,* 113; *V,* 445.
Fairfax Deed Books: B, 336; *G,* 39-42.
Fairfax Liber D, No. 2, 25.

Chapter 15. THE BENJAMIN DULANEY HOUSE.

[1]Fitzpatrick, *Writings,* III, 114. Letter to Burwell Bassett.
[2]Fitzpatrick, *Diaries,* II, 339 and 344.
[3]*A Stranger in America* (Anonymous), 212.
[4]Contributed by Mr. W. B. McGroarty.
[5]Courtesy Mr. and Mrs. John Howard Joynt.
Alexandria Deed Book T, 508.
Fairfax Deed Book O, 75.

Chapter 16. DR. JAMES CRAIK AND HIS DWELLING.

[1]From an address on James Craik, Physician General, by Major General Robert A. Patterson in *The Military Surgeon,* February 1932.
[2]Will Book A, 128, April 13, 1803. Alexandria.

[3]Ford, *Writings of Washington*, XIV, 245-258; Callahan, *Washington: the Man and the Mason*, 188-191.
[4]Prussing, *The Estate of George Washington, Deceased*, 58.
Alexandria Deed Book BB, 349.
Fairfax Deed Book Y, No. 1, 224.

Chapter 17. ALEXANDRIA'S OLD APOTHECARY SHOP.

Chapter 18. SPRING GARDENS.

[1]*Order Book*, 1753. Fairfax Court House.
[2]Fitzpatrick, *Diaries*, IV, 279.
[3]Washington's Cash Memorandum Book, Toner Transcript in Library of Congress.
[4]Baker, *Washington After the Revolution*, 361.
[5]Fitzpatrick, *Diaries*, IV, 309.
[6]Baker, *op. cit.*, 383.

Chapter 19. WILLIAM FITZHUGH AND ROBERT E. LEE.

[1]Fitzpatrick, *Diaries*, IV, 269.
[2]*Ibid.*, 301.
[3]*Ibid.*, 301.
[4]*Ibid.*, 318.
Alexandria Deed Books: 13 (1883-1884), 399; K, No. 2, 234; M, 162; M, No. 2, 343; O, No. 2, 231.
Alexandria Will Book C, 308, 318.

Chapter 20. GEORGE WASHINGTON'S TENEMENTS.

[1]Fitzpatrick, *Diaries*, *sub.* April 28, 1760, I, 157.
[2]Powell, *Old Alexandria*, 76-78.
[3]Fitzpatrick, *Writings*, II, 448.
[4]*Ibid.*, XXVIII, 25.
[5]*Ibid.*, XXXIV, 503-504. George Washington to Tobias Lear.
[6]Papers of George Washington, 245. Library of Congress.
[7]Fitzpatrick, *Writings*, XXXV, 496.
[8]*Ibid.*, XXXVI, 25.
[9]Prussing, *Estate of George Washington, Deceased*, 73 (page 30 of Will).
[10]*Ibid.*, 81 (page 40 of Will).
[11]*Liber M. Folio 140* (1804). Deed recorded June 17, 1805. Fairfax Court House.
Alexandria Deed Books: 4, 206, 209; 8, 459; 19, 10; 45, 205; 120, 464; 218, 532, 550; G, 256; I, No. 3, 165.
Alexandria Liber F, No. 3, 190-192; M, 140; X, No. 2, 524.

Chapter 21. THE GEORGIAN COTTAGE.

[1]*Liber M*, 103. Alexandria.
[2]*Deed Book W*, 10 and 103. Alexandria.

Chapter 22. THE VOWELL-SNOWDEN HOUSE.

[1]Powell, *Old Alexandria*.
Alexandria Deed Books: B, 195, 485; B-3, 329; L, 209; Q-2 (1826), 195.

Chapter 23. THE EDMUND JENNINGS LEE HOUSE.

[1]Lee, *Lee of Virginia*, 374; Lee, *Recollections and Letters of General Lee*, 24.
[2]Lee, *Recollections and Letters*, 28.
Alexandria Deed Books: A (1801), 264; *H*, 460.
Alexandria Will Book 4, 320.

PART THREE: FIVE SKETCHES OF THE NINETEENTH CENTURY.

Chapter 24. THE YEATON-FAIRFAX HOUSE.

[1]*Deed Book K*, 264. Alexandria.
[2]Information contributed by Mr. Worth Bailey. The author is indebted to the Mount Vernon Ladies' Association for permission to quote Yeaton's letter which follows in the chapter text.
Alexandria Deed Books: D, 81; *S-2*, 669.
Alexandria Liber V-3, 470.

Chapter 25. THE LA FAYETTE-LAWRASON-CAZENOVE HOUSE.

[1]*Alexandria Gazette*, October 19, 1824.
Fairfax Deed Books:G, 358, 383; *K*, 181.

Chapter 26. ENTER THE QUAKER PEDAGOGUE: BENJAMIN HALLOWELL.

[1]Hallowell, *Autobiography*, 99 and 100.
[2]*Ibid.*, 104.
[3]*Ibid.*, 105.
[4]*Ibid.*, 108.

Chapter 27. THE ALEXANDRIA LYCEUM.

[1]Hallowell, *Autobiography*, 128-129.
[2]*Alexandria Gazette*, December 2, 1876.
[3]*Liber Y, No. 3*, 410. Alexandria.
Alexandria Deed Book 45, 406.
Alexandria Will Book 10, 414.

Chapter 28. THE SEA CAPTAIN'S DAUGHTER AND HER HOUSE.

[1]The material for this sketch was contributed by Mrs. George R. Hill, Sr., daughter of Mrs. Melissa Hussey Wood.

Bibliography

I. MANUSCRIPTS

Alexandria Court Records; Deed Books, Will Books.

[Alexandria], *Custom Record Journal of the Port for the Year 1816-1817.* Privately owned.

[Alexandria], *Minutes of the Trustees and the Council,* 1749-1780; 1792-1800.

[Alexandria], *Minutes of the Sun Fire Company.* Privately owned.

[Alexandria], Personal Tax List, 1782. *Virginia State Library and Archives.*

Fairfax County Court Records; Deed Books, Will Books, Minutes and Order.

[Fairfax County], Census and List of Tithables for 1749; Personal Tax List, 1782-1793. *Virginia State Library and Archives.*

[Fairfax County], Liber K. *Library of Congress.*

[Fairfax County], Truro Parish Vestry Book. *Library of Congress.*

Lawrason Family Bible. Privately owned.

Letter, Olney Winsor to his wife. *Virginia State Library and Archives.*

Letters of J. A. Pearce to Dr. A. M. Toner, his great-grandfather. Typescripts prescribed by Mr. William B. McGroarty to the author.

Mount Vernon Ladies' Association, Miscellaneous manuscripts.

Mutual Assurance Society of Virginia. Microfilm records. *Virginia State Library and Archives.*

Presbyterian Historical Society, Philadelphia, Pa., Dr. Muir's Report; *Minutes* of the Session (210); Committee Minutes.

Ramsay Family Records.

Stabler-Leadbeater Apothecary Shop, Archives. Courtesy of the Alexandria Landmarks Association.

Washington, George, Accounts, Cash memoranda; Ledgers A and B. *Library of Congress.*

Washington, George, Papers. *Library of Congress.*

Washington, Lund, Ledger in the collection of the *Mount Vernon Ladies' Association.*

Washington, Martha, Letter to Miss Betsy Ramsay, dated December 30, 1775. *Pierpont Morgan Library.*

II. PERIODICALS

Alexandria Gazette, established as *The Virginia Journal and Alexandria Advertiser* and underwent many changes of proprietors and names.

American Turf Register and Sporting Magazine, March, 1830.

Carne, William E., "Tiny Town Notes," *From Ramsay Family Records.*

Carne, William E., "Washington As a Burgher," *Harper's New Monthly Magazine.* February 1880.

The Magazine Antiques, special issue devoted to Alexandria, February 1945.

Maryland Gazette, Annapolis, Md.

Records of the Columbia Historical Society, Washington, D. C.

Tyler's Quarterly Historical and Genealogical Magazine, Richmond, Va.

Virginia Magazine of History and Biography, Richmond, Va.

William and Mary College Quarterly Historical Magazine, series I and II. Williamsburg, Va.

III. PUBLISHED SOURCES & GENERAL WORKS

[Alexandria], *The Charter and Laws of the City of Alexandria, Va., and Historical Sketch of Its Government,* published by the city council, Alexandria, 1874.

Baker, William Spohn, *Washington After the Revolution,* Philadelphia, 1898.

Blanton, Wyndham B., *Medicine in Virginia in the Eighteenth Century.* Richmond, 1931.

Brockett, F. L., *The Lodge of Washington, 1783-1876,* Alexandria, 1890.

Burnaby, Rev. Andrew, *Travels Through the Middle Settlements in North America, 1759-1760,* London, 1775.

Callahan, Charles H., *The Memorial to Washington: an Historical Souvenir,* Alexandria Memorial Committee, c.1923.

Callahan, Charles H., *Washington: The Man and the Mason,* published under the auspices of the Memorial Temple Committee of the George Washington Masonic National Memorial Association, 1913.

Cary, Wilson Miles, *Sally Cary, A Long Hidden Romance of Washington's Life. With Notes by Another Hand.* New York, 1916. Privately printed.

Caton, James R., *Legislative Chronicles of the City of Alexandria, or Jottings from the Annals of Alexandria,* Alexandria, 1933.

Conway, Moncure D., *Barons of the Potomack and the Rappahannock,* New York, 1892.

Custis, George Washington Parke, *Recollections and Private Memoirs of Washington,* New York, 1860.

Davis, Deering, Stephen P. Dorsey, and Ralph Cole Hall, *Alexandria Houses, 1750-1830,* New York, 1946.

Dictionary of American Biography. Edited by Allen Johnson and Dumas Malone, New York, 1928-36. 20 Vols. and supplement.

Fairfax, Thomas, *Journey from Virginia to Salem, Massachusetts, 1799,* London, 1936. Privately printed.

Fitzpatrick, John C., ed., *The Diaries of George Washington 1748-1798.* Published for the Mount Vernon Ladies' Association. New York, 1925. 4 Vols.

Fitzpatrick, John C., ed., *The Writings of George Washington. Bicentennial Edition.* Washington, D. C., 1932. 37 Vols. and index.

Ford, Worthington Chauncey, ed., *The Writings of George Washington.* New York and London, 1889-93. 14 Vols.

Freeman, Douglas Southall, *R. E. Lee,* New York, 1934. 4 Vols.

Hamilton, S. M., ed., *Letters to George Washington,* Boston and New York. 5 Vols.

Harrison, Constance (Cary), "Mrs. Burton Harrison," *Crow's Nest and Belle Haven Tales.* New York, 1892.

Harrison, Constance (Cary), "Mrs. Burton Harrison," *Recollections Grave and Gay.* New York, 1916.

Harrison, Fairfax, *The Background of the American Stud Book.* Richmond, 1933. Privately printed.

Harrison, Fairfax, *Early American Turf Stock, 1730-1830.* Richmond, 1934. 2 Vols. Privately printed.

Harrison, Fairfax, *The Equine F.F.V.'s,* Richmond, 1928. Privately printed.

Harrison, Fairfax, *Landmarks of Old Prince William,* Richmond, 1924. Privately printed. 2 Vols.

Harrison, Fairfax, *Virginia Land Grants,* Richmond, 1928. Privately printed.

Hayden, Rev. Horace Edwin, *Virginia Genealogies,* Washington, D. C., 1931.

Hening, William Waller, comp., *The Statutes at Large Being a Collection of All the Laws of Virginia, from the First Session of the Legislature in the Year 1619.* Richmond, 1810-23. 13 Vols.

Hallowell, Benjamin, *Autobiography,* Philadelphia, Pa., 1883.

Jackson, Rev. Eugene B., *The Romance of Historic Alexandria.* Alexandria, 1923.

Janson, Charles William, *The Stranger in America.* London, 1807.

Kettell, Russell Howes, ed., *Early American Rooms . . .* Portland, Me., 1936.

Knox, Katharine McCook, *The Sharples, Their Portraits of George Washington and His Contemporaries,* New York, 1930.

Lee, Edmund Jennings, *Lee of Virginia, 1642-1892.* Philadelphia, 1895.

Lee, Robert E. Jr., *Recollections and Letters of Robert E. Lee,* New York, 1905.

Lindsey, Mary, *Historic Homes and Landmarks of Alexandria, Virginia.* 1931. Privately printed.

Lipscomb, Andrew Adgate, ed., *The Writings of Thomas Jefferson.* Washington, D. C. *(Memorial Edition)* 1903-04. 20 Vols.

Lossing, Benson J., *Mount Vernon and Its Associations.* New York, 1859.

MacDonald, Rose Mortimer E., *Mrs. Robert E. Lee,* Boston, 1939.

McGroarty, William Buckner, *The Old Presbyterian Meeting House at Alexandria, Virginia 1774-1874.* Richmond, 1940.

McIlwaine, H. R., ed., *Journals of the House of Burgesses of Virginia.* 11 Vols.

McIlwaine, H. R., ed., *Legislative Journals of The Council of Colonial Virginia,* Richmond, 1925-28, 3 Vols.

Morrison, A. J., ed., *Travels in Virginia in Revolutionary Times,* Lynchburg, Va., 1922.

Morse, Jedidiah, *The American Geography,* London, 1792.

Mount Vernon Ladies' Association, *Annual Reports, 1938-48.*

Neill, Edward D., *The Fairfaxes of England and America.* Albany, N. Y., 1868.

Norfleet, Fillmore, *St. Memin in Virginia,* Richmond, 1942.

Powell, Mary G., *The History of Old Alexandria, Virginia.* Richmond, Va., 1928. Privately printed.

Prussing, Eugene E., *The Estate of George Washington, Deceased,* Boston, 1927.

Ramsay, A. M. H., *A Short Life of Sir Alexander Ramsay of Dalhousie.* From Ramsay Family Records.

Ritson, Mrs. A., *A Poetical Picture of America Being Observations Made During a Residence of Several Years at Alexandria and Norfolk in Virginia,* London, 1809.

Scott, Sir Walter, *Historical Passages in the Life of Sir A. Ramsay.* From Ramsay Family Records.

The Scottish Tartans, Edinburgh and London, 1886. From Ramsay Family Records.

Shepperson, Archibald Bolling, *John Paradise and Lucy Ludwell,* Richmond, Va., 1942.

Slaughter, Rev. Philip, *The History of Truro Parish in Virginia,* Philadelphia, 1907.

Smoot, Mrs. Betty Carter (McGuire), *Days in an Old Town,* Alexandria, Virginia, 1934. Privately printed.

Snowden, Samuel, *The Laws of the Corporation of The Town of Alexandria from 1779 to 1811.* Alexandria, 1811.

Snowden, W. H., *Some Old Historical Landmarks,* Philadelphia, 1894.

Spencer, Richard Henry, *Carlyle Family,* Richmond, Va., 1910.

Swem, Earl G., *Virginia Historical Index,* Roanoke, Va., 1934-36. 2 Vols.

Wedderburn, Alexander J., *Historic Alexandria, Va., Past and Present, Souvenir of Virginia Tercentennial,* 1907.

Wilkes, Marion R., *Rosemont and Its Famous Daughter,* mimeographed edition, 1947.

Wilstach, Paul, *Mount Vernon,* Garden City, N. Y., 1916.

Index

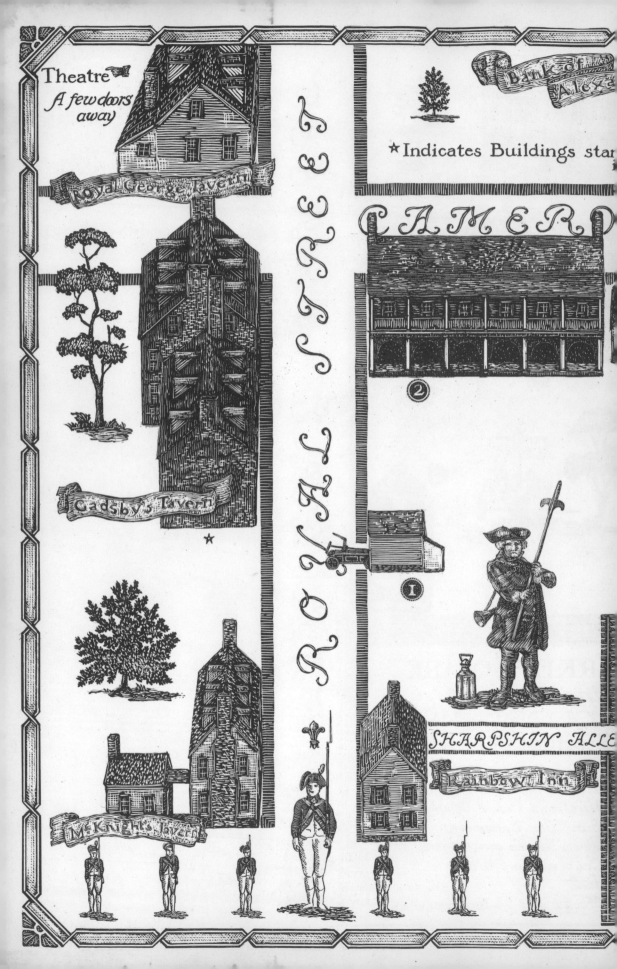